Power Play

For Mum, Dad and Noelle (RB)
For Susan and Alice (RH)

Power Play

Sport, the Media and Popular Culture

Raymond Boyle and Richard Haynes

Stirling Media Research Institute
University of Stirling

An imprint of **Pearson Education**

Harlow, England · London · New York · Reading, Massachusetts · San Francisco
Toronto · Don Mills, Ontario · Sydney · Tokyo · Singapore · Hong Kong · Seoul
Taipei · Cape Town · Madrid · Mexico City · Amsterdam · Munich · Paris · Milan

Pearson Education Limited
Edinburgh Gate
Harlow
Essex CM20 2JE
England

and Associated Companies throughout the World.

Visit us on the World Wide Web at:
www.pearsoneduc.com

———————————————

First published 2000

ISBN 0-582-36939-8

British Library Cataloguing-in-Publication Data
A catalogue record for this book can be obtained from the British Library

Library of Congress Cataloging-in-Publication Data
A catalog record for this book can be obtained from the Library of Congress

10 9 8 7 6 5 4 3 2 1
05 04 03 02 01 00

Typeset by 35 in 9¹/₂/13pt New Aster
Printed by Ashford Colour Press Ltd., Gosport

Contents

Preface   *ix*

1   **Sport, Media and Popular Culture: Questions of Theory**   *1*
Introduction • Sport in sociology and history • Media
Studies sport • Television and sport • Mediated sport and
identity • Mapping the field and the structure of the book
• Conclusion

2   **All Our Yesterdays: A History of Media Sport**   *22*
Introduction • Origins of sport and the media: the sporting
press • Sport on newsreel • Sport on radio • Origins of
televising sport • Conclusion

3   **A Sporting Triangle: Television, Sport and Sponsorship**   *46*
Introduction • The good old days? Sport and sponsorship
• Global sports sponsorship: branding sport • The Olympics
and the 'Hamburger Games' of 1984 • The media marketing
of World Cup USA 1994 and France 98 • Global sport:
changing the rules • Where only the sponsored survive
• Conclusion

4   **Power Game: Why Sport Matters to Television**   *67*
Introduction • What television needs from sport •
Reinvented for television: the case of snooker • Screening
sport: terrestrial and satellite versions • Sports commentary:
codes and conventions • Conclusion

5   **Who Wants to be a Millionaire? Media Sport and Stardom**   *89*
Introduction • A star is born • The origins of the sports
celebrity and the sports agent • Michael Jordan and the
NBA brand • Stars and transformations in sports labour
• The trouble with fame • Conclusion

6   **The Race Game: Media Sport, Race and Ethnicity**   *111*
    Introduction • Sporting and media representations of race
    • Prince Naz • Sectarianism, sport and popular culture
    • Sport, ethnicity and media bias • Conclusion

7   **For Men Who Play to Win: Media Sport and Gender**   *127*
    Introduction • Representing female sports and
    sportspeople • Masculinity and sport • Boxing and being
    a man • Conclusion

8   **Games Across Frontiers: Mediated Sport and**
    National Identity   *143*
    Introduction • Media, discourse and identity • Media
    sport and national identity • Political football: Euro 96
    and the Auld Enemy • France 98: a nation once again?
    • Globalization and the local • Conclusion

9   **Sportspages: Journalism and Literature**   *165*
    Introduction • Sports journalism • Constructing the
    sports page • The new sports writing • A whole new
    ball game? • Conclusion

10 **Consuming Sport: Fans, Fandom and the Audience**   *187*
    Introduction • The masculine ritual of sport • Male
    spectatorship and televised sport • Men viewing boxing •
    Tribal instincts: fandom and the media • Tradition and
    history among football fans • Conclusion

11 **Conclusion: The State of Play, Sport in the New Media Age**   *206*
    Introduction • Power play: regulating media sport •
    Power play: convergence in media sport • Power play:
    public-service sport and the BBC • Power play: digital
    and pay-per-view sport • Power play: cricket's last stand
    • Power play: no pay, no play; rugby union • Power play:
    the Internet: a new sporting superhighway • Endgame

Bibliography   *225*
Index   *236*

Sport, is of course one of the very best things about television; I would keep my set for it alone.

Raymond Williams, *The Listener*, 1 August 1968

A truly international field, no Britons are involved.

David Coleman, BBC Television's athletics commentator, 1988

A subject need not be intrinsically important to be sociologically informative.

Professor Patrick Reilly writing about Scottish football and society, *The Herald*, 23 March 1998

In my time, it was the army generals running Brazil who tried to pick the team. Today, it's the sponsors, the businessmen, the media moguls. The World Cup Final is the world's biggest tv show.

Carlos Alberto Perreira, Brazil's 1994 World Cup winning coach

Preface

Sport absolutely overpowers film and everything else in the entertainment industry.

Rupert Murdoch (quoted in 1996)

A decade of change: media sport 1989–99

Considering the shuddering impact it would have on the world of broadcast sport, it seems appropriate that a new stage in the media–sport relationship should have been announced by the launch of a rocket. It's February 1989 and as the Ariane space rocket carrying the Astra satellite, which is about to beam back to earth Rupert Murdoch's Sky channels, soars into the atmosphere, the landscape of UK broadcast sport is about to change beyond recognition. In Britain that year if you wanted to watch sport on television you paid a licence fee and watched the four publicly regulated terrestrial channels who provided you with 2800 hours of television sport.

Ten years on, and football alone now receives over 5000 hours of television coverage, with the total sports television output closer to 25,000 a year. You can watch sport on the five – substantially less regulated – terrestrial channels or invest in a satellite or cable delivery system, pay various subscription fees and watch three additional all-sports channels aimed at a UK audience and a host of others carrying sport from around the globe. Most of the major sporting events you can watch live from the comfort of your armchair. For those willing to pay, there has never been a better time to be a television sports fan.

Over the weekend of 10/11 April 1999 it was possible to construct your weekend viewing around television coverage of top sporting action. This was available across eight channels (both terrestrial and satellite) and included Five Nations rugby, the Grand National horse race, the English and Scottish Cup football semi-finals, the Brazilian Grand Prix, a one-day cricket international between England and India, the final two rounds of the US Masters Golf tournament and a WBO World Featherweight title fight involving a British world champion.

In addition to this sporting televisual feast there were also available, live, tennis from Portugal, curling from Canada, snowboarding from Switzerland or the possibility of settling down to watch the stars of tomorrow as Costa Rica played Germany in the World youth football championship taking place in Nigeria.

Little wonder that broadcaster and writer Archie MacPherson could note:

> This weekend has suggested to those of us who became television troglodytes over the last 48 hours what it must be like to be holed up in a nuclear bunker. (*The Herald*, 12 April 1999)

Even if you could drag yourself away from the couch and actually attend one of these events, things would also look different ten years on.

Football fans, many from the middle class, now sit in all-seater stadia and watch football teams such as Rangers – managed by a Dutchman and containing virtually no Scottish players, most of them earning more in a month than their counterparts a decade ago did in a year – playing a Scottish cup semi-final staged for the benefit of live satellite television at 6.05pm on a Sunday evening.

In 1999 there is more sport, more hype, more money and more media coverage (across newspapers, radio, television and the Internet) than at any other time in recent memory. A host of reasons lie behind this explosion and most are rooted in developments in the media industries in general, and in broadcasting in particular. By the end of the 1990s television exerts a stranglehold over sports.

There are other key agents of change, with the revolution in British football owing much to the Taylor Report which followed the Hillsborough disaster of 15 April 1989 when 96 Liverpool supporters lost their lives at an English FA Cup semi-final, and compelled the sport to address the crumbling infrastructure of football grounds and rethink its relationship with supporters. Without these changes it is doubtful whether television, and the money which flowed from it, would have shown the interest in the game it did in the early 1990s.

Nor are these changes confined to the UK. Sport's relationship with media organizations has developed apace across national borders, with many of these boundaries themselves having been redrawn since the fall of the Berlin wall in 1989. Nor indeed is this process of change new. Sports have always had a relationship with media and commerce; what is significant is the scale and the intensity that now exists within this relationship and the rapid pace of change which characterizes the media and sporting industries.

Media Studies sport

One of the problems faced when setting up an undergraduate university unit looking at *Sport and the Media* in the late 1980s was the dearth of material – outside of the US experience and the issue of football hooliganism – that existed in the academy which focused on sport and the media. In the ten years since it has become difficult to keep pace with the tide of books both academic and non-academic examining facets of the increasingly close links between sport and the media. In part this reflects the growth in Media and Cultural Studies and the realization that the sport–media nexus offers particularly rich pickings for those interested in the study of mediated popular culture and the interplay between culture, identity and power.

It also demonstrates the extent that sport, more than at any other time in its history, has been explicitly pulled into the orbit of commerce and business. Sport, and the media themselves, are now integral components of what are often called the entertainment or cultural industries. This section of the economy has become increasingly important over the last decade as the revenue streams and the employment opportunities offered across the creative industries of sport, music and media have mushroomed.

Sport has become important to those working within Media Studies and beyond even if they have little actual interest in sports *per se*. The business of sport and its linkage with the media industries mean that today sport matters to those whose primary interest may lie in the economics of the media industries and the political issues which relate to regulation and media policy.

Another key driver in the upsurge of interest in media sport has been the extent to which issues of identity – ethnic, racial, regional, national and international – have moved centre stage in both academic and political public debate. The extent to which globalization is eroding distinctive national traditions and identities has seen sport, with its universal appeal, being examined for evidence of this economic and political process.

We have been fortunate in that as sports fans and media academics our twin interests neatly collide with each other and we hope that this background is reflected throughout the book.

There is little doubt that the advent of digital broadcasting heralds the next phase in the evolution of the relationship between sport and the media. What we wish to look at in this book is how the sport–media nexus has evolved to its present state and examine what have been the implications of this for sporting and media organizations and their supporters and consumers.

For some, sport appears to be a massive triviality and in essence when the games of sport are looked at in isolation this may well be true. However, for the millions of fans around the world who invest financially and emotionally in these games, sport has always mattered. What is different as we enter a new century is that sport also matters to big business and to those who drive the increasingly commercial and global media and entertainment industries. The power play involving the control and meaning of sport which began this century shows every sign of intensifying as we enter the next.

Acknowledgements

Thanks are due to a number of people who reassured us that sport was worth treating seriously, among them are Neil Blain, Hugh O'Donnell, Simon Frith and Philip Schlesinger. Some of the material in chapters 7 and 10 draws on original research carried out by the authors while working on the *Men Viewing Violence* project commissioned by the Broadcasting Standards Commission.

Over the last ten years thanks are due to the various students who have taken the sport and media course offered first at Glasgow Caledonian University and later at Stirling University, by the Film & Media Studies department. While we hope the students learned something from the course, we also learned much through our discussions with them.

Thanks also to Sarah Caro who commissioned the book, and to both Jane Powell and David Harrison at Pearson Education for their support in seeing the project through.

We are grateful to the following for permission to reproduce copyright photographic material; Action Images for the front cover Cantona kick photograph, Hulton Getty for photographs on pages 23, 40, 81, 84, and 94; *The Daily Record* for allowing us to reproduce two front covers, pages 108 and 149; Graham Brown of Media Services at the University for his help with pages 178 and 183, and Sky Sports for the image which appears on page 192.

CHAPTER 1

Sport, Media and Popular Culture

Questions of Theory

> Sport is at once both trivial and serious, inconsequential yet of symbolic significance . . . Sport in many cases informs and refuels the popular memory of communities, and offers a source of collective identification and community expression for those who follow teams and individuals.
>
> **John Sugden and Alan Tomlinson, Soccer culture, national identity and the World Cup, in Sugden and Tomlinson (eds.) (1994) p. 3**

> . . . where *Il Sole* was available most of the prisoners, including politicals, read *La Gazzetta dello Sport*.
>
> **Observations made while in prison in Milan by Antonio Gramsci, in David Forgacs (ed.) (1988) *A Gramsci Reader*. London: Lawrence and Wishart, p. 376**

Introduction

Without question one of the great passions of the twentieth century has been sport. It has mattered to thousands of players and fans across the globe, with differing sports playing a particularly important role in the cultural life of countries and people. While football is the global game, others sports such as baseball occupy a central position in American popular culture; cricket and Aussie Rules in Australian life; gaelic games and football in Ireland; cricket and basketball in Caribbean culture, while rugby union is important in constructions of Welsh and New Zealand national identities.

However, the history of the twentieth century has also been to a large extent both dominated and documented by the mass media. Newspapers, film, radio and television broadcasting have all had a profound effect on shaping the popular and political culture of this century. While sport has always mattered beyond the confines of the pitch or the stadia, it has as the century progressed become increasingly intertwined with various media and television in particular.

Something, however, has begun to happen to this relationship towards the end of the century which has resulted in sport becoming increasingly important within the worlds of business and politics. This is illustrated by taking a snapshot of sports media stories moving in March 1999. We had extensive news media coverage of the hugely controversial World Heavyweight boxing match between Britain's Lennox Lewis and the American Evander Holyfield – a fight which ten years ago would have been available on terrestrial television to a massive UK audience, but was watched by a minority audience on a British pay-per-view channel.

BBC television screened a documentary on British football's new millionaire players, highlighting the massive wealth which players such as Michael Owen and David Beckham can accumulate through their media stardom, which stands in marked contrast to the financial rewards secured by the previous generation of players. This financial revolution has been funded by satellite television's annexation of the game and the extensive media coverage given to the top players.

In the world of business, newspapers were leaking rumours of the Monopolies and Mergers Commission's decision relating to the proposed takeover of one of the biggest football clubs in Europe, Manchester United, by one of the world's most powerful media moguls, Rupert Murdoch. It appeared that the decision to block the takeover would have political repercussions for the New Labour government who were keen to keep the support of Murdoch's influential British newspapers.

Meanwhile in Switzerland, the President of the International Olympic Committee was frantically attempting to cling to power as key members of that organization were being sacked amid accusations of corruption in the awarding of the Olympics to particular host cities. Due to the massive media coverage and exposure given to host cities, becoming an Olympic city is something which offers extensive commercial opportunities to whichever city is selected.

The President of the world governing body of football (FIFA) was also coming under fire for suggesting that the World Cup should be held every two, rather than every four years, in order to maximize the media exposure of the game on a global stage. It had little support among players and fans, although unsurprisingly some media organizations (including Rupert Murdoch) and commercial sponsors thought it was a good idea. While, back in Britain, three of the top football administrators in both England and Scotland had either resigned or been sacked. The former over the way that consultants had been appointed to advise on the negotiations of television contracts, the latter after a vitriolic newspaper campaign to unseat him.

All of these stories were covered in the sports, business and news pages of the print media, and given an extensive airing on both mainstream radio and television news. It appeared, certainly in Britain in 1999, that sporting issues, inevitably bound up with the media, had never mattered more and appeared to extend into areas of society previously immune to engaging in such a high-profile manner with the business of sport.

How and why has this has come about is something which this book seeks to explore. As will be evident from Chapters 2 and 3, there has always been a relationship between sport and the media, but we would argue that the ties between two of the great forces of twentieth-century popular culture have never been closer and this tell us much about wider cultural and social shifts in society. This chapter seeks to trace briefly the previous academic work that engages with aspects of the relationship between sport, media and identity and provide the reader with a context within which to place the book. We examine the treatment of sport in sociological and historical encounters and then focus specifically on academic writing directly concerned with what we call 'media sport'.

Finally we outline the specific areas the book covers, identifying both the key themes addressed in the chapters which follow and how they interact with each other. In so doing we discuss our own broad theoretical approach to studying the complex relationship between media and sport and argue for an interdisciplinary awareness which locates this relationship within the specific wider economic, political and cultural contours of society. In so doing we hope that it invites the reader to engage and think about sport and the media in a more critical manner than they may have previously done. As will be clear from the discussion of previous academic approaches to sport and society, sport – and its media context – have increasingly mattered to academics.

Sport in sociology and history

An excellent overview of the position of sport within social theory is provided by Jarvie and Maguire (1994). In their book they trace the influence that major sociological traditions have had on the sociology of sport and leisure. In the context of this work, while sociological encounters with sport are discussed, specific attention here is paid to the position of sport within the particular field of media/cultural studies.

Until recently, sociology has been largely indifferent to suggestions that the position of sport, and indeed leisure, in modern society was worthy of serious and sustained investigation. Leisure was viewed as unimportant, or at its most simplistic, as the antithesis of work. Sport was perhaps one of the last major areas of human activity to be subjected to rigorous examination by sociologists.

The last ten to fifteen years has seen a sea-change in attitudes towards the sociological study of sport and leisure (see Critcher, 1992). Accompanying the movement of sport from the periphery of sociological enquiry has been a debate between sociologists and those working within media/cultural studies regarding the most suitable theoretical paradigms within which this work should be located. There is little doubt that the rise in popularity of Media Studies courses and the media's increased interest in sport have also focused the minds of scholars.

Chris Rojek (1992), in an overview of the position of theory within the field of sport and leisure studies, highlighted how much of the writing in this area has been situated within either an agency or structure paradigm. The former approach characterizes society as a pluralistic system, in which individual choice is the key determining factor in the pattern of leisure development. While admitting that power is not equally distributed among all groups in this plural society, they view the relations of power as shifting unproblematically between groups and that ultimately it is the individual and the choices that he/she will make which shape the environment.

Sport and power

In contrast, those working from within the structure paradigm draw upon a Marxist analysis, which posits sport and leisure activities as being determined by the economic and political contours of society. In addition, they cite the centrality of class and capital in shaping the choices open to individuals, and present the arena of sport and leisure as a terrain on which dominant and subordinate groups produce and reproduce power relations that exist elsewhere in a capitalist society. In short, sport and leisure became vehicles of social control which both exploited workers and expanded the hold of capital on all areas of human activity.

It is a far from monolithic theory, however, and feminists such as Hargreaves (1994), and Creedon (1994) have highlighted the importance of gender relations in shaping leisure patterns, while Cashmore (1982) emphasizes the important role that race plays in determining the patterns of sporting behaviour among ethnic groups in Britain. The work of Hargreaves and Cashmore is closer to a process approach adopted by neo-marxists (also referred to as the 'cultural studies' approach). Horne *et al.* (1987) sum up the strengths of this neo-marxist approach as being threefold:

> it takes seriously the idea that sport and leisure practice must be understood as relations of power; it emphasises the role of the state and the economy in structuring sport and leisure activity in contemporary society; and it applies an open-ended approach to sport and leisure studies so that new developments can be examined in a non-dogmatic fashion. (Horne, Jary and Tomlinson, 1987, p. 188)

While Rojek (1992, p. 8) recognizes that this 'cultural studies' approach is useful because of its recognition of leisure and sport as 'deeply rooted social processes', he also attacks this approach as being too deterministic and overtly concerned with class and capital. In addition, he quite rightly points out that all the case studies and fieldwork, despite their location within British cultural studies, have been centred on England and English society, failing to recognize the cultural differences that exist elsewhere, for example between Scotland and England.

Rojek places himself within another process paradigm, that of the 'figurational sociology' approach to the study of sport and leisure (Dunning and Rojek, 1992). Drawing heavily on the work of Norbert Elias, the 'figurational' sociologists view society as a series of interlocking and dependent groups whose interplay is in a constant state of development and change. In other words, they place the individual at the centre of a series of configurations which, as they move outwards, become more complex, with no one factor overtly determining the relationships between the individual and society, but a multiplicity of factors and social groups such as the family, schooling, housing and such like all influencing the individual.

Rojek argues that much of the difference between the cultural studies approach and the figurational sociologists has been over-emphazised. He acknowledges that a fundamental difference between the two approaches centres on the figurational sociologists' assertion that all social science research should aspire to 'the conditions of detachment, a methodology of self-consciously distancing oneself from the object of study' (Rojek, 1992, p. 28), rather than what Rojek views as the politically motivated drive of cultural studies. However, he concludes that:

> The common respect for history, the common emphasis on the
> historical and social dimensions of the 'natural' and the 'obvious', the
> common application of cultural diversity and richness – these are not
> insignificant common denominators. (Rojek, 1992, p. 28)

There is much of value in this assertion. However, the fundamental difference between the approaches as to the location of power in society remains. Cultural studies researchers are accused of over-emphasizing class as a determining factor in social relations, while figurational sociologists are accused of underplaying its centrality.

In addition, the subjectivity of the researcher in any research process, and his/her ability to 'detach' themselves from that work remains a point of disagreement. Perhaps the most significant agreement between the scholars is that the various patterns of sport and leisure development should be viewed as a continual process, although they may disagree on the determining influences that shape this development.

Much of this debate has moved the study of sport and leisure from the margins of sociology and sociological enquiry. In his concluding remarks in Dunning and Rojek (eds.) (1992), Eric Dunning notes how he hoped that the book would: 'persuade more sociologists that the sociology of sport is a field that is vibrant and alive' (Dunning and Rojek, 1992, p. 277). A point that is also emphazised in the work of Jarvie and Maguire (1994).

Sport and historians

In addition to the body of work concerned with the sociology of sport, another area, that of social history, has also engaged with the study of sport. The need to place sport within a broader economic and political perspective has been recognized by social historians who have contributed much to the elevation of the study of sport within the academy, viewing it as a legitimate and fruitful scholarly activity, which highlights the cultural, economic and political significance of sport to society. As Jones argues:

> sport in industrial societies is an important economic, social and
> political activity in its own right, able to provide the specialist with vital
> evidence about labour markets, capital investments, class, gender and
> even international relations. (Jones, 1992, p. 2)

The interchange between historians and sociologists working within the field of sport has been dogged by debates surrounding the role of theory in any investigation. Put at its simplest, historians claim that sociological encounters with sport suffer from the weight of ideological baggage that scholars carry to the subject. They argue that sociologists use sport to legitimize particular theoretical positions. In addition, they suggest that these positions are in fact untenable due to a neglect in adequately historicizing the sporting and cultural context.

Sociologists claim that historians lack theoretical rigour and in addition that historical analysis is of limited use in understanding contemporary culture. (The 'figurational' sociologists and those working within cultural studies are exempted from the latter criticism.)

Those working within the cultural studies tradition outlined above, who in particular view the historicizing of the sporting cultural context as of central importance, also claim that much historical analysis, important as it is, fails to place the work within a theoretical framework (Clarke and Critcher, 1985). As a result, much of the work of social historians becomes simply descriptive analysis. It is from within cultural/media studies, both multi- and inter-disciplinary subjects, that the most fruitful engagement with sport as a cultural form has taken place. It offers a commitment to understanding contemporary sporting culture by historicizing sport as a cultural form, and also offers a serious theoretical engagement with the subject.

For all this academic growth remarkably little sociological work has focused directly on the relationship between the media and sport or, more complex still, the relationship between the media, sport and questions of identity formation. While the neo-marxist approaches have been more alert to the lacunae that have existed, it has only been relatively recently that a sustained engagement with the sport/media/society nexus has taken place (Goldlust, 1987; Hargreaves, 1986; Whannel, 1992; Blain *et al.*, 1993).

Much of this work has originated from within the emerging multi-disciplinary cultural/media studies field, and has quite rightly viewed sport as an area of study through which wider issues can be addressed and examined. These issues, all of which are central in the broader cultural/media studies field, are a concern with the role of media institutions in society, the production/consumption of culture and the ideological significance of popular culture in modern society.

Media Studies sport

A good deal of the sociological theorizing on sport has focused on the particular dynamics and ideologies embedded in sporting culture and the societies in which they are played. However, the media, television and the press in particular, are playing a central role in producing, reproducing and amplifying many of the discourses associated with sport in the modern world. It is this process and its ideological fallout that has been of particular interest to media/cultural scholars. John B. Thompson argues that:

> Pop music, sports and other activities are largely sustained by the media industries, which are not merely involved in the transmission and financial support of pre-existing cultural forms, but also in the active transformation of these forms. (Thompson, 1990, p. 163)

Understanding this process of transformation and its implications is what has interested many key writers who focus on media sport (Goldlust, 1987; Whannel, 1992; Rowe, 1995 and Wenner, 1998). There has been an increasing recognition of the importance of examining both the political and economic structures of the media–sport relationship as well as its mediated representations – for example the way in which television increasingly dictates when sporting events take place (moving Saturday football matches to a Sunday evening and such like). Barnett (1990) remains a good example of an empirical strand of the former; however Whannel (1992) was not only concerned with the political economy of media sport but also has an equal interest in text and ideology. In other words, he was interested in looking at how media sport helped to promote particular ways of thinking about sport and society, for example the notion that politics has nothing to do with sport, and that black athletes are 'naturally' more gifted than white athletes.

Whannel is an important figure in media sports scholarship: he was one of the first in the UK to write in a sustained and critical manner about the relationship between sport and the media and has always retained an equal concern with both the political economy and ideological dimension of media sport. Thus not only does his work examine the increasingly complex relationship that exists between capital, television and sport (through sponsorship, advertising and international marketing), but is also concerned with the ideological implications that such a process has on the sporting representations. One of Whannel's objectives is to examine:

> What are the cultural and economic relations between television and sport, and how, if at all, has television transformed sport? What relationship is there between the cultural and economic level in this particular instance? (Whannel, 1992, p. 4)

– a research agenda which still remains valid as we enter a new millennium and seek to track the continually evolving relationship between these two institutions.

Key media sport writers

Goldlust (1987), Whannel (1992), Blain *et al.* (1993) and more recently Wenner (1998) all examine the role that mediated sport plays as a form of symbolic ritual in many modern industrialized societies. They examine the transformation of sport in the televisual age and argue that the study of media sport provides a particularly incisive insight into the commodification of popular culture by capital. They also investigate the pleasures that television sport offers to its audience and the way that it constructs 'fields of representation' which comment on society and the position of groups (such as women) within that society. In addition Blain *et al.* (1993) have stressed the relationship between the domains of sporting and political discourse, particularly as it relates to the construction of national characteristics and identities. Thus the Scots are passionate, the Italians fiery, the Swedes are cool and so on.

Whannel (1992) is keen not to take an overly deterministic view of the power of television over its audience, and ultimately argues that not only is the television/sport/sponsorship axis reshaping sport as a cultural form, but it is also reflecting deeper economic and cultural shifts in society.

> Sports now stress the need to be businesslike and efficient, offer sites
> for the celebration of corporate capitalism, provide executive boxes and
> hospitality tents to serve the needs of commercial sponsors, and in
> general have become prime sites for the construction and reproduction
> of an entrepreneurial culture. Television has not itself produced this
> reshaping but, in enabling the rapid growth of sponsorship, it provided
> the key element in the process. (Whannel, 1992, p. 208)

While alert to the possibility of economic determinism, this work draws both on political economy and on the Gramscian concept of hegemony which has so informed much media/cultural studies work on popular culture during the last couple of decades.

Perhaps one of the most important books to draw on the Gramscian tradition in the study of sport has been *Sport, Power and Culture*: A Social and Historical Analysis of Popular Sports in Britain (1986) by John Hargreaves. He places Gramsci's concept of hegemony at the centre of his study of the development of popular sports in Britain. The historicizing of sporting culture, and its interplay with the economic and political development of the British state, is placed within the paradigm of the hegemonic struggle between dominant and subordinate groups within British society.

> By hegemony we mean the achievement by a class, or by a class fraction or alliance, of leadership over the rest of society, in accordance with its perceived interests . . . Power resides more in the ability of the hegemonic group to win consent to, and support for, its leadership . . . Hegemony is achieved through a continuous process of work . . . groups are won over to sports rather than forced into, or manipulated into, involvement in them. (Hargreaves, 1986, p. 7)

Hargreaves' prime concern is to show how the development of popular sports has been a site of struggle between groups in society, the outcome of which has helped achieve and maintain a bourgeois hegemony in British society. He argues that sport was a key site in the fragmentation of the working class (and other subordinate groups), and their reconstitution under a bourgeois hegemony (Hargreaves, 1986, p. 209). He is keen to point out that this was not achieved by one all-powerful agency, but rather by a sometimes contradictory political process.

Interestingly, Hargreaves devotes just one chapter to media sport, and it remains an underdeveloped part of his thesis. The centrality of hegemony in Hargreaves' work has been criticized as being too limiting, given the diverse and complex activities encompassed in sporting culture. However, this scepticism of the applicability of hegemony to a study of sports and sporting culture is not shared by many working from within the political sciences. Their primary concern has been to examine the relationship between sport and political culture and, while they may be criticized for their neglect of the role of the media in this relationship, their arguments provide an entry point into wider debates about the role of sport in the process of identity-formation.

Television and sport

As an academic field of enquiry and cumulative knowledge, the study and research into the relationships between television and sport is relatively new. Apart from the sporadic appearance of media or cultural studies of televised sport during the 1970s, the literature on the subject did not gain momentum until the 1980s and find a more systematic approach until the 1990s. Considering the amount of literature given over to other television genres (in particular news, current affairs and popular drama) or to other aspects of sporting configurations (specifically football hooliganism) it is surprising that academic research has taken so long to recognize one of the most pervasive aspects of our popular culture. Televised sport not only provides our main connection to sport itself, but also our ideas about nationality, class, race, gender, age and disability. It therefore presents a rich seam of material from which to investigate and understand our social, cultural, economic and political lives.

As Whannel (1992) has highlighted, the relative dearth of material on televised sport in the growing field of media studies was largely due to a schematic split in the academic analysis of television: first, textual or semiotic critiques that drew upon film theory; and second, socio–economic analysis that focused on production practices and the political organization of the media. The former approach is most recognizable in the British Film Institute (BFI) publication *Football on Television* edited by Buscombe (1975) that incorporated a series of textual readings on the televising of the 1974 World Cup. This exploratory work has proved very influential within subsequent research on televised sport, specifically related to the ideological components of sports broadcasts.

Analysis of the structural aspects of the sport–television nexus provide the alternate trajectory in the media study of sport which can be identified in the work of Rader (1984), Goldlust (1987), and Barnett (1990). These studies investigate the transformation of sport by television, in particular how such changes relate to the economic imperatives of television and sponsorship or the cultural policies of nation states in pursuit of public-service criteria.

Other major studies, most notably Wenner (ed., 1989), Whannel (1992) and Blain, *et al.* (1993), have variously attempted to bridge this analytical gap through a mixture of political economy, textual readings and aesthetic concerns. These studies have a clear connection to the interdisciplinary agenda of British Cultural Studies which had its roots in the Centre for Contemporary Cultural Studies at Birmingham University.

The issues of power have also been raised by feminist critiques of sport and the media that in Britain have been sustained by J. Hargreaves (1994) and in North America by Creedon (1994). Research on the issues of race and ethnicity in televised sport have largely gone under-researched, with a cultural study on the basketball megastar Michael Jordan by Dyson (1993) and Afro-American athletes by Hoberman (1997) notable exceptions.

From within the expansive sociological and cultural study of football, the investigation of televised football has only recently received attention. This is due to a preoccupation with fan violence as the theoretical concern of studying the sport. While certain discrepancies have been rectified in recent years in the work of Redhead (1991, 1997), Williams and Wagg (1991), Taylor (1992), Sugden and Tomlinson (1994) and King (1998), to name but a few, any in-depth research on the interrelationship between television and the sport before our own research has not been forthcoming. The only exceptions to this have been produced by the UK's leading football research group, the Sir Norman Chester Centre for Football Research at Leicester University. In particular, Williams (1994) has produced an excellent overview of the shifts in the television–football nexus during the early 1990s.

Non-academic work on televised sport has emerged among popular titles on football which have benefited from the explosion in sports literature kick-started by the football fanzine sub-culture (Haynes, 1995) and the success of the fan-autobiography of Nick Hornby (1992). In particular, Fynn and Guest (1994) uncover some of the inner workings of the football industry and how television is gaining control of the sports' future, and have since been followed by Conn (1997).

From within the world of television accounts of the codes, conventions and practices of televised sport are revealed in a numbe of biographies. The best of these are by Teddy Wakelam (1938) on early rugby union broadcasts by the BBC, Kenneth Wolstenholme (1958) on the programme *Sports Special*, Brian Johnston (ed., 1968) on cricket commentary, Sid Waddell (1979) on darts, Frank Bough (1980) on anchoring *Grandstand*, Dan Maskell (1988) on tennis, Christopher Martin-Jenkins (1990) on cricket and, from Scottish football, Archie MacPherson (1991). These all offer insightful material on the elements of production in broadcasting from sport, in particular the art of running commentary. Aspects of the production codes and practices of televised sport also appear within media studies of television that have looked at British broadcasting more generally.

Mediated sport and identity

The connection between sport and identity has also generated interesting work which, while not directly addressing the role of the media, alert us to the importance of taking a broad-based approach to media sport. The historical dimension of national sporting identities and their interplay with political culture is well demonstrated in the collection of essays *Tribal Identities*, edited by Mangan (1996). While the anthropological approach taken by MacClancy (1996) traces the close ties between ethnic collective identities and their expression and reinforcement through sporting forms.

The recent research by one of the authors (Boyle, 1995), which focused on the relationship between football and collective identities in the cities of Glasgow and Liverpool, also argued that media representations are often an important factor but not necessarily the most influential in individual and collective identity-formation. Thus a variety of factors such as schooling, family socialization, religion and traditional patterns of behaviour and belief are all central in the process of identity-formation among and within groups, as well as in the process of boundary-marking between groups. These aspects vary in their importance so that, for example, religion and religious labelling are important among supporters in Glasgow, but deemed to be virtually non-existent as a force in contemporary Liverpool.

Of central interest is the extent to which educational and religious patterns shape allegiances to various clubs in the cities which in turn become part of process of identity demarcation. To follow or support a particular club becomes a badge of identity which connects with other cultural markers of identity such as religion and nationality. In turn, support of clubs connect personal identity to collective identity, larger groups which enjoy a shared passion and sense of loyalty to a team or club, a city or even to a larger political or cultural entity such as Scotland, England or Ireland.

Thus what the research suggested was that, while the media may reproduce, amplify and even reconstitute parts of the identities associated with clubs, cities and supporters, many of these will already exist within and among members of that social group (in this instance supporters of specific clubs). This is not to suggest that people are simply acted upon by external forces, but while they of course make choices and decisions many of these in turn are influenced by the environment in which they have grown up. The fact that football support in Glasgow is broadly divided along particular religious lines in a way that it is not in Liverpool is not determined by the media, but rather a range of social and cultural factors.

The media are important, in the sense that they help to foster a wider feeling of collective identification among members in the social group, and may even put different members in touch with each other. This process can also be complex. Many Celtic fans have their sense of collective identity as supporters heightened by sharing the common assumption that their club is unfairly treated by sections of the media (Boyle, 1995). Thus any process of boundary-marking by the media may be both intentional or accidental and is continually subject to changes in the political and economic climate.

What we would argue is that the media can become one part of a complex relationship that helps link an individual to a larger collective grouping. At certain moments the media are important in legitimizing and giving a profile to groups of supporters, such as in the coverage of a successful Cup Final victory, or the aftermath of a tragedy such as Hillsborough. At other times and in specific social circumstances their importance may be less. We suggest that even in a book about media sport we must be alert to the wider pressures, often political, economic and cultural which frequently set the parameters in which media sport and its relationship with collective identities are being shaped. We will return to this below as we outline the structure of the book.

Finally, within this initial overview of literature concerned with sport it is worth noting the growing body of work on the globalization of televised sport, related to both the pan-global reach of mega-events like the World Cup and the localized effects within individual nations. Again the work of Blain *et al.* (1993) is significant, as is research from within figurational sociology by Maguire (1991, 1993 and 1994), from Australia by Rowe, Lawrence, Miller and McKay (1994) and the special edition of *Media, Culture and Society* on 'Sport, Globalization and the Media' edited by Rowe and Wood (1996). Globalization is also a growing theme in the study of football including Sugden and Tomlinson (eds., 1994; 1998), Giulianotti and Williams (eds., 1994) and Wagg (ed., 1995).

Mapping the field and the structure of the book

Any study of the increasingly symbiotic links between sport and the media should offer an entry point into wider debates and concerns which we feel are central in media studies. The study of media sport provides an arena in which students can investigate some of the wider issues concerned with media, power and ideology. In this book we are particularly interested in:

- the political economy of media sport
- the relationship between sport, media and identity-formations of gender, race and nation
- the consumption of sport and the role of audiences in the communication process.

To understand any of these political, economic and cultural processes involves placing both sporting and media institutions within a
larger frame of reference – a field of play which recognizes that sporting forms and mediated versions of these forms are continually being
shaped by and in turn shaping culture as a whole. While the media are
becoming increasingly powerful in driving the form and content of
modern sport and its relationship with its supporters they are not doing
this in isolation from wider economic or cultural shifts in society. In
other words, we argue that to examine the sport–media relationship we
need to encompass a broader range of vision beyond simply focusing on
the mediated discourses of sport circulated by the media.

Despite the usefulness of some aspects of postmodern theory in
examining mediated textual representations of sport, we suggest that a
more rooted concern with the economic, political and social structures
which remain central in determining our lives is also more likely to
increase our understanding of the role of media sport in contemporary
society.

Historical perspective

The early part of the book identifies the key role of a historical perspective on the relationship between various media and sport when attempting to understand the contemporary situation. Historian Martin Polley
(1998, p. 9) has argued that not only does a historical approach allow us
to understand the broader political and economic factors shaping sports
events in the past, but 'it can offer a sense of long- and short-term trends
that are not always visible to present-centred disciplinary approaches'.

Broadly speaking we argue that, while sporting and media institutions have evolved and developed individually with their own distinctive
traditions, practices and ideologies, there has always been some interface between these cultural forms. Initially the press, then newsreel and
radio and more recently television have not only used sport as media
content, but often helped to change and reconstruct the position of
sport within society. For example, we see newspapers helping to facilitate the commercial development of sports such as football in Britain
through sponsorship and media exposure, or radio amplifying sporting
contests such as gaelic games in Ireland during the 1920s into truly
national sporting events.

Thus Chapter 2 examines the origins of modern sport and mass
communications, focusing on the early sporting press and how the
relationships established between radio broadcasters and sporting
authorities in Britain during the early part of the century helped mark

out the relationship which would evolve between sport and television later in the century. It also highlights the extent to which tensions in the relationship between sport and various media are not new, and are characteristic of each new stage of technological development.

Political economy

In Chapter 3 we turn our attention to what we call the sporting triangle of media sport: the relationship between television, sponsorship and sport. For much of the later part of the century this interrelationship has constituted the key drivers which have shaped and continually re-shaped sport as a cultural and ideological form and as a commercial/ business entity. The media in their various forms have increasingly become the economic underwriter of modern sport. In many ways this has become more explicit in recent times.

Thus, when Australian cricketer Shane Warne became embroiled in a betting scandal in 1998, almost immediately the sportswear giant Nike, sponsor of Warne to the tune of £500,000 a year, made it known that it was seriously considering withdrawing its support of the player. It emerged in 1999 that the same company has considerable influence in the running of the Brazilian national football team, with which it has a lucrative sponsorship contract (see Chapter 3); while the Nationwide building society, newly acquired main sponsors of the England national football team, quickly made public their dismay (along with other groups) at comments made by the national coach Glenn Hoddle in a newspaper article, remarks which subsequently resulted in him leaving that post.

We argue it is impossible to understand fully the relationship between mediated sport and forms of representations which are discussed later in the book without a grasp of the underlying economic structures which have increasingly intertwined sporting and media forms and institutions both nationally and internationally.

One of the aspects that a historical analysis of media sport highlights is the extent to which the relationship between sporting and media forms is continually being driven by wider economic and cultural shifts in technology and broadcasting regulation. Thus, while Chapters 2 and 3 highlight the historical and economic developments in media sport, the final chapter focuses on sport in the new media age. It suggests that we are embarking on yet another stage of development in a relationship which seeks to reconcile the tensions between continuity (one of the media appeals of sport is its 'traditional' character and history) and change (both in media regulation and in new technological innovations).

Sport and media sport

In Chapter 4 we turn our attention to the key role that television in particular plays in transforming sporting forms into media events. There is an equal concern here with examining both why television needs sport, as well as how it constructs the mediated version of sporting contests. In other words, there is a recognition that, at times, sports coverage can provide both ideological and economic benefit to particular media systems.

Thus the ability of the BBC to call itself a national broadcaster is reinforced, or undermined, by its ability to deliver national sporting events to the country. This becomes increasingly problematic not simply because of commercial competition, but because broadcasting has to reflect the new political realities of a devolving UK state. Too often broadcasters, and indeed some academics studying media sport, have not been aware that, for people in Glasgow or Edinburgh, the Football Association is actually the *English* football association and 'national' sporting events may be understood or viewed differently by the Scottish, English, Welsh or Irish.

On the other hand, a commercial broadcaster such as BSkyB may view sport simply as a key 'media product' to be used to attract and sustain a subscription base among viewers. As we argue in Chapter 4, this does not of course mean that it will necessarily be ideologically neutral. In other words a broadcaster may mobilize established ideological discourses of Scottishness (passion, grit, determination) for commercial reasons in order to sell Scottish football to a predominately English audience (Boyle and Haynes, 1996).

Chapter 4 also focuses on the ways in which production codes and practices of television sport have become established, including areas such as modes of address – commentary, highlights and action replays. Central here is the way in which sport gets constructed by various media into narrative forms which not only make sense of particular sporting stories, but often reinforce and reconstruct wider values and attitudes in society.

This chapter also examines whether stylistic differences in the treatment of sport on television exist between terrestrial and satellite broadcasters. Both this and the following chapter build on the historical and economic analysis outlined in the earlier part of the book. Chapter 5 demonstrates the close ideological and business links between sport and the media in the promotion of sports stardom. We examine how transformations in the media–sport relationship have highlighted tensions between amateurism and professionalism.

Building on Chapter 3 we explore the key role that the sports agent plays in creating the sports star with both commercial and ideological spin-offs for the structure of sport and our understanding of its position in society. Case studies of the ground-breaking golfer Arnold Palmer and the more recent basketball and media phenomenon Michael Jordan are used to highlight some of these trends in celebrity star-making. They also remind us of the important role that media sports stars play in sustaining aspects of the mythical dimension of sport in society and creating both heroes and villains whose appeal extends beyond the confines of the sports field.

Media sport and representations of race, gender and nationality

As we noted above, we do not take a media-centred view of social development. However, it remains true that mediated discourses of sport play an important part – at times more crucial than others – in reproducing, naturalizing and even constructing values, attitudes and sometimes prejudices, which circulate in wider society. It is also important to recognize that often particular ideological formations of identity exist in and around sporting sub-cultures, for example the often masculine culture which surrounds sports such as football. Mediated versions of sport may choose to ignore or amplify certain aspects of this culture for a range of reasons. Thus any sectarian overtones surrounding a Celtic v Rangers football match may be played down by television coverage, keen to highlight 'the atmosphere' at a match, but less happy to examine some of the more unsavoury elements which exist in and around such matches.

This part of the book examines the ideological role that mediated coverage of sport plays in constructing and reproducing various discourses centred around race, gender and nationality. Chapter 6 looks at sport and social inequality; stereotypes and discourses of race in media sport; black and Asian athletes and media sport; and sectarianism and sport. The following chapter asks is media sport a male preserve? It examines stereotypes and discourses of gender in media sport and the extent to which female sports journalists and presenters are challenging professional ideologies of gender.

We would argue that often the intersection of media–sport representations and issues of identity are not clearly demarcated, so issues of gender, race and nationality often collide. Thus, when the black English boxer Frank Bruno enters a boxing arena to the strains of 'Land of Hope and Glory', we witness a range of ideological discourses being mobilized which connect with wider issues of race, gender and nationality. However, for the purposes of the book we examine them separately while aware of the complexity and interplay between them.

Chapter 8 focuses on media sport and the civic nation, looking at how international sports coverage often carries with it a broader political agenda. This can also operate at the national level, where sport and its attendant coverage often become a focal point for an expression of a range of collective identities. This process can call into question the complex relationship that exists between discourses which circulate in the media about sport and its collective power.

For example, when Ulster played the French club Colomiers in the final of rugby union's European Cup in Dublin in 1999, British media coverage of the match focused on the extent to which it was bringing together both communities in the province, and uniting both the north and the south of Ireland. While not disputing the excitement generated by the match, the complexities of ascribing too much power to sporting identities was neatly illustrated by the broadsheet newspaper *Scotland on Sunday* (31 January 1999). In its sports section it could proclaim ALL IRELAND REJOICES FOR ULSTER, while its news section told us that VIOLENCE HEIGHTENS TENSIONS IN ULSTER, as paramilitary violence continued to escalate, threatening the Peace Agreement.

This is not to suggest that, at certain moments in the political and cultural life of communities, sport does not offer an important forum for collective expression and identity. Rather, that caution is required in simply reading media representations (and interpretations) of events as accurate indicators of political and cultural realities. Put simply, we would argue that sometimes they are, and sometimes – often depending on who is telling or re-telling the story – they are not.

The burden of expectation placed on sport (often by the media) and the treatment events are given by media institutions is closely related to deeply rooted historical, political and economic factors (Blain and O'Donnell, 1998; Puijk, 1997). This approach remains alert to the range of influences (social, economic and political) which continually construct aspects of personal identities and in turn connect these to wider patterns of collective experience.

Media consumption: fans and audiences

We are not suggesting that the media simply deposit various ideas on an audience which in turn unproblematically absorbs them. Nor do we think that the various media institutions are simply constructing or creating various discourses. As we argue in the latter part of the book, these discourses are of course themselves influenced by wider social, economic and political pressures. For example, different versions of a country's national character may be used for differing political, economic or cultural reasons.

A UK national newspaper such as *The Guardian* (13 December 1998) will mobilize the importance of football in Italian life in its travel section to sell to its readers the glamour, designer style and excitement of combining football and shopping on a weekend visit to Milan; while a political story about the growth of right-wing extremism in Italy may note how football has become a recruitment ground for some of these groups. In other words, particular configurations of discourses drawing on sport and national character can often be used for differing reasons in differing media. This is not, however, a 'media-centred' view of society, where the media are the origins of all discourses that circulate within society at any given time. Rather we argue that they are part of a complex interrelationship between groups in a society who come to understand themselves in part through internal group dynamics, and in part by defining themselves against 'others'.

Chapter 9 examines the key production role that journalism and sports writing plays in both imposing narratives on sporting contests and developing the mythic aspects of sports' wider appeal. When England football coach Glenn Hoddle resigned from the post in 1999, it was partly as a result of comments made in an interview with *The Times* newspaper. The story made the front and back pages of most UK newspapers and the lead in television news broadcasts. If nothing else it testifies to the importance placed by the media, and a media-obsessed government, on a national (English) sporting figure such as Hoddle. Once again the complexities of broadcasting in the nationally differentiated UK state were brought to the fore when some Scottish viewers complained that BBC Scotland had interrupted its news programme to go live to a press conference announcing the resignation of the *English* football coach.

In Britain the recent explosion in sports writing appears concerned with documenting the private world of the British male, while in America, sports writing with a longer literary pedigree often appears more concerned with using sport as a way of defining and understanding aspects of American myth and identity.

The consumption of media sport through broadcasting and print media is discussed in the following chapter, particularly against the backdrop of changes in the ecology of media sports outlined earlier in the book.

Conclusion

Our final chapter on sport in the new media age both pulls together some of the issues raised, while also setting out some of the structural changes and implications of the latest stage in the evolution of the sports–media relationship. We would argue for a multi-disciplinary approach to the subject, one which recognizes the importance of the political economy of media sport as well as the ideological and political dimension to media coverage of sporting forms. By political in this context we mean the ways in which power is organized in society, and the ways in which formulations of power are both maintained and often challenged by groups and individuals.

To shed some light and understanding on how the media function within the wider political, economic and cultural contours of society appears to us to be one of the tasks required of media studies. Drawing freely from the social sciences we hope this examination of the complex relationship between the media and sport will go some way to increasing our understanding of how two of the great forces of the twentieth century – sport and the media – have become intertwined in a global business relationship, which brings both pain and pleasure to many and increasingly generates profit for a select few.

CHAPTER 2

All Our Yesterdays

A History of Media Sport

Sport . . . is probably the biggest thing in the land.
It occupies the thoughts, and empties the pockets,
of countless millions.

Trevor Wignall, sports journalist, *Daily Express,* 1936

A glance at the world showed that when the common
people were not at work, one thing they wanted was
organised sports and games.

C.L.R. James (1983), *Beyond A Boundary* (originally published in 1963), p. 153

Introduction

Mediated versions of sport are one of the key areas of culture which give
us a sense of a lived history. One of the particular appeals of sport, for
both the media and supporters, is the extent to which the narratives or
stories which surround sport act as a bridge between the present and
the past. Sporting events need to have a history and a longevity to feel
important. In Australia, international cricket is dominated by the Ashes
series with England, a competition given extra impetus by the long
rivalry between these two countries. As we argue in Chapter 4, television
increasingly helps to create – and at times even invent – this historical
dimension for more recent sporting events. However, it is important
that we have some historical perspective on the institutional relationship that has evolved between the media and sport, particularly as it is
the former that has told the history of sport for much of the twentieth
century.

   This chapter aims to highlight some of the major transformations
in the historical relationship between sport and the media: from the
emergence of a popular press to the beginnings of an international

Broadcasting History – The twinning of royalty and sport has always been a feature of the BBC's outside broadcasts, as with the televising of the 1948 Olympic Games from Wembley Stadium, London.   © *Hulton Getty*

sports–media nexus. We shall explore this relationship by investigating various media in turn: the press; cinema and newsreels; radio; and finally television. However, it is important to stress that each new mode of communication did not develop in isolation from the other.

It is unquestionable that mass communications have transformed sport from what Holt (1989, p. 12) refers to as an 'orally transmitted popular culture' to a mass culture with mass spectatorship. However, oral traditions continue to pervade through sport and the interplay between sport as popular culture and various media forms is historically complex. There is no simple linear transformation of sport by modern communication systems and technologies. Neither, of course, is this a one-way street – sport has also played its part in the transformation of media industries. Therefore, there is much to be learnt from the historical relationship between sport and the media.

Down the years how the media have affected the way in which sport is played, spectated and organized, and the importance of sport in the social and economic history of media industries, offers an insight into the current transformations and tensions that arise in the sport–media nexus which are examined later in the book.

Origins of sport and the media: the sporting press

Media sport is a product of modernity, that phase of western civilization which transformed European societies, 'resulting from the explosive interaction between capitalism, technology and human linguistic diversity' (Anderson, 1991, p. 45). It is no coincidence that the institutions through which 'print-capitalism' was diffused in the late seventeenth and early eighteenth centuries, namely the church, the armed forces, the public schools and the universities (Mann, 1992), are the very same media through which modern sporting practices emerged in the late eighteenth to mid-nineteenth centuries (Holt, 1989).

It is during this latter period that folk games, played under the patronage of the aristocracy, started to be transformed and codified, swept up by the spread of industrial capitalism and urbanization in an era of unprecedented change (Hargreaves, 1986). In Britain these processes set in motion the morphology of the modern nation and gradually led to the ascendancy of a powerful middle class which appropriated many aspects of popular sporting custom. Previously, sport had developed as an integral part of localized ritual amusements quite often associated with religious festivals.

Early industrial society, motivated by the tenets of modernism, led to the rational belief that sport represented 'progress' and 'moral improvement' (Real, 1998, p. 17). However, as Holt has argued, the Victorian transformation of sport, particularly in the public schools, does not suggest that modern sport's antecedents were either crude or met with a rapid decline (Holt, 1989, pp. 12–14). Commonly known rules and the dissemination of results or victories were well established in some areas by the late eighteenth century and, as we shall see, a fledgling sporting press had begun to emerge during this period.

Sports print media

Contrary to popular belief, sport has a rich literature which stretches back into the eighteenth century. One of the earliest chroniclers of traditional sporting pastimes was J. Strutt, whose publication *The Sports and Pastimes of the People of England* was published in 1801. From bear-baiting to knur-and-spell* Strutt recorded for posterity a vivid picture of the English at play. Where Strutt documented some of the more esoteric

---

* A game played in the north of England where the object was to hit a ball as far as possible.

and brutal aspects of pre-industrial popular recreations, other writers turned their attention to emerging codified sports.

As early as the 1720s and 1730s the first accounts of village cricket were captured in heroic verse. These romantic visions of pastoral England were written in Latin and provide a pre-Georgian impression of one of the oldest team games. Later, in the early 1800s, reports of village cricket were serialized in *The Lady's Magazine* by the sketch artist Mary Russell Mitford. Her prose was critical of a growing professionalism in the sport which she viewed as the antithesis of the gentlemanly art. In one issue she is noted as saying: 'Everything is spoilt when money puts its ugly nose in' (cited in Martineau, 1957, p. 98) – a romantic sentiment that is wholly recognizable and an early indicator of the ideology of amateurism.

Sport was very marginal to the news agenda of the respectable press of the late eighteenth century and the early nineteenth century. The cost of producing daily or weekly newsprint, due to restrictive pressures of censorship and stamp duty ('taxes on knowledge') meant that sport could not compete for space in a copy-scarce environment. Even the cheap journalism of the radical press, which by the 1830s challenged the hegemonic control of ownership and licence enjoyed by the respectable press, as well as appealing to a predominantly working-class audience, could not find room for urban recreations. Instead, a wholly separate sporting press emerged to cater for genteel interests in horse-racing, prize-fighting and blood-sports.

One aspect of the sporting press was to communicate and help legislate the organization of sport. For example, horse-racing had long enjoyed the patronage of the aristocracy, and in 1751 a group of socially élite owners joined to form the Jockey Club which remains the administrator of the sport. The Jockey Club's rules of racing were published in its own official organ, the *Racing Calendar* (Vamplew, 1988, p. 47). The publication allowed both the policing and capitalization of the racing programme. Any races not advertised in the *Racing Calendar* were not recognized by the ruling body, enabling a strict control of the sport's administration. It can be seen, from this example, that the dispersion of rules was crucial to the reform of traditional sporting forms from pre-industrial popular culture and reflected the broader shifts in the economic and the political spheres of early industrial capitalism.

Gambling and advertising

The growth of popular gambling was a second, and more economic focus, for the growth of a sporting press. Sports-minded gentry required a forum from which to wager their bets, and the press became 'full of little calls to combat' (Clapson, 1992, p. 16). Daily newspapers like *Bell's Life in London* (orig. 1822) were stakeholders for the aristocratic 'fancy' on prize-fighting and were full of news and gossip about 'the ring'. By the mid-nineteenth century *Bell's Life* enjoyed a circulation of more than 30,000 (Mason, 1988, p. 46), although censure and regulation of illicit betting began to gain ground, spurred on by the liberal press and evangelical campaigns of the National Anti-Gambling League.

However, the use of the telegraph from the 1860s reinvigorated off-course betting on horse-racing, enabling sporting newspapers to develop a national average from the transmission of racing odds and results from the 'Tattersall's Rings' (exclusive betting enclosures at race-courses) and deliver to an expectant working-class betting market.

As Clapson (1992, p. 28) has illustrated, from the 1870s the sporting press expanded in its range and tenor. In Britain, Manchester became the provincial capital of the sporting press, dominated by the publisher Edward Hulton. During this period Hulton published two major daily sports newspapers, *Sporting Life* (orig. 1859, replacing *Bell's Life*) and the *Sporting Chronicle* (orig. 1871). For those opposed to gambling such papers represented the 'cheap and the sensational' and, by popularizing gambling and the commercial dimension of sport, had irreparably damaged the spirit of sport.

If gambling had opened up the commercial potential for a sporting press from the early 1800s to the 1870s, it was the sporting evangelists who forged another wave of sporting publications designed for the burgeoning recreations of the English middle class. Lowerson (1993) has traced the rise of some of these specialist sporting publications during a wave of middle-class enthusiasm for sport from 1870 to 1914. The view of sport as 'improving', providing spiritual as well as bodily virtue, was central to this movement. The growing popular press provided an essential vehicle for disseminating the evangelical zeal of a section of the middle class who promoted the therapeutic value of sport.

Through the patronage of the sporting press both traditional and modern sport enjoyed an unprecedented promotional boom. Economically driven by advertisements the sporting press developed a more graphic layout afforded by cheaper block printing. Hunting, which had long received the patronage of the socially grand *Field* magazine, was joined by the more commercial *Shooting Times* (orig. 1882) and *Horse and Hound* (orig. 1884), which were heavily laden with advertising for manufacturers of tack and firearms among other essential hunting and shooting equipment. *The Field* had also transformed itself to incorporate

ball games, specifically the summer pastimes of lawn tennis and croquet. Here was an instance where the sporting press moved directly into
the business and administration of sport – the proprietors of *The Field*
offered a silver trophy to inaugurate the Wimbledon Championships
held by the All England Croquet Club in 1868 (Lowerson, 1993, p. 253).

For those in positions of power in sports administration the rapidly
expanding sporting press was a means to communicate the social and
cultural parameters of sport. For example, the weekly *Athletic News*
(orig. 1875), another of Hulton's publications from Manchester, disseminated the unofficial, but authoritative, 'voice of football'. The paper
was closely allied to the northern-based Football League and enjoyed
an impressive circulation in excess of 180,000 at its prime (Mason,
1988, p. 48). Edited by J.J. Bentley from 1892 to 1900, who would go
on to be President of the Football League, the *Athletic News* took a
strong view on any moral transgression of football's codes and etiquette.
This was particularly true where gambling by players and officials was
concerned and the paper eschewed any 'tipsters' or horse-racing results
from its pages.

The Edwardian era saw pressure on daily newspapers to increase
their sporting coverage. The newspaper industry had seen a rapid accel-
eration of newspaper chains, with press barons such as Northcliffe and
Beaverbrook shaping the content and layout of their papers. Economic
pressures to boost circulation to satisfy the demands of advertisers led
to a more universal outlook on content, and sport fitted into a broader
magazine miscellany.

The sporting press had proved very successful in tapping into the
nation's captivation with sport. The establishment of regular fixture lists
and seasonal events within many spectator sports provided a steady
flow of stories and results for the sporting press to report. Tipping
sheets and football coupon papers had emerged in the 1880s, albeit on
an ephemeral basis. However, by 1900 local newspapers were beginning to employ their own specialist 'tipsters' and conduct variants of
what became the football pools, whose lead was soon to be followed by
the national press, including the *Daily Mail*, the *Daily Mirror* and the
Daily Express, as well as the Sunday editions.

As we have already mentioned, newspapers began to sponsor sporting occasions for the promotional effect association with new professional sporting heroes might bring. For example, the *News of the
World* sponsored the first Professional Golfers Association (PGA)
matchplay championships with £200 in prize money after professional
golfers had threatened a strike over inadequate payments (Lowerson,

1989, pp. 203–4). As the PGA tournament grew in the 1920s and 1930s the championship began a long association with the *Daily Mail* in 1936. The growth of sports coverage in the national popular press spelt the death-knell for many of the independent daily and weekly sporting papers that by the 1930s had dwindled to just a handful of publications predominantly catering for horse-racing.

Europe's sporting press

The demise of a specific sporting press in Britain contrasted with the growing strength of daily sport newspapers in continental Europe. The *Gazzetta dello Sport* in Italy was launched on the eve of the first Olympic Games held in Athens in 1896. The paper was born of a merger between two newspapers *La Tripletta* and *Il Ciclista* that had supported an early Italian passion for cycling.

As with its British counterparts, the *Gazzetta* began to sponsor sporting events, the inauguration of the cycling race, Giro Ciclistico, fostering closer ties between sport and the press. Today the *Gazzetta* enjoys an unprecedented position in the Italian press having embedded itself in the daily culture of Italian newspaper readers and it has gained in recognition abroad with the spread of interest in Italian football which has been facilitated by increased television coverage.

Cycling and motorsport also played a key role in the establishment of a French daily sports paper *L'Auto-Velo*, later to become *L'Équipe*. Established in 1900 by Henri Desgrange, founder of the Tour de France, *L'Auto* changed its name to *L'Équipe* on the Liberation of occupied France and was integral to the re-establishment of the Tour in 1946 as well as instigating new European competitions in football, basketball and athletics. *Gazzetta*, *L'Équipe* and the Spanish sports newspaper *El Mundo Deportivo* (founded in 1906) have been the guardians of the meaning of sport in their respective national cultures, developing distinctive forms of sports journalism from that developed in Britain (see Chapter 9).

The sports journalist

Sports writers themselves were emerging as a specialist breed of journalist. Cricket had long enjoyed a level of serious writing about the game. The Cricket Reporting Agency had been established in the mid-nineteenth century as had several statistical compendiums on cricket, the most famous being John Wisden's *Cricketers' Almanac*, first published in 1864. *Wisden*, characterized by its 'yellow half-brick' appearance became an essential read for cricket enthusiasts and was the most visible example of a growing interest in sporting minutiae.

More elaborate prose on cricket emerged in the 1920s and 1930s through the writing of Neville Cardus of the *Manchester Guardian*. Formerly a music critic, Cardus had turned to cricket after suffering a breakdown and recuperating at Old Trafford, home of Lancashire County Cricket Club. Cardus used his self-taught musicology to express the rhythms of the game and the performance of the men who played it. A more detailed examination of the sports journalist's craft is made in Chapter 9; however, in this historical context, it is important to note the break from the rather cursory and formulaic tradition of sports writing that emerged during this period.

The 1921 Ashes tour by Australia caused an outpouring of new journalism on cricket and prompted several national newspapers, including *The Observer*, to take its coverage of the sport more seriously. However, this brand of journalism did not have a wide appeal. Less highbrow newspapers, such as the *Daily Mirror*, turned to a brasher mode of address in the coverage of sport in a clear attempt to attract a young working-class readership. Sport was entertainment that was kept separate from 'hard news'. As Trevor Wignall – quoted at the top of the chapter – a sports journalist from the *Daily Express*, reflected in 1936:

> Football had a place of its own in newspapers, and even Test cricket was regarded as something that should not be mixed with politics or a readable murder. Sport, as this is composed, is probably the biggest thing in the land. It occupies the thoughts, and empties the pockets, of countless millions. (Wignall, 1936, p. 6)

As with today, the coverage of sport from the turn of the twentieth century was highly selective. Heavily dominated by men's sporting achievement, often associating the manliness or courageousness of a performance with a fervent patriotism, sports coverage was schematically divided into 'naturalized' seasons of sport: football, rugby and steeplechase horse-racing in winter, and cricket, tennis, golf, athletics and flat horse-racing in summer. In this way, the press socialized their readers into the place of sport in society, setting parameters for the communication and significance of sport.

The press rarely questioned the politics of sport, and only where scandal and corruption arose did it remind its readers of the sanctity of sport founded on the amateurist values of its administrative leaders (Inglis, 1987). Until the press was faced with the competition and immediacy of broadcasting, newspapers could rely on a voracious appetite for sports news and results, from a largely male audience.

Sport on newsreel

It is interesting and significant that the period in which sport gained mass popularity as a form of entertainment coincides with the invention, innovation and commercial exploitation of the moving image. Although sport can engage all the senses it is perhaps the sight of the élite sports performance that most catches the imagination and stirs the emotions. It is fair to say that film has rarely contributed to the wider popularity of sport. Rather, sport has been used by film as a device for exploring human emotion and form, with all its sense of achievement, failure, courage, athleticism, ritual and occasion. However, in return, film has captured and reproduced the often mesmeric and heroic moments of sport, as well as the corporeal aspects of people at play.

Film and sport

In the 1890s the Lumière brothers, Thomas Edison, Robert Paul and others had begun to show actualities or 'topicals' as a way of exhibiting their versions of a mechanical eye that would capture a moving image. Exhibiting short sequences in travelling fairs and music halls the pioneers of film engineering were more interested in the intellectual challenge of manufacturing equipment than the images they created. However, some films did focus on specific subjects and sporting events featured prominently in the productions of this band of inventors and scientists.

An early illustration of this practice was Robert Paul's film of the 1896 Derby from Epsom Downs where his camera, located twenty yards behind the finishing-post captured the winning horse owned by Edward, Prince of Wales named Persimmon, later to be screened at the Alhambra Theatre, London (Fielding, 1972, p. 18). Other sporting events were staged deliberately for the camera, for example Thomas Edison captured a boxing match featuring Billy Edwards in his New York studio in 1895, later to be exhibited in peep shows. Boxing, moreover, became a staple of these early films.

On one occasion in 1899 both the Edison and Biograph companies produced films on a prize-fight between Jeffries and Sharkey that was later re-created in a more successful 'fake' film produced by Sigmund Lubin for the Vitagraph company that used two impersonators instead of the actual pugilists (Fielding, 1972, p. 16). The exercise of 'faking' actual events for film indicated the intense rivalry that grew among the competing companies as each sought to promote their own technological achievements. The subject matter appeared to take second place behind the technology, 'intended simply as short-lived novelties, designed to demonstrate the convincing qualities of their projectors and cameras' (Puttnam, 1997, p. 27).

Newsreel began in earnest in Paris when Charles Pathé started the *Pathé Journal* in 1908. Newsreel gave order to the 'topicals' that had previously entertained the patrons of travelling fairs and sideshows. Pathé had understood that the renting of film was the most economical method of reaching wider audiences than hitherto possible. The rise of newsreel coincided with the process of industrialization of film production. The expansionist building programme to house film exhibition led to the construction of cinemas across Europe.

Newsreels helped to fill cinema programmes, and were commercially circulated. The French companies Pathé and Gaumont dominated the market and built up economies of scale through extensive distribution networks. With locally fixed audiences the demand for film content rapidly increased. The same film could be screened in several countries at once, with amendments to captions to suit the localized needs of different language communities. The system of weekly releases went a long way to satisfy the hunger for film entertainment from mushrooming cinema audiences.

Sporting entertainment and 'exclusives'

Although the First World War had produced a fillip to the craft of newsreel production, in terms of camera operation, direction and editing, the market demand for entertainment drove its expansion during the 1920s. Traditional values of objective journalism were forgone for the principles of storyline and dramatic effect. Sport matched the industrial need for entertainment, providing ready-made spectacles for the newsreel companies to capture and release to mass audiences.

During the 1920s, photo-journalism of sporting events was underdeveloped and technically poor. Moving images of sport filled this niche with an array of popular sporting events. Boxing, football, cricket and horse-racing were staple favourites, and reels on large sporting occasions, like the Henley Regatta or yachting from Cowes, provided the mass audience with a window on culturally exclusive worlds of sport that were demarcated by class and social distinction.

As power in the film industry shifted to Hollywood during the interwar period, American companies expanded their operations in Europe with the introduction of sound in 1929. British Movietone News, owned by Twentieth Century Fox, headed this audio-visual revolution in newsreel, famously interviewing the Prime Minister, Ramsay MacDonald

(Aldgate, 1979, p. 22). The entry of American corporations promoted vociferous competition among newsreel producers and distributors. Sport was at the centre of these rivalries that reached their height during the 1930s.

The intense rivalry between newsreel companies led to an escalation of 'exclusives', where film of individual events were secured through payment to the various governing bodies of sport. Gaumont paid up to £2000 for the rights to the Grand National alone (Aldgate, 1979, p. 24) and other events such as the Cup Final, by the 1930s well established at Wembley Stadium, warranted similar fees.

Reflecting on the 'golden age' of newsreel, cameraman Ronnie Noble recalled the practice of 'pinching' in the highly competitive environment for film footage from sport. The war for coverage led to all manner of pirate activities in order to 'get one over' the opposition. Scaffolds were erected around perimeter fencing, cameras were smuggled into stadiums by a variety of cunning strategies and aeroplanes were deployed to capture remote footage with long-focus lenses. 'Pinching' was an essential quality for the newsreel cameraman and was deliberately used to spoil the value of rival newsreel companies:

> A really first-class pinch is one that remains undetected until the story hits the screen. The satisfaction is not only in getting pictures of the event, but in putting the story on the screen simultaneously with the 'rightful' company's claim of EXCLUSIVE PICTURES. (Noble, 1955, p. 100)

Pirating certainly enlivened the working day of those cameramen who travelled the length and breadth of the country to deliver the best pictures for cinema audiences. However, because sports rights cost newsreel companies dear for film they could not guarantee was exclusive, there was a pressure to pool resources and access to events. The main reason for this tendency was the sense that sporting authorities were overtly capitalizing on the newsreel war, causing much grievance and resentment.

The filming of Test Match cricket, for instance, proved notoriously difficult to police. Test grounds were not only large, with many possibilities for smuggling cameras through the gates, but also were surrounded by buildings that overlooked the arena offering numerous vantage points for clear, uninterrupted and legally secure coverage. Attempts to prevent such 'pinching' led to extreme measures of balloon barriers and spotlights to blind cameramen. Unfortunately, the projectionist's moves also interfered with the crowd's enjoyment of the game and even distracted the players themselves.

Newsreels continued to cover sport into the 1960s; however, with the decline and fragmentation of the cinema-going audience, due, in the main, to the rising popularity and ubiquity of television, the newsreel lost its resonance and ability to tell truly the whole story of events. Radio commentaries had given instantaneous reception from sport, and television then added the moving image in people's homes, with the comfort and ease of turning the switch. Nevertheless, newsreels stand as a significant historical document on sport from the turn of the twentieth century to the immediate post-war years. They capture the wider feel of the event itself, with as many shots of the crowd as the play on the field and, for this alone, are valuable anthropological texts.

Sport on radio

> Britain was still frayed and shaken by a war it had won, and ration books still mattered more than any written by Shakespeare, but sport helped provide the promise of a better tomorrow in one heady and irresistible package.
>
> **Bryon Butler (1997), radio sports commentator, p. 18**

The immediacy of radio

The introduction of radio in 1922 posed an immediate threat to the dissemination of news by the local and national press. Radio enjoyed the power of immediacy and the ability to go out and about to deliver on-site accounts from sport. Even the most efficient of the Saturday specials run by many local newspapers were pushed to turn the day's news around and distribute their publications to their agents before 7pm in the evening. Radio news, therefore, posed a real threat to the livelihood of many journalists, printers and salesmen and women who relayed the afternoon events to the hundreds of thousands of eager readers waiting to gain information on the day's results, whether it be in football, rugby union, rugby league, cricket or horse-racing.

One of the most vociferous opponents of radio was Lord Riddell, who represented the Newspaper Proprietors' Association (NPA) before the Sykes Committee of 1923 that had looked at the regulation of radio in the UK. It was believed that a results service and running commentaries from sport would seriously damage the sale of newspapers and between 1922 and 1926, before the BBC became a Corporation by Royal Charter, the results service from sport was restricted to bulletins after seven o'clock (Briggs, 1961, p. 172; Whannel, 1992, pp. 13–14).

BBC radio sport

On becoming a Corporation in 1926, the BBC was given the freedom by the Postmaster-General to provide outside broadcasts (OBs) from sport. The BBC soon developed a sequence of firsts from sport in a portfolio of programming that included a results service, eye-witness accounts, running commentaries and talks. The results service fed the appetite not only of the sports enthusiast but also the rapidly growing number of households that completed a pools coupon in the hope of getting rich quick.

This posed some ethical problems for the BBC whose conservative moral tone was compromised by indirectly supporting the rapid rise of mass gambling through the pools during the inter-war period. Eye-witness accounts and running commentaries offered the sports fan a new engagement with sport. The immediacy of radio outside broadcasts provided the sports fan with an unparalleled access to sport. Central to the ideology of programming from sport was the rhetoric of public-service broadcasting championed by the BBC's first Director General, Lord Reith. Enshrined in this concept was a belief in the power of broadcasting to enlighten its audience culturally, informing them of important political events, as well as providing entertainment during the 'lighter' moments of programming.

Sports programming clearly fitted into the latter definition of the BBC's cultural mission under Reith's direction. Sport provided a way of broadening the BBC's appeal to a wider audience, reminiscent of the way in which it is used to introduce new communicative platforms like pay and digital television at the dawn of the twenty-first century. In response to criticism of the place of sport in the serious agenda of broadcasting the growing constituency of BBC listeners soon began to make their voice heard, as this reply to a letter of criticism to the *Radio Times* from 1930 makes clear:

> Sport is not a plague to be avoided, and one must be very bigoted to switch off whenever it is mentioned. Even an 'Indiscriminate Listener' should understand that the average healthy-minded man be as keenly interested in the latest cricket score as in (say) a revolution in Mexico. Something must come first, and whether news or sport matters little to the ordinary listener – I enjoy both. Your correspondent should learn to be tolerant; after all, narrow-mindedness has done more harm to the old country than sport. (J.W. Coxon, letter to the *Radio Times*, 20 June 1930)

BBC radio and sports rights

By the early 1930s the BBC soon had a portfolio of sporting events placed in a broadcasting calendar that resonated with the winter and summer seasons of sport (Scannell and Cardiff, 1991).

Now well-established events, the Scottish and English Cup Finals, Test Cricket, the Boat Race, the Grand National, the Derby, the Five Nations rugby union internationals, Wimbledon and the Open Golf Championship, were the portals to a shared national culture, and radio gave them a wider audience and significance. However, the arrangement to broadcast some events was reliant on the good will of the various governing bodies of sport concerned.

The BBC had taken the Corinthian principle that business and sport did not mix and that, because it was promoting such events to a national audience, it had a right to broadcast without payment. The BBC's principled defiance hid a wider agenda to gain dominance in the coverage of sport, feeling that, because the press did not have to pay for access into sports arenas, neither should they (Haynes, 1999). The sports' authorities were not of the same opinion, and believed the BBC's attempt to gain universality of reception and access to sport was proving a threat to their own status as providers of entertainment. In particular, the authorities and the NPA were afraid of the possible effects public broadcast of running commentaries would have on attendance at sporting events and the circulation of newspapers.

The intransigence of some sporting bodies to adhere to the public-service rhetoric of the BBC included the English Football Association which prohibited access to the 1929 Cup Final between Bolton Wanderers and Portsmouth. Here, the BBC resorted to a series of eye-witness accounts by a number of reporters who had paid for entry into Wembley and then rushed to a flat in Chelsea where they delivered a summary of events (Haynes, 1999).

A further ban by the FA in 1930 brought matters to a head and the BBC conceded to pay a facility fee of £1000 for entry into the stadium. However, the director of OB's Gerald Cock was far from satisfied with the FA's conflation of sport and business:

> [It] is a dismal prospect when the governing body of a sport originated, built up, and entirely supported by amateurs, should be captured by professionals whose whole interest apparently is commercial.
> (*Radio Times*, 28 March 1930)

Cock's view hints at the socio–cultural background of BBC personnel, many of whom held Oxford or Cambridge 'blues' and carried the sporting ethics founded in the amateurist origins of organized sport during the nineteenth century.

The sporting rivalries of the two universities figured highly in the early OBs from sport, not only the annual 'Boat Race', but also the Varsity rugby union match from Twickenham, athletic events with American universities Princeton and Cornell in 1931, and football from Highbury.

Producing sport on radio

When radio outside broadcasts from Britain's sporting arenas began in 1927 the technical and logistical problems greatly outweighed any concern with the structure and quality of the programmes. The early years of the BBC's promotional arm the *Radio Times*, and its annual review of the year the *BBC Handbook*, are full of references to the technical difficulties of broadcasting from sport. Experiments with OBs brought some humorous results as the following recollection of a pioneering broadcast from the Derby suggests:

> In the now distant days of 1926, while a contract with the newspapers
> precluded the broadcasting of one word of descriptive matter of events
> as they were taking place, attempts were made to broadcast some
> Derby 'atmosphere' from Tattenham Corner . . . Listeners will
> remember that terrible Derby. From early in the morning to late
> afternoon the rain came down in torrents, and during the Race, not
> only were there no sounds from the hoofs in the soft going, but even
> the bookies, tipsters and onlookers were more occupied in taking
> shelter under their umbrellas than in speeding home the winner.
> (*BBC Handbook*, 1928, pp. 143–4)

Similar experiments were made at speedway tracks, where all that could be heard was the roar of the bikes as they neared the microphone. It became clear that in order to convey the sporting scene a new form of narrative speech needed to be introduced.

Radio sports commentary

Running commentaries from sport became the mainstay of BBC Radio's sports production. Before the innovation of the lip-microphone, that isolated and shielded the commentator's voice from the surrounding roar of the crowd, running commentaries were conducted from small huts erected near the pitch, racecourse or track. The commentators themselves invariably came from an 'Oxbridge' background, were ex-sportsmen themselves, and were employed through a network of friends and acquaintances, largely developed at University or in the Armed Forces.

Commentary was a craft that had to be learned. A mellifluous delivery of words was a central feature of good commentary, the guidelines for which were set by the BBC's second director of OBs Seymour Joly de Lotbiniere. De Lotbiniere set the parameters of good practice, and devised a way of sound-testing potential commentators, as well as keeping a rigorous check on the quality of broadcasts with a regular meeting of his staff following the weekend's sport where his critiques began with the ominous phrase: 'Programmes since we last met'.

Running commentaries from sport produced some of the most popular household names on British radio. From the inter-war years names such as George Allison (football), Captain Teddy Wakelam (rugby union and cricket), Graham Walker (motorsport – and father of Murray Walker), Wynford Vaughan-Thomas (rugby union) and Howard Marshall ('The Voice' of cricket) educated and entertained a rapidly growing audience. In the late 1940s, John Arlott (cricket), Max Robertson (tennis), Raymond Glendenning (football, horse-racing and athletics) and G.V. Wynne-Jones (boxing), fresh from their experience of war, provided a new vigour and artistry to sports commentary, more professional in the rudiments of broadcasting than the previous generation of practitioners.

The BBC also introduced new sports programming in the post-war era, most notably, *Sports Report* in 1948. Produced by the Scot, Angus Mackay, *Sports Report* was the flagship results service of the BBC's Light Programme, which 'brought in reports from no fewer than 15 towns up and down the country within the space of 30 minutes' (Mackay, 1997, p. 13).

With television not yet established, the programme introduced new stars of broadcasting and sport, in particular the Irish presenter and commentator Eamonn Andrews, and attracted more than 12 million listeners in the 1940s and 1950s (Butler, 1997, p. 18). The programme flitted across the country, and in some cases across the world, to on-the-spot reporters who had been given chapter-and-verse by Mackay to keep their summaries concise and articulate. The demands of producing a programme so quickly after the event are captured in the following words from Mackay himself:

> *Sports Report* goes out so soon after the end of the day's sport that, far from having a complete rehearsal, we are usually working from hand to mouth while it is being broadcast. (Angus Mackay, Producer, 1997, p. 13)

The other outstanding element of the BBC's sports programming became *Test Match Special*. In the formative years of sports commentaries, cricket was not considered to be a viable option for extensive coverage, not only because it took up a lot of airtime, but because it was thought the listener would get bored with a ball-by-ball account. Therefore, cricket was largely restricted to eye-witness accounts from Tests until regular commentaries began on *Test Match Special* in 1957 with England's series against the West Indies (see Johnston, ed., 1968 and Martin-Jenkins, 1990 for comprehensive historical accounts of cricket on radio and television).

The key to cricket commentaries was the wider picture magically and majestically captured by the likes of John Arlott, Rex Alston and, latterly, Brian Johnston during a lull in play. As producer Robert Hudson argued in 1968:

> It is in the filling of these pauses in play that the commentator really reveals his quality; his timing must be as precise as the batsman's in the middle – so that he rounds off the point he is making just as the bowler wheels round to bowl the next ball. (Hudson, 1968, p. 35)

By the time television sports programming began in earnest during the 1950s radio had already set the codes and practices of OBs from sport and, most importantly, the standards the audience had come to expect from the BBC's sports service.

Origins of televising sport

Of all the media discussed in this chapter, and indeed this book, television has shaped our contemporary view of sport more than any other. The history of sport that television often presents to us is, in fact, a history of televising sport. All the 'golden moments' of sport are worked and reworked by television to re-present the 'world of sport' in new ways and combinations.

However, as we have already reviewed, modern sport had existed long before television entered our homes and communities. To understand this state of affairs fully we need to analyse critically the origins of this relationship, to ask how and why this relationship began, and to decipher what this history means in an omnipresent world of televised sport.

Continuities of radio and televised sport

The history of televising sport in the UK is intimately related to the history of radio outside broadcasts from sport. Technically, many of the people involved in BBC radio were also the pioneers in television sport. The first Director of Television at the BBC was Gerald Cock, previously head of Outside Broadcasts in radio. Such ties meant that sport became a key instrument in the promotion of television as a new form of entertainment.

Institutionally, the connections between BBC producers and the administrators of sport were also of value. The new-found engagement between broadcaster and sports administrator allowed a honeymoon period for television sport to develop on an experimental basis. As with radio, a major fear had been the possible effect television broadcasts would have on actual attendance at sports events. This remained an issue that would never go away, and would ultimately cost television dear.

As this suggests, the relationship between sport and television has not always been sanguine and throughout their historical association the struggles over the representation of sport through the lens of the camera and the microphone, who this mediation is for, and when or how it is delivered, have often proved volatile. The main causes of these disruptions and altercations have been a set of conflicting agendas that reflect the historical infrastructures of sport and the unique political economy of British broadcasting formed by an uneasy marriage between public-service broadcasting and publicly regulated commercial (otherwise labelled 'independent') television.

Any history of televised sport should, therefore, consider the political economy of this 'match made in heaven' (Goldlust, 1987, p. 78) as well as those technical innovations that have helped to transform the way in which sport is delivered to our homes.

BBC television sport

When the BBC Television service began broadcasting in November 1936 there was a great scepticism about what the medium could achieve. Certainly, with regard to sport, there was no sense that sport would be dominated by this new form of entertainment. BBC radio was still consolidating its position in the British living room, and television was nothing short of a frivolous gimmick. For Gerald Cock, sport and outside broadcasts in general offered the most effective way of attracting an audience for what was a considerable unknown entity.

In order to promote the new medium the *Radio Times* introduced a new column under the pseudonym 'The Scanner' that showed a preoccupation with promoting the technological dimension of outside broadcasts from sport. For example, preceding the first televising of a rugby

The First Televised football Match – Arsenal, the most successful English club of the 1930s, made frequent appearances in the early days of radio and television outside broadcasts, and were captured here after their first match in front of the cameras.   © *Hulton Getty*

union international between England and Scotland from Twickenham in London during March 1938, there appeared an early indication of the logistical difficulties facing the BBC technicians in their attempts to provide the clearest possible 'depictive form' of the play. Twickenham was to become the first sports stadium to be permanently equipped for television, and the *Radio Times* informed its readers that three cameras were to be positioned within specially constructed wooden huts in the West Stand, thirty feet from the ground placed level with the half-way line and the two twenty-two yard lines.

The *Radio Times* gave an expectant impression of what viewers might see:

> With skilful use of the telephoto lens the ball or the forwards on top of
> it should be seen the whole time. A 'sticky' pitch slowing up the game
> will probably make a better picture. (*Radio Times*, 11 March 1938)

The fragility of the image can be sensed from this account, and the positioning of the cameras was clearly viewed as the optimum use of the telephoto lenses to capture the play in each third of the field. The sheer bulkiness of the technology required to transmit from sport, specifically the mass of cable involved, severely restricted the mobility of the equipment. The problems of economically marshalling the technology needed on location took many years to resolve.

This, inevitably, enforced certain time constraints. For example, in 1938 the coverage of England against Scotland from Wembley on Saturday, 9 April, was preceded by a Light-Heavyweight title fight between the boxers Len Harvey and Jock McAvoy on Thursday, 7 April, which left twenty-nine hours between the broadcasts. As The Scanner suggested, 'come behind the scenes, and you will see that, far from being ample, the twenty-nine hours' interval is giving something in the nature of a rush job' (*Radio Times*, 22 April 1938).

This relative immobility is symbolic of the transitional period in media technology. It was a time-consuming (and labour-intensive) process and virtually pre-Fordist in comparison to other forms of communication at this time (radio reached over ninety per cent of the population by 1938). Processes and techniques had yet to be fully standardized and programmes had yet to be formalized in any coherent, recognizable way. The mass consumption of television was still some way off.

Sports rights and competition

For the duration of the Second World War BBC Television was put on hold. On resumption, the first major sports broadcast came from the London Olympic Games in 1948. This event kick-started a whole series of innovations during the immediate post-war period. New, more sensitive, CPS Emitron cameras were introduced, providing a higher degree of depth of field and focus (Whannel, 1992, p. 64).

Allied to this innovation was the introduction of 'zoom lenses' mounted on turrets giving OB directors the ability to focus on individual players instead of actual play. First used in the coverage of horse-racing from Ascot in 1951, the new lenses brought a five-to-one ratio, which was a vast improvement on the previous two-to-one system, allowing a process of personalization, to give the viewer a 'privileged insight' into the sport (Clarke and Clarke, 1982, p. 72).

Transformations in sports programming were also emerging in the early 1950s after a series of decisions on broadcasting policy. Firstly, issues of copyright had led governing bodies to restrict access to sport.

In 1944, led by the Greyhound Racing Association, many of Britain's leading sports organizations formed the Association for the Protection of Copyright in Sport (APCS). The APCS were fearful of the 're-diffusion' of televised sport in public places and attempted to enforce their own copyright on the performance of sports women and men, much akin to the legal rights of an author, composer or playright (Haynes, 1998, pp. 215–18).

These cool relations thawed after the Labour government's Committee on Copyright announced in 1952 that the rights to television sports performance should be vested in the broadcaster on agreement of remuneration to sports promoters for any loss of revenue incurred. This opened the way to a series of deals between the BBC and sport, including the rights to the 'Matthews Final' of 1953 for £1000.

The second major shift in broadcasting policy was the introduction of commercial television in 1955. The Independent Television Authority reflected broader shifts in British popular culture after the austerity of the immediate post-war years. It also broke the broadcast monopoly of the BBC and introduced more lively, populist forms of programming.

As Whannel (1991) has highlighted, the BBC was initially slow to respond to its new competitor in most areas of programming except, that is, for sport. From 1954 to 1958 the BBC introduced three new sports programmes that came to be the staple diet of sports broadcasting in Britain. These were the mid-week sports omnibus *Sportsview* (1954); the Saturday evening highlights package *Sports Special* (1956); and the star in the BBC's portfolio of sports programming, the Saturday afternoon sports magazine *Grandstand* (1958), still running in 1999.

All three programmes placed great value on winning the 'family audience', appealing to both the sports lover and the uninitiated. *Sportsview*, introduced by Peter Dimmock, was designed to combine filmed material with studio comment and interviews, with much emphasis placed on sporting personalities. *Sports Special*, the forerunner of *Match of the Day* later to be launched on BBC 2 in 1964 after the introduction of videotape, was introduced by Kenneth Wolstenholme and was built on the back of the BBC's exclusive deal with the Football League for edited filmed highlights.

Finally, *Grandstand*, introduced by David Coleman, brought together previously disparate live outside broadcasts from sport under one umbrella programme, and was invariably structured around horseracing. Together, the BBC's portfolio of sport made it very difficult for the disparate ITV franchises to gain a foothold in the televising of sport market.

ITV sport

The first ITV companies to introduce sport into their schedules faced an upward struggle to gain the confidence of suspicious governing bodies and restricted funds for sports rights. ITV managed to poach some talent from the BBC, like producers Bill Ward and John Graydon, and also recruited from within sport itself, including Wolves and England skipper Billy Wright who joined the Midlands-based Associated Television as chief sports advisor in 1956.

ITV sought new avenues of televised sport including a mobile unit to film the Monte Carlo Rally for the Associated Rediffusion (AR) programme *Calvalcade of Sport*, 'behind the scenes' interviews with sport personalities in *Sportstour*, and the Wednesday evening programme *Sports Formbook* that discussed the following weekend's sport with racing journalist John Rickman giving the latest tips from the racecourses and stables. ITV also famously introduced wrestling to its sports programming, screened twice a month by AR in 1956.

Transformations in sport were also delivering new experiences for the viewer. Until the 1950s the Football Association and the Football League had resisted the introduction of floodlighting. However, many games had been played under floodlight outside the auspices of the FA Cup and League programme. Specifically, clubs such as Wolves began to pit their skills against international competition, invariably under floodlight in front of the TV cameras (Haynes, 1998, pp. 218–21). Both the BBC and ITV companies revelled in the opportunity to show international stars like Ferenc Puskas on British screens, introducing viewers to a new era of mid-week European football that would blossom in the late 1960s with the triumphs in the European Cup of first Celtic and then Manchester United.

Global TV sport

Other international sporting occasions like the Olympic Games and the World Cup were also gaining wider recognition during this period. Television helped bring such events into the living rooms of the nation. The introduction of a cross-continental association of broadcasters in 1954 called 'Eurovision', allowed viewers the first live pictures from the World Cup in Switzerland (1954) and Sweden (1958), followed by the Rome Olympics in 1960. Through the amalgamation of public-service broadcasters under the auspices of the European Broadcasting Union (EBU) the internationalism of sport was disseminated to a wider public, the philosophy of which resonated with the desire of broadcasters to bring new exotic experiences into people's homes on a trans-continental basis.

These exchanges relied upon some four thousand miles of connecting land lines, with forty-four transmitters. The ideological motivation for the exchange, from the British perspective, is identifiable within the following quote published in the *Radio Times* from the BBC's Chief Technician, M.J. Pilling:

> We have tried to advantage the universality of the picture as a way of overcoming the language barrier. This has led us to develop much more along the lines of shared programmes. (*Radio Times*, 21 May 1954)

The World Cup of 1962 from Chile and the Olympic Games of 1964 from Tokyo were beyond the reach of land lines and denied British viewers any live action from these events. However, the BBC and ITV companies went to extreme lengths to provide pictures as soon as they could from the other side of the world.

For the Tokyo Games this meant the first use of satellite technology, although only to restrict the delay of recorded material. Using the Syncom III satellite of the US Navy which covered the Pacific region, the EBU recorded three hours of action in the United States then flew video tape to Europe for transmission on the same day. The true immediacy of satellite broadcasts of sporting events from around the world did not arrive until the Olympic Games from Mexico in 1968. Both ITV and BBC sent out their own camera crews and presenters to provide on-site 'unilateral' broadcasts, to compliment the universal EBU broadcasts. This allowed far more focus on British athletes, and has since become the standard way of covering such global sporting events.

The 1970 World Cup from Mexico added colour to the immediacy of live satellite transmission. With England looking to retain their World Championship and the brilliance of the Brazilian team that included Pele, this tournament inaugurated a new era of global television, capturing the imagination of millions of viewers worldwide. As the 1970s progressed, other sports entered the global playing field, most notably boxing. The 1974 fight between George Forman and Muhammad Ali, known as the 'Rumble in the Jungle', raised Heavyweight boxing to unprecedented heights, both as global spectacle and the efficacy of sports superstardom. The fight, thanks to television, is legend in twentieth-century popular culture, and was recently revisited in the film documentary *When We Were Kings*.

In many respects, the 1970s and early 1980s were the 'golden years' of British sports broadcasting. Operating as a duopoly, the BBC and ITV companies enjoyed the fruits of a highly limited spectrum for television in the UK. The introduction of Channel 4 in 1982 opened up some new vistas for sports broadcasting, providing an outlet for previously marginalized sports such as American Football from the NFL in the United States, and previously unseen sports like Sumo wrestling from Japan. However, the dominance of the BBC as the national broadcaster of sport would be sustained until the late 1980s and early 1990s when, under challenge from new cable and satellite broadcasters, the Corporation began to be outpriced in the battle for inflationary sports rights and the relatively settled landscape of television sport would be dramatically altered for broadcasters, sporting bodies and viewers and supporters.

Conclusion

What we have suggested in this chapter is that there has always been a relationship between various media and sport. At an institutional level this is a relationship that has evolved and developed, often accompanied by a substantial degree of tension. Sport and the media were two cultural forms which simply proved to be irresistible to each other as the century progressed.

The remainder of the book looks at how this history has informed the shape of modern media sport. Chapter 4 examines in detail what exactly television wants from sport in the 1990s, while the sporting stars and heroes which the media help to create are scrutinized in Chapter 5.

In this brief historical context we have examined two sides of the triangle which constitutes modern sport, television and sport itself. The third, sponsorship, and its interplay with the other two is an absolutely vital component in the story of the evolution of the contemporary media–sport experience and it is to this area which we now turn our attention.

CHAPTER 3

A Sporting Triangle

*Television, Sport and
Sponsorship*

Listen buddy we're ABC Television. We bought the
Olympics, and we can do what the hell we like.

ABC cameraman, The Winter Olympics, Sarajevo, February 1984

NIKE V ADIDAS: Battle of the brands gets hotter.

Financial Times, 27 May 1998

Introduction

An indicator of the major shifts which have taken place in the relationship between sport and commerce over the last thirty years was the
volume of reporting surrounding the premier global sporting event, the
FIFA world cup of 1998, which focused not on the football, but on the
increasingly close and complex links between professional sport and
business. It appeared that to the people who fund international sport in
the 1990s the crucial battle of France 1998 was not between Ronaldo
and Zidane, but the global sportswear companies Nike and Adidas.

In the intensively competitive sportswear market of the 1990s, companies such as Nike will pay up to $400 million over ten years to the
Brazilian national team to help promote its brand around the world.
As part of this deal the team play five exhibition matches a year, thus in
the run up to the World Cup in France the greatest footballing country in the world and defending champions were often referred to as
Team Nike. When details of their contract with Nike were leaked to the
Brazilian press a year later it emerged that Nike could dictate the team's
opponents in friendly matches as well as demand that at least eight
regular first-team players turn out in these arranged Nike fixtures (*The
Guardian,* 2 February 1999) – another symbolic example of the extent

to which the balance between sporting and commercial interests has become increasing blurred in the media-centred world of professional football.*

In this chapter we attempt to make sense of the complex relationship which has evolved at the very centre of national and international sport – a triangular relationship between, sport, sponsors and television which now increasingly drives the shape and development of sporting contests. Building on the previous chapter we focus on the historical link there has always been between sport, the media (television in particular) and sponsorship. As we point out, this relationship is not new and, as Cashmore (1996, p. 163) has noted, its roots date back to the initial growth of professional sport:

> The development of the sports goods industry dates from the last
> quarter of the nineteenth century, paralleling the growth of organised
> sport.

However, what also becomes clear, is that the last thirty years or so has witnessed a tightening of the stranglehold that sponsors in conjunction with television exert on major sporting events.

Later, we examine the centrality of this sporting triangle in shaping the contemporary national and international sporting experience. Here we look at recent events such as the 1994 and 1998 FIFA World Cup finals held in the USA and France respectively, and examine the extent to which funding from sponsors and television underpin their economic structure. Finally, we ask what are the tensions and contradictions inherent in such a relationship for all the parties involved. In particular, how will, what Gary Whannel (1992, p. 151) has called the increasingly powerful 'interlocking forces of television and sponsorship' shape the future of sport and its audiences as we enter a new century?

The good old days? Sport and sponsorship

A triangular relationship has developed in recent years that has come to dominate the economic structure of modern sport. Sports governing bodies, sponsors and television have become intertwined in an alliance that has transformed sport in Britain and throughout the world.

---

* A BBC Television investigation for *Panorama* entitled 'Who Wins the World Cup' (8 June 1998) examined the extent to which business and political interests have fundamentally reshaped the world game of football. The sportswear company Nike even felt it necessary to publicly deny rumours that it had any role in ordering that an obviously unfit Ronaldo should play in the World Cup final against France.

Professional sport in Britain today relies on commercial sponsorship and money from the sale of television rights for its financial survival.

Sponsors are keen to secure media exposure, the most desirable being television, thus sports are desperate to achieve a television space for their sport and their sponsor(s). As this pattern develops it seems that sport is increasingly becoming an adjunct of the advertising industry. Why has this come about?

Martin Polley (1998, pp. 63–84) convincingly argues that sporting activity has always had a contact of sorts with commercial sponsors. Initially this took the form of aristocratic patronage. By the nineteenth century it involved members of the landowning classes becoming involved in popular recreation through forms of patronage. This was perceived as a means of promoting the social order, as well as providing an opportunity to increase the standing of the landowner among the lower classes.

In Britain, the later part of that century saw a fundamental reorganization of sporting activity along both professional and commercial lines, with mass spectator sport as we understand it today evolving during this period (Holt, 1989). Many of the governing bodies of sport that exist today were founded around this time. As the commercialization of popular activities increased, reflecting the commercial opportunities that the new industrial urban environment offered to some, so the business opportunities offered by sport increased also.

As patronage declined due to the economic and social dislocation caused by the development of industrial capitalism, so commercial sponsorship increased. Two of the most popular spectator sports in Britain, football and cricket, enjoyed varying degrees of contact with commercial sponsors. As early as 1896 for example, Nottingham Forest were sponsored by Bovril when they appeared in that year's FA Cup final, while elsewhere in Europe the origins of the modern Tour de France cycle race date from a commercial sponsorship deal which used the race to promote the newspaper *L'Équipe*. However, this level of sponsorship involvement would seem minuscule when compared with the expansion in this area that was to occur during the 1960s.

1960s: the sponsorship game

A number of currents and cross-currents were responsible for the sudden growth in the level of sports sponsorship that was to occur from this period onwards. One major factor was the financial crisis that professional sport found itself in as a result of the falling revenue that accompanied the decline in attendances. During the early 1950s over

40 million people regularly watched professional football in Britain. By the 1960s this had declined to under 30 million and, despite a brief resurgence after the English World Cup victory in 1966, attendances continued to drop. This pattern was repeated in all the major spectator sports in Britain. Gate receipts provided the main source of revenue for these sports.

The shift away from spectator sport was part of a wider shift in the leisure pattern of post-war Britain. As the suburbs grew, leisure activities were becoming increasingly domestically orientated, a trend accentuated by the growth in the popularity of television. In addition, as the British economy enjoyed a period of relative buoyancy, the increase in discretionary income resulted in the development of a more aggressively commercial pattern of leisure activity. Sport suddenly found itself competing for the public's attention in an increasingly competitive marketplace.

Allied with this was the internal structure of the sports governing bodies themselves. Most of the organizations were still run along amateurish and paternalist lines and were incapable of dealing with the problems that the changing nature of leisure activity posed to their sports. Against the backdrop of these changes, it was the banning by television of cigarette advertising in 1965 that provided the incentive needed for major corporate involvement in sports sponsorship.

Many of the initial corporate sponsors of televised sport were those companies who viewed sponsorship as a way of securing television exposure, not only on commercial television, but also on the 'advertising-free' public-service BBC TV. During this period sport was particularly vulnerable to the overtures of the commercial sponsor. A sport's ability to secure television coverage thus became a key factor if it wished to attract potential sponsors.

As we argue in the next chapter, television has always viewed sport as an important part of its schedules. Historically, sports programming proved to be cheap, popular and easily scheduled. The fees that sport receives from television, although initially disproportionally small, have in recent years mushroomed with increased competition in the television marketplace with the result that governing bodies of sport are keen to go to any lengths to accommodate television.

In 1966, sports sponsorship accounted for less than £1 million of the revenue received by sport in Britain. By the mid-1970s this figure had risen to £16 million (1976) with a further growth to £46 million by 1980. By the early 1990s the amount of money generated by commercial sponsorship had jumped to over £250 million and in 1998 it was estimated to be worth £350 million (Kolah, 1999). Globally it has been estimated that expenditure on sports sponsorship grew between 1989 and 1996 from $3 to $11 billion (*The Economist*, 6 June 1998), while the latest figure (1999) puts the global figure at around $19.5 billion (Kolah, 1999).

Initially, cigarette sponsors such as Benson and Hedges (cricket and snooker), and John Player (cricket and motor-racing), used sponsorship of televised sport as a means of evading the television ban on cigarette advertising, and obtaining 'piggy-back' exposure on the advertising-free BBC television. Such was the success of these arrangements for the sponsors involved, that the range of corporations involved in televised sport began to grow.

Why sponsor sport?

The reasons why companies choose to sponsor sport vary. They can be looking to achieve an increase in the public profile of the company, as well as increasing public awareness of the product/services that the company offers. The association of the company/product in the minds of the consumer with a particular sporting image is also a factor in determining which sport companies may choose to sponsor.

When Luciano Benetton, the creator of one of the largest knitwear companies in the world, was considering how to raise the profile of his company he realized that sports sponsorship offered potential exposure to millions through television coverage. As Jonathan Mantle comments:

> at a global level . . . the attraction had to be glamorous and exciting, as well as appealing to the competitive instinct. There was only one sport which was capable of satisfying these criteria. This was the most expensive, glamorous and dangerous sport of all: Formula One.
> (Mantle, 1999, p. 50)

Benetton got involved in the 1980s in sponsoring the Tyrell Formula One team and later extended their interest in the sport by buying a team and creating Benetton Formula One.

During the 1970s the condom manufacturer Durex became involved in the sponsorship of motor-racing as part of the company's strategy to 'normalize' their product. Sports sponsorship has also proved a very cost-effective means of achieving these aims. Major corporations also use sport as a place at which clients can be entertained. The growth of corporate entertainment through the 'tented villages' that now accompany most major sporting events is another manifestation of the increasing links between business and sport.

By the early 1980s it became increasingly clear that sport was be-coming firmly positioned within the broader communication strategies of corporations. Whitson (1998), focusing on North America, clearly demonstrates how the linkages between professional sport and the media industries have evolved in the 1980s and 1990s to such a degree that he identifies 'a new kind of corporate integration in the media and entertainment industries' (p. 59).

Not only does high-profile televised sport offer a range of marketing, public relations and advertising opportunities which extend the range of public awareness for particular companies, but increasingly in North America this also involves media corporations not simply providing the television channels which deliver this 'sports product', but also owning the sports clubs involved. Thus through vertical integration media corporations can control both distribution and content. The extent to which this pattern is emerging in the UK is examined in more detail later in the chapter; however, it does mark a significant development in the ever closer links or increased synergy between sports, media and sponsors.

While for corporations involved in the sports–leisure industry the benefits for brands of a close association with a sporting élite are clear (note how both Nike and Reebok during the 1980s overtook rivals such as Adidas in market share by aggressively pursuing such a policy see Chapter 5 for more details). At a national level non sports-related com-panies can benefit hugely from close involvement with sporting teams and individuals. The current sponsorship of the Republic of Ireland international football team by a car corporation highlights the increas-ing interplay between business and sport at an important structural level.

Opel's Ireland

Sports sponsorship often offers multi-national companies the opportun-ity to claim that they have integrated into local and national commu-nities. The evolution of one of the largest sports sponsorship deals in Irish sport involving the Football Association of Ireland (FAI), Media Sports and Leisure Ltd and General Motors (Opel) (in the UK they trade under the name Vauxhall) serves to illustrate the fusion of multi-national capital and sport that is now occurring across the globe.

In 1985 the Irish government lifted restrictions on car imports into the Republic of Ireland, with the result that the market became increas-ingly vulnerable to Japanese penetration. General Motor's European sales began to be adversely affected in Ireland. To counteract this trend

G.M. (Ireland) drew up a corporate strategy that would attempt, in their words, to 'achieve a deep level of integration into the community, socially, culturally and economically'. G.M. (Ireland) saw a need to increase the public awareness of what the company perceived as their key role in the Irish economy. This strategy to emphasize success and increase community identity with the company was an integral reason for the company's involvement with sports sponsorship.

The move was facilitated and arranged in 1986 through Trevor O'Rourke's management consultancy agency, Media Sport and Leisure Ltd. With Ford Motors already involved in a Gaelic Athletic Association sponsorship deal, as part of its public relations drive to undo some of the PR damage inflicted on the company with the closure of its Cork assembly plant, Opel looked elsewhere. The deal they were seeking had to be one which in their eyes highlighted the 'social responsibility of industry', a multi-national phrase that was viewed internally as particularly important in the light of the Ford/Cork closure.

While Opel turned to soccer, they made sure that the FAI would be capable of dealing with the money involved (in 1985 such had been the financial crisis, that the FAI had literally been on the verge of going out of business) by encouraging the setting up of a commercial division within the organization. The eventual deal with the FAI was worth initially £400,000 and crucially allowed the FAI to appoint Englishman Jack Charlton to the post as national manager. As a result of this the team embarked on a period of unprecedented success on the European and World stage bringing in massive revenues to the FAI and national and global exposure for Opel Ireland. Not content to sit back and watch their money being spent, Opel have been closely involved in encouraging the FAI's commercial manager in his drive to commercialize and rationalize the Association's outlook.

Central to the new regime is profit maximization. Soccer, it appears, must compete for its share of the sponsorship cake in the increasingly competitive market place. Recent protests from fans about the allocation of tickets to corporate sponsors and clients, at the expense of other less powerful supporters, as well as questions about the exact distribution of the massive increase in FAI revenue have largely gone unaddressed. The danger looms that, as the FAI becomes increasingly dependent on its sponsors, it is likely that it will be to them, not the fans, that they will have to be accountable. Within this sport/sponsorship axis television exposure is crucial.

The national television rights to show the Republic's international matches – secured by RTE – also generates substantial revenue for the FAI. Foreign television rights also boost revenue, while perimeter advertising space provides a substantial income thanks to the television exposure.

Over the last decade Opel, Ireland's self-proclaimed Number One supporter, have seen car sales increase by over 60 per cent. In 1997 it announced that it was once again extending its sponsorship of the national team until 2003. Irish soccer success on the pitch had, it seemed, been accompanied by a corporate success story of another kind.

The sports broker

As we have seen corporations have clearly defined aims in sponsoring sport. As capital penetration of sport has increased, there has been a corresponding growth in the consultancy agencies, such as the one mentioned above, which link the sponsor with the sport. These agencies have become the new power brokers in the alliance between sport and commerce, helping to provide the linkage points in the television/ sport/sponsorship axis.

World-wide one of the largest of these agencies is Mark McCormack's International Management Group (IMG). McCormack's initial interest in sports management evolved around golf. Gary Player, Arnold Palmer and Jack Nicklaus were three of his first clients (see Chapter 5). Soon his organization began to diversify into other sports such as tennis, while he used his sporting and business contacts to help facilitate the development of the television arm of his empire, Trans World International (TWI).

This company is now the largest independent producer of sports programming in the world. Today IMG is a global marketing and management consultancy operation. Not only does it manage top sportspeople, but through its tv arm, TWI, it creates televised sporting events for over a hundred corporations worldwide. However, they were by no means the only players in the game.

In the UK one of the main trailblazers in the development of sports brokers was Patrick Nally, whose WestNally pioneered the model of sports marketing which would be put to good effect in the world of both the Olympics and the FIFA World Cup by ISL (International Sport and Leisure Marketing) which exclusively marketed both events globally.

As we examine below, governing bodies of sport employ such agencies to find exclusive sponsors for their sporting events, and to sell both the television and arena advertising rights to potential clients. Television exposure becomes of central importance both in generating substantial rights revenue and providing global exposure for sponsors who in turn pay handsomely to have their company linked with a premier sporting event.

Global sports sponsorship: branding sport

As a result of television becoming the driver of élite professional sport, it has come to dictate when, where and in what form sport can take place. The list of such examples of the economic stranglehold that television has over some sports would prove exhaustive if reproduced here. However, one example is World Heavyweight boxing title fights which take place in London that are often staged at midnight in order to suit the American networks which are showing the fight live. In the global fight to secure the television rights for sport the American networks dominate. The east coast of the USA is the most densely populated part of the country, thus offering the audience that advertisers are anxious to reach and television can deliver.

Major sporting events are staged to suit American television networks anxious to secure a return, through advertising revenue, on their capital outlay used in buying the television rights. In the case of the FIFA World Cup, it has been European television that has dictated even when the finals have been played in America. Both the 1986 finals in Mexico and the 1994 finals in the USA saw some of the matches being played during the hottest time of the day in order to provide European television with prime-time live football.

At a national level, sports such as cricket have changed due to television's insatiable appetite for more 'entertaining' forms of sports programming. This has resulted in the development of the one-day game, to the detriment some would say of the longer, more traditional Test matches, while in Australia television was instrumental in the initiation of the floodlit day/night matches. The sport now has one-day internationals, a one-day World Series and a limited overs Sunday League competition, all initiated by television and supported by sponsors keen to secure exposure.

Such is the importance that sports place on their ability to secure television exposure that rules are changed or altered to suit the needs of television. Barnett (1990) notes how American Football is overtly tailored to fit neatly into the pattern of advertising breaks on American television. Indeed, such is American television's desire to guarantee a resolution of the sporting contest, that a number of rule changes in various sports ensure that the matches cannot end in a draw.

In snooker, a sport largely re-invented by BBC television in the 1970s, matches are now shorter to suit television. Domestic football matches in both England and Scotland which traditionally took place on a Saturday afternoon, now, thanks to exclusive television deals, are played on any day of the week at any time, much to the inconvenience of the actual travelling supporter.

Europe's premier football club tournament the Champions European Cup which was a home and away knock-out competition has metamorphosed into the Champions League format to maximize the financial benefits for the top clubs and to provide more content for television companies. Central in this process has been the intention of the governing body of European football (UEFA) to secure the greatest monetary gain through the marketing of television rights and sponsorship opportunities of this new tournament through The Event Agency and Marketing AG (TEAM) formed in 1991 (Sugden and Tomlinson, 1998, pp. 93–7). However, it is wrong simply to cast television as the villain of the piece as is often done. More often than not any finger of blame must be pointed at the governing bodies of sport which hold the rights for sporting events and often choose to sell them to the highest television bidder.

The model of international sports sponsorship and marketing which dominates in the late 1990s owes much to perhaps the most important Olympics of recent times. These were not necessarily the most important in athletic and sporting terms, but signified a new era had arrived in the commercialization of global sport. The games in Los Angeles in 1984 set new benchmarks in the marketing and sponsorship relationships which have now become an integral part of international sport.

The Olympics and the 'Hamburger Games' of 1984

The growth of televised international sport is inexorably bound up with the developments in satellite and video technology, and how the medium has used these developments to enhance the spectacle of sport on television. With the launching, in 1962, of the first communication satellite Telstar, a new era of international sport was about to begin. The 1964 Tokyo Olympics were received, via satellite, in 39 countries. Developments in colour television during the 1960s, and video technology also, enhanced the quality of picture that television could offer the viewer thousands of miles from the event.

The battle between the American television networks to secure the rights to screen these major events has resulted in an upward spiral in the amounts of money each network is willing to bid for the event. Such are the massive costs incurred by the host city in staging the games (Montreal is still paying off the debt it incurred during the hosting of the 1976 Games), and with the realization that the spiral in television fees was levelling out, the organizers targeted alternative sources of revenue.

Select corporate sponsors would become official Olympic sponsors marketing their products/services under the Olympic logo. In LA there were 30 official sponsors paying between $4 and $15 million for the privilege. Among the largest of this élite group were, Coca-Cola (official Olympic drink), McDonalds (official caterers), Kodak (official film), Levi-Strauss (official clothing), Visa (official credit facilities), Anheuser Busch (Budweiser, official alcoholic drink) and so on.

Allied with this, the sponsors involved also bought much of the advertising space available throughout ABC's television coverage of the games. For instance Coca-Cola and Levi-Strauss between them bought $70 million worth of air time in addition to their sponsorship deals. The Olympic stadia are one of the few international sporting arenas that do not carry perimeter advertising. While the International Olympic Committee (IOC) feel that this helps to preserve the 'pure' athletic atmosphere within the stadium, one wonders how long the IOC can resist the pressure from sponsors to relinquish this policy.

This contradiction between overt commercialism and the mythical aura of sporting activity presents an interesting dilemma for television, sports governing bodies and potential sponsors. The apolitical 'world of sport' full of mythical unsullied heroes that television likes to portray becomes increasingly difficult to substantiate as capital penetration of sport becomes more overt. For many the 1984 LA Games were a celebration of corporate capitalism, an arena where human activity was transformed into an economic process that fuelled the consumption of corporate goods and services. It was a process that television both mediated and played a crucial role in sustaining. Sport has become synonymous with corporate image, television entertainment and consumer capitalism and, for sponsors and marketers, global sporting events would never be the same again.

Global sponsorship strategies

Much of what LA achieved through its private selling of the Games has been adopted by other organizations around the world. The 1996 European Football Championships played in England had eleven official corporate sponsors arranged by ISL who were working on behalf of UEFA. Sponsors paid £3.5 million for the exclusive rights to advertise in the stadia and up to £10 million on related advertising and marketing.

In addition official suppliers such as Microsoft provide free of charge goods and services worth in or around £10 million (Abel and Long, 1996, p. 19). As an evaluation report of the sponsorship opportunities offered by 1996 concluded:

> An event such as the European Football Championship is a major media occurrence and can provide a superb marketing platform for brand and image communication worldwide. In particular, if sponsor companies are willing and able to underpin and support their headline sponsorship with other marketing activity, these opportunities are further enhanced. (Easton and Mackie, 1998, p. 113)

The global marketing strategies of these multi-nationals have become an integral part in the staging of an international sporting event. Such is the size of the financial undertaking involved in staging these events, and the inability of the organizers to find alternative sources of funding, that this concentration of a cluster of corporate sponsors involved in sport will continue.

Expenditure on such events is not deemed a legitimate area for state involvement, especially in the prevailing economic climate where market forces dominate, and there are considerable reductions in state expenditure on welfare provision. Sports organizers have firmly set out their stall (and are being encouraged by governments to do so) to woo the private sector.

The media marketing of World Cup USA 1994 and France 98

Increasingly sport is strategically managed and marketed to produce maximum commercial yields for sports federations, media corporations, sponsors and advertising concerns. The depth of this commercial activity is witnessed in the media marketing of the 1994 World Cup held in the United States. After an official pledge of assistance in February 1988 from US President Ronald Reagan to FIFA President Joao Havelange the United States was chosen in July 1988 as the host of the 1994 World Cup, receiving more than half of the total votes from FIFA's Executive Committee.

No more than four months after the 1990 finals, FIFA announced a marketing structure in readiness for the three and a half year countdown to USA '94. The strategy was jointly drawn up by International Sports and Leisure Marketing (ISL) a Swiss-based company established

in 1982 by the FIFA President Joao Havelange and the late sports manufacturer and owner of Adidas, Horst Dassler. Even before we knew
who the 24 finalists would be, American Airlines, one of the 'official'
sponsors, had beckoned us to travel to our ultimate dream destination,
a rendezvous with fate, a dream ticket to the World Cup Final.

From its inception ISL secured itself a marketing partnership with
FIFA for the foreseeable future of the tournament, a deal which now
spans the last five World Cup finals (1982–98). The joint marketing
strategy enabled the provision of an economic base upon which international football, now being sold as a highly commercialized entertainment industry, could feed into the multi-national and trans-national
corporate world.

Furthermore, the willingness of FIFA to market the game on a com-
pletely new level at the beginning of the eighties, a decision based on
both Havelange's admiration of Dassler and the recognition that the
World Cup was selling itself short in comparison to the Olympics, led to
Dassler enticing further trans-national companies, most notably Coca-
Cola, into sponsoring what was increasingly marketed as the 'world game'.

As Alan Tomlinson (1986, 1994) has highlighted, the dramatic
changes in the marketing strategy of international football ironically
have their roots outside of the historically powerful footballing nations
of Europe. By the 1980s both the established and developing football
nations of South America, Asia and Africa were being led by the charis-
matic Havelange (with the technical assistance of Dassler) in a challenge to the advanced footballing world on the global, televisual and
commercial football field.

However, the transference of political power to Havelange and his
followers did have its broader and contrary ramifications as Tomlinson
suggests:

> The Third World had been aroused and in footballing terms was on the
> ascendancy; in power terms, the alliances within FIFA combined the
> political and cultural interests of emergent nations with the market
> aspirations of multi-national and trans-national economic interests still
> based firmly in the first world of capitalism. (Tomlinson, 1994, p. 23)

Élite sport, élite sponsors

The unprecedented move of signing up only a handful of primary sponsors was an attempt to spread the financial risk of the finals and move
FIFA's income away from an overdependence on revenue derived from
television rights. The rights holders, the broadcast channel ABC and
its sports cable station ESPN, were confirmed as the US World Cup

networks in June 1992 after negotiating a deal worth $11 million, a relatively small sum given the escalating prices for large US sports events like the Superbowl, The Masters golf tournament, the US Open tennis championship, and the forthcoming 1996 Olympic Games in Atlanta, Georgia.

The deal was struck only after support and assurances were given by three of the eleven official sponsors: Coca-Cola, M&M/Mars (represented by the Snickers brand) and MasterCard International. In an attempt to capture the interest of a wide American public, ABC was scheduled to air 11 live matches over weekends and on 4 July (Independence Day) and ESPN would pick up the remaining 41 matches in a mix of live and recorded coverage with a potential reach of 60 million US households, or 65 per cent of all US TV households (*Cable and Satellite Europe*, July 1992).

After two years of negotiation ISL, as the marketing partner of the Organizing Committee, had managed to find a commercial balance that suited not only FIFA but the primary sponsors and US television networks. Before the deals were finalized fears that the US networks would not be interested in covering the World Cup had posed a serious public relations problem outside of the States, adding fuel to arguments waged by European pessimists who could not foresee any merit in holding the Finals in a country without its own professional football league.

But by claiming exclusive rights to sell all international sponsorship worldwide to a select few corporations (Canon, Coca-Cola, Energizer, Fuji Film, General Motors, Gillette, JVC, MasterCard, McDonald's, Philips and Snickers) ISL provided a sponsorship package costing $15 million per company which ensured that these 'blue chip' investors had the right to market their products worldwide on what was called 'a product-category-exclusive basis' (World Cup USA '94 News Kit, February 1994).

It is clear that 'blue chip' companies, like Coca-Cola and McDonald's, now see sports sponsorship as an additional medium of persuasive communication within which they can integrate a marketing mix of advertising, public relations, sales promotion and personal selling. Sports sponsorship, while dependent itself on the media, is increasingly a part of marketing strategy for companies that traditionally have relied upon television, radio and newspapers to convey their symbolic messages.

The 1998 Football World Cup in France was simply the latest example of the process kick-started in LA in 1984. In France, the 45 companies which collectively paid £300 million to be involved in the tournament included the key 12 official sponsors, as well as host of equipment and service suppliers. In addition, companies such as

McDonald's and Coca-Cola would supplement their sponsorship packages by spending between £60 and £80 million in marketing support.

Central in any strategy is the global nature of the event which highlights the centrality of television in the process. The Director of Communications for the Gillette company views France 98 as worth the promotional spend: 'We've been involved with the event since 1970, and if the World Cup was not a powerful global marketing tool we would not be involved today. You are raising brand awareness' (*Financial Times*, 3 June 98).

Global sport: changing the rules

Unsurprisingly perhaps, recent upheavals in the broadcasting environment have had a significant impact on the relationship between sport and sponsors outlined above. Within a UK context the rise of satellite and cable delivery systems and the Rupert Murdoch-controlled BSkyB in particular have altered not only the media landscape in this country, but mark another stage in the ever closer corporate synergy between the media and sporting industries (see Chapters 4 and 11).

The regulatory framework within which broadcasting in the UK has historically operated has loosened considerably since the 1990 Broadcasting Act. One notable change has been in the rise of sponsored programming particularly within the commercial television sector. Sponsors no longer simply sponsor sporting events which are broadcast by television, in addition they also sponsor the programmes themselves. This has become a particular feature of entertainment, drama and sporting output on both terrestrial commercial television and satellite themed sports channels.

In the UK, money for sports rights from BSkyB has become a major revenue stream for professional sport; in return that company dominates the television coverage of a number of major sports, in particular English Premiership football (Horsman, 1997; Williams, 1994). The securing in 1992 of exclusive live coverage of English Premiership football marked the dawn of a new stage in the development between sport and television in the UK. While this is examined in more detail in Chapter 11, what is of particular interest here is how these developments are changing the relationship between sports and the sponsor.

As television becomes the major sponsor of sport in the UK, commercial sponsors increasingly are having to make arrangements not solely with the sports with which they wish to associate, but also with the television companies which control the exposure of that sport on either a free-to-air or subscription basis.

For example in the coverage on the ITV commercial network of Formula One racing, the petrochemical company Texaco is not only involved in sponsoring the sport, it also sponsors ITV's coverage. By embedding itself in the opening credits and ad break intros and exits, Texaco achieves a distinctive position in the television coverage of a sport cluttered with a host of brands and sponsors. Having a core sponsor such as this paying up to £1 million a year also lowers the production cost for ITV in covering the sport.

This linkage by sponsors into the actual on-screen identity of television coverage is a particular feature of the aggressively marketed BSkyB's sports coverage. An increased reliance by television on sponsors is not surprising given the vast amounts of money being ploughed into securing sports rights by the likes of BSkyB. In 1993 the English Premiership Champions received £2.4 million from BSkyB; by 1998 this had risen to £9.7 million. Thus satellite television is also keen to recoup its investment through increasing its revenue streams not only from its subscription base, but also through programme sponsorship.

In the fast-moving commercial world of television sport, sponsors' logos are not simply confined to the field of play or sports stadium, but are increasingly central in the actual coverage of the event itself. In a competitive deregulated media market where channels are busy branding themselves in order to stand out in a crowded marketplace, exclusive sports coverage has become increasingly important as a revenue generator for television.

Bellamy (1998) has surveyed the ties between television and sport in North America where the next logical step in the ever-closer linkage between sport, commerce and television was for media corporations owned by the likes of Ted Turner and Rupert Murdoch to actually buy and control sports clubs such as baseball's Atlanta Braves and the LA Dodgers.

The attempted takeover in 1998 at a cost of £625 million of one of the biggest clubs in Britain, Manchester United, by Murdoch's BSkyB television operation was an effort to merge two of the most aggressively marketed brands in the UK sports–media arena. While globally relationships between television companies and sports clubs have existed for some time, most notably in North America, but also in European countries such as Italy through entrepreneurial figures such as Silvio Berlusconi, what the Manchester United deal signified was the beginning of new phase in the continually evolving sport–media–sponsorship axis in the UK (further explored in Chapter 11).

What we wish to do now is to examine some of the implications for sport of the developments that have been outlined above.

Where only the sponsored survive

> We are winners, we win in a very professional manner, we
> intend to keep on winning. Exactly what you want your
> company to be.
>
> Barry Hearn, sports entrepreneur, interview with one of the authors, 1988

Commercial sponsorship wants to be associated with success. Sponsorship of this type is not patronage and companies expect a commercial return on their involvement in sport. Despite the claims made by many 'socially responsible' companies that they sponsor non-televised community events, this aspect of commercial sponsorship remains minimal when compared with the total revenue allocated to sponsoring televised sport. In Britain it has been estimated that sponsorship of youth sporting events accounts for 0.5 per cent of the total sponsorship budget.

What the sponsor gives, the sponsor can take away. Money tends to follow the successful high-profile sports. Image becomes all important to the sport, with its financial survival becoming dependent on its ability to attract favourable media coverage. As the sponsor becomes more important, the need to sanitize the televised image of the sport increases as does the desire to distance sports from anything which may be deemed political or controversial.

Sports also go in and out of fashion partly driven by the media. The 1990s boom in football, which has changed the profile of the fan, has led to companies refocusing their sponsorship strategies on that sport to the detriment of others with which they may have previously been involved. Commenting on the failure of English cricket to secure eight top sponsors for the World Cup held in England in 1999, Andrew Jameson, a sports sponsorship consultant noted how:

> Ten to fifteen years ago sponsors trying to target a more mature, higher
> class audience would have gone to rugby or cricket, but the kind of
> people now watching football has changed and now serves the same
> purpose. (*The Guardian*, 20 April 1999)

Even sports which still attain extensive television coverage, such as snooker, can have trouble attracting sponsors if they appear to be suffering adverse publicity arising from internal administrative conflict.

One of the key problems facing many sports in the UK is the decline in the level of sponsorship from tobacco companies and the need to attract other sponsors as the UK government bans future arrangements between sport and tobacco.

Conflicts of interest

As patterns of cross ownership increase, the issue of accountability within media coverage becomes important. During the proposed takeover of Manchester United in 1998, two of the most vociferous advocates of the move were *The Times* and the *Sun*, the former operating in the broadsheet newspaper market, the latter the biggest selling popular newspaper in the UK. Both are part of Rupert Murdoch's media empire, which stood to gain if the takeover was successful and both clearly had vested interests in supporting the deal. The *Sun* (8 September 1998) even had the arrogance in its editorial column to suggest that those opposed to the deal were either 'brain dead, or editors of rival national newspapers'. Media commentator Martin Kelner urged caution when reading sports stories relating to the take over of Manchester United as reported in the print media:

> given the cross-media nature of Murdoch's tentacles it was necessary to embark on some heavy and tedious deconstruction before accepting anything that was said on the subject. (*The Guardian*, 14 September 1998)

Thus, as the links between sport, sponsors and the media become ever closer, it also becomes more difficult for media which are party to particular relationships to be clear sighted in their reporting of events involving key sponsors, clubs and such like.

It is perhaps ironic that any decline in the levels of critical scrutiny of sport by either the print or electronic media is occurring at a time when, given the massive amounts of television-generated money now circulating in the higher echelons of sport, the temptations to cheat or to get involved in corrupt dealings has never been greater.

The winner takes it all

While winning has always been an aspect of sporting activity, the increasing commercialization of sport has amplified the importance that has become attached to success. Sporting success has become equated with financial solvency.

Television's thirst for 'entertainment' has also led to an infatuation with élite and successful sporting individuals and teams. Sponsors target their resources towards the top of the sporting tree. The concern over the use of drugs in sport has tended not to connect this alarming growth industry with the increasing commercial incentives on offer to the top sportspeople who succeed.

The increasing linkages between sport, television and commerce have also coincided with a converging in the values that are supposedly held to be dominant in sport. The close relationship between sport and television inhibits the space available for critical debate about the effects on sport and sporting subcultures of television's commodification of this aspect of popular culture into another area of light entertainment.

Television's treatment of sport as an activity that occurs in some apolitical vacuum is increasingly being challenged by the very process it has helped facilitate. As links between the 'world' of business and the 'world' of sport become more overt, so the separation of these worlds becomes more difficult to sustain. Rather than being an arena free from the economic structures that dictate our working environment, sport is also seen as being subject to these self-same influences.

While sport has always operated within the economic parameters of the social system that it finds itself in, television has denied this in its representation of sport. As capital penetration of sport, both amateur and professional increases, this façade becomes more apparent.

Sports organizations have never seen themselves as purely profit-maximizing businesses; however this is changing. As the importance of television money and commercial sponsorship increases so does the ability of the TV/sponsor to, if not push, then certainly nudge the sport in particular directions.

Significantly, while the rallying cry of many of the key players involved in reshaping the television/sponsorship/sport axis has been the need to loosen regulation or open up the market to competition, either in the media or commercial marketplace, what is actually emerging are new patterns of control which restrict open competition.

Who's in control?

In Formula One motor racing, a sport built on money from sponsors and television, the governing body is the Fédération Internationale de l'Automobile (FIA). Bernie Ecclestone is its vice president for marketing; in 1996 the FIA signed over the rights to market the sport and sell it around the world until the year 2010 to companies owned by Ecclestone.

As Williams (1998, p. 9) notes, he is also chairman of the Formula One Constructors' Association which represents the competitors 'and also chairman of something called Formula One Administration – a company which collects, divides and distributes the revenues from the circuit owners, race sponsors, television companies and trackside advertisers . . . he is in an unique position: poacher, gamekeeper and lord of the manor too.'

In addition, according to *The Economist* (6 June 1998), he can offer one-third discounts to broadcasters around the world who 'agree not to show other "open wheeler racing" – which is doubtless why America's IndyCar series gets relatively little exposure outside the United States'.

Such are the powerful links between corporate business and political culture that politicians are often reluctant to get involved in disputes which may harm important political/media relations. Occasionally politicians do step in, such as in the United States in 1992 when, due to political pressure, the Supreme Court exempted the sport of Baseball from its antitrust laws. More recently the European Union has attempted to eradicate tobacco sponsorship of sport by the year 2006.

However, increasingly the allegiances being forged between television (media corporations) and sponsors do present a powerful challenge to those bodies which have traditionally run sport, either at national or international levels.

With regard to the global sport, football, Sugden and Tomlinson (1998, p. 98) are alert to oversubscribing to a particular deterministic notion that global economic developments unproblematically mean the destruction of local or national identities by a global culture (an issue developed in Chapter 8), while at the same time aware of the important structural changes taking place which are changing the nature of the sport.

> Football is a cultural product, and its meanings and significance are not wholly defined by its political economy. People in pubs or domestic lounges, as well as at live games at various levels of performance, can chant sing, shout, speak and respond in their own appropriate ways as, with varying degrees of freedom and choice, they negotiate the expression of a particular cultural identity through the public culture of the game. But at the top level, football represents more and more graphically the triumph of the universal market, and whenever it is watched – live or in its transmitted forms – it is an increasingly commodified cultural product in a structured environment of an intensifyingly exclusive type. (Sugden and Tomlinson, 1998, p. 98)

At an international level we also see the major sporting sponsorship deals increasingly becoming concentrated in the hands of a number of trans-national companies.

To these companies the sponsorship of sport and the arts is part of a wider strategy to diversify into new markets and seek new areas of profitability. Television and sports sponsorship have helped pull élite performance sport into the mainstream of consumer capitalism.

Conclusion

Sporting cultures, while always linked with commercial forces, have never been more intertwined given the growth of the sports media. While this has been noted in the UK, in the more commercial broadcasting climate of Australia, over ten years ago John Goldlust was noting that:

> In the process they (TV and Business) arrogantly sweep aside any consideration of the organic significance of these games (cricket and Australian Rules Football), as collective social and cultural resources, representing to many people deeply meaningful community traditions, identities and relationships. To those who appropriate sport as their own property, it is just another potentially lucrative entertainment commodity. (Goldlust, 1987, p. 171)

In more recent years, British sport has undergone a series of rapid and dramatic transformations.

One has been the introduction of more sophisticated marketing and promotional strategies both by sporting bodies keen to attract the interest of television and by the television companies themselves who want to maximize the return on their investment in the rights to broadcast sports. This reflects a mode of organization which is more akin to the long-standing consumer-oriented configuration of sport in North America.

The cultural critic Reuel Denney (1989) recognized this media-led process during the 1950s in what he termed 'the decline of lyric sport' and the rise of 'spectorial forms' which function like 'rationalised industries' where the codes of spectatorship for sport and the media are virtually one and the same. Such an argument leads us to ask if there is a difference, and if so how can we any longer discern this?

Television views sport as another part of its entertainment programming that delivers potential audiences to advertisers, and attracts subscribers to new delivery systems. The economic environment in which television finds itself helps to shape the nature and character of the programmes it broadcasts. It also dictates what sports should be shown and how they should be presented. It is this particular aspect of the sport–media relationship to which we turn our attention in the next part of the book.

CHAPTER 4

Power Game

Why Sport Matters to Television

It is always difficult to explain the point of sport to those who do not like it. Non-*aficionados* will never be persuaded to take pleasure from ball skill or pace.

But the level at which sport can be understood by anyone is as a story: as a narrative which must build to a decisive climax and in which character is revealed through actions.

Mark Lawson, Forever England, *The Guardian*, 2 July 1988

Introduction

Television to all intents and purpose controls large sections of contemporary sport. What we want to do in this chapter is examine some issues centred around the reasons why television is so interested in sport (in some sports more than others) and how this relationship alters what appears on our screens from that which we may witness in sporting stadia. Part of this involves what Garry Whannel (1992) calls the transformation of sport by television, and we highlight some of these key practices below.

However, as was evident from the previous chapter, a central element in the sport–television relationship revolves around the economics of the broadcasting industry, and its use of sport as 'television product' in the drive to secure audiences and subscribers.

The first part of the chapter examines what television demands from its sports and the economic benefits which this strand of programming can offer television. Then we briefly examine the case of snooker, a sport largely reinvented for television in the late 1960s and early 1970s. How did television transform this sport to such an extent that it became the most exposed sport on television during the 1980s, and what does its decline as a television sport a decade later tell us about the television–sport relationship?

Next we draw on the pioneering work of Whannel (1992) and look briefly at some of the visual transformations that turn a sporting event into television sport. Given the fast-changing nature of televisual techno-logy, we examine the extent to which, at the end of the 1990s, the treatment of sport differs when covered by terrestrial as opposed to satellite broadcasters.

Finally we focus on the key – and often underestimated – role that commentators play in this process of transformation. In so doing we broaden out our argument to suggest that sports commentary has played a key role in shaping how we come to think and talk about sport and its position in contemporary society.

What television needs from sport

Audiences and advertisers

Economically sport matters to television, be it public-service broad-casters or commercially driven terrestrial and satellite companies. At certain times, such as during football world cups, it delivers large audi-ences outside peak-time viewing, something which is becoming rarer as the audience continues to fragment in a multi-channel environment. During 1998, for example, the largest audience achieved by ITV was 23.8 million for the Argentina v England World Cup match. On the BBC it was 19 million for another England game, this time against Colombia.

As Mark Lawson noted above, the commercial value of these tele-vision events is their ability to appeal both to the committed sports fan, and also the peripheral sporting viewer who becomes interested partly due to the narratives which television, in conjunction with the press, construct around the event. People also get interested for reasons of an ideological nature connected with national pride, and an identification with a wider collective experience (see Chapter 8).

However, outside football, which in 1998 was without doubt *the* television sport in the UK with over 5300 hours (almost 20 per cent of all television sport) broadcast across both terrestrial and satellite chan-nels, certain sports can attract respectable ratings for mixed program-ming channels such as ITV's coverage of Formula One motor racing (between 4 and 8 million for a Sunday afternoon), or the BBC's cover-age of the Grand National steeplechase (11.4 million in 1998). Early figures in 1999 also indicate that football looks set to remain the most covered sport on UK television (Sports Marketing Survey, April 1999).

Where sport becomes of crucial importance in terms of a chan-nel's portfolio, however, is in its ability either to deliver a small, but advertisingly lucrative group of viewers to the screen (Channel 4's coverage of Italian football on a Sunday afternoon was regularly attracting over a million viewers in 1999, mostly young and male) or to entice committed television sports fans to subscribe to a dedicated channel (as in the case of BSkyB in the UK).

At other times during high-profile football games, advertisers will pay a premium to reach the young males who generally watch little television. When Manchester United played Juventus in the European Champions league semi-final in 1999, it cost £150,000 to buy air time for a 30-second advert during half time. ITV generated up to £2 million pounds in advertising revenue during the 15 minute half-time break (*The Observer*, 25 April 1999).

The popularity of specific sports may differ across Europe where in 1997 sports programming accounted for 26 per cent of the Top 20 rated programmes in 23 European countries (the only larger category is Fictional Drama programming at 29 per cent) (Television 98, p. 37). However, as we outline in Chapter 1, football remains the dominant television sport throughout Europe, and the driver in attempts to establish pay-per-view television both in the UK and elsewhere in Europe.

As Robert McChesney (1998, p. 36) points out:

> Sport is arguably the single most lucrative content area for the global media industry, a point understood best of all by Rupert Murdoch, CEO of News Corporation. Sport was crucial in making his British Sky Broadcasting (BSkyB) the most successful satellite TV service in the world and in making the US Fox TV network a fully-fledged competitor to ABC, NBC and CBS.

Due to the emergence of dedicated subscription sports channels, these broadcasters are interested, where possible, in offering the popular sports exclusive and live to the consumer. As we noted in the previous chapter this has resulted in increased competition for sports rights, and as a result sports programming involving the most popular sports, such as football, cricket and rugby, is no longer the cheap form of programming it once was. While the economics of making money out of television increasingly view sports 'product' as vital, it isn't the only reason why sports matter to television.

Prestige and profile

As we argued in Chapter 2, the BBC's historical image of itself as *the* national broadcaster owes much to the centrality of its sporting coverage. National sporting events such as the Scottish and English FA Cup finals have been projected by the BBC as part of the national fabric of

British life down through the years. However, as we examine in more detail in Chapter 11, the BBC and public-service broadcasting (PSB) in general is struggling to redefine itself as the ecology of broadcasting in Britain rapidly alters in the late 1990s (Goodwin, 1998).

The BBC has seen many of its key sporting events such as English live football, the golf Ryder Cup, Formula One motor racing and key rugby coverage all lost to rivals. Despite BBC protestations, part of these losses have stemmed from a reluctance to divert licence money away from other programme areas such as the expanding TV news and current affairs empire, and poor policy decisions including entering into relationships with BSkyB in a doomed attempt to shut out its terrestrial rival ITV, failing to realize that in the long term its real rival would prove to be the satellite channel. Sport should matter to the BBC because the corporation's ability to deliver to a national audience key sporting events is one of the cornerstones of its PSB remit.

Sport is important to other channels because it gives them a credibility and profile in the marketplace as well as delivering lucrative audiences to advertisers. Channel 5 have successfully targeted bidding for one-off international football matches and European games involving English clubs and in so doing not only have they achieved some of the Channel's largest audiences, they have also considerably raised the profile of the fledgling station.

The extent to which sports historically anchored to one channel are shifting from their moorings was perfectly illustrated in 1998 by the England and Wales Cricket Board's decision to award the rights to screen home test matches at a cost of £104 million (1999–2002) to Channel 4 (in association with the ubiquitous BSKyB), thus leaving the BBC after an association of almost half a century.

The ability of BBC Scotland (both television and radio) to offer extensive coverage of football in that country is a crucial element of its attempt to create a legitimate and distinctive Scottish broadcasting identity in the eyes of the Scottish footballing public. While audiences are important, there are also wider ideological and political reasons why national broadcasters must carry national sporting events to remain credible.

While in 1998 it was true to say that the BBC covered almost fifty sports, increasingly these are sports which exist at the margins of the television schedules. Ironically, at a moment in the history of sport on television when there has never been more of it on our screens (particularly if we are willing to pay extra for it), it remains the case that there are in reality a small core number of mainstream sports which television is particularly interested in, with football and its fan base number one in the eyes of the television executives.

There are economists (Hoskins, McFadyen and Finn, 1997, pp. 91–2) who argue that in a multi-channel environment the main rationale for public-service broadcasters should be to offer programmes which carry an 'external benefit' to the citizen. While they include news and current affairs in these programme categories, they see no reason to include sport, arguing that this should be left to the private sector. We would disagree with this analysis and indeed suggest it appears illogical given that part of the argument they advance for including drama within a PSB remit, is that this programme category 'may provide external benefits in the form of an increased sense of identity and awareness of national/regional themes and values' (p. 91).

We would strongly argue that this is exactly one of the functions which certain sporting events provide for a broad audience. One can imagine a lively debate if viewers in Scotland were asked to choose between having access to a television drama or a major international football and rugby match involving the national team. These issues and the extent to which governments should intervene in the operating of the sports–television marketplace are developed in more detail in Chapters 8, 10 and 11.

It is also worth noting at this juncture the extent to which sport has come into contact with other areas of television output, in particular game shows (such as the BBC's long-running *A Question of Sport*). Programmes such as this are often a vehicle for sports stars (see next chapter) and, as we suggest below, firmly locate sport within the light entertainment sphere of television output.

Reinvented for television: the case of snooker

As we suggested in Chapter 2, the development patterns of particular sports are heavily influenced by shifts and changes in broadcasting institutions and technological innovations. Of course, how broadcasting responds to changing economic and cultural shifts in society and its use of technology are closely related.

For example, snooker owes much to the fact that it allowed the BBC to demonstrate its new colour service in the late 1960s, and sports have often been among the first areas of television programming to be used to show off technological innovations, which as often as not are driven by a range of commercial and industrial interests such as the electronics industry.

Televised snooker allowed the BBC to show off its new colour service and, with the launch in July 1969 of *Pot Black* on BBC 2, the game had a permanent slot in which it could build a following. Before this, snooker had been used as a 'filler' during the racing coverage on BBC's *Grandstand*. However, *Pot Black* with its single-frame match began the transition of the game from back-street snooker halls to the living rooms of millions of people.

This transition was aided by Ted Lowe, who became the established 'voice' of television snooker and used his contacts to help arrange the series. From television's viewpoint snooker fulfilled a number of its key requirements: the action took place within a confined space easily covered by television cameras, it could be packaged to fit into a flow of programmes in a television schedule and it was cheap television programming.

However, it wouldn't be until the late 1970s that snooker's television potential would be fully developed. A television producer Nick Hunter thought that the audience for *Pot Black* of between 2–4 million could be extended if tournament play was brought to the screen. At a time when what we understand as day-time television didn't exist, it was relatively easy to secure air time, but what interested Hunter was not simply the game itself, but the players who played. Put simply, Hunter and his team transformed television coverage of the game.

They changed the lighting, to allow players sitting away from the table to be seen; introduced cut-aways and reaction shots of players supposedly at rest (Hunter wanted the viewers to see up close the pressure that players experienced during a match); repositioned the cameras so that balls were potted into camera and established a pace of cutting which, while offering a range of viewpoints on the event, didn't disrupt the flow of the coverage.

Hunter recognized that sport was about drama and people and wanted to amplify the characters playing the game and create a range of narratives partly resolved as each frame concluded and the match progressed. The televising of the 1978 Embassy World Championship from the Crucible Theatre in Sheffield changed the sport forever. Television now dictated that matches were shorter and Hunter's tele-visual style set the standard for how the sport is covered on television (in 21 years a few extra camera angles have been added and a selective use of slow-motion replay, but the production principles remain the same). The verbal commentary was informative, but unobtrusive, gently adding to the drama unfolding on and around the table.

Snooker soap

Viewing figures grew, as snooker, with its television cast of heroes and villains attracted a large female viewership – the analogy with television soap opera has been made elsewhere (Boyle and O'Conner, 1993). By the 1980s snooker was the most covered and most popular sport on British television. Its high point occurred in 1985, when a record viewership of 18.5 million were watching BBC television after midnight as the World Final between Dennis Taylor and Steve Davis reached its final black ball resolution.

While never to achieve this level of ratings again, snooker remained a staple diet of television's sporting menu into the 1990s. By this stage the game, driven by commercial interests and television, had become global, establishing enormous popularity, particularly in the Far East. Ironically, this occurred at a time when its popularity began to wane with television audiences in the UK.

There are a number of reasons for this, including over-exposure on television, a multiplying of the tournaments around the globe, the dominance of a handful of players – notably Steve Davis in the 1980s and Stephen Hendry in the 1990s – the resurgence in the popularity of football from the turn of the decade, and the move away from alcohol and tobacco sponsorship (the mainstays of the game during the 1980s), which all helped contribute to viewers, advertisers and television executives becoming jaded with the sport.

In addition ITV was concerned with the demographics of the audience (too many working-class and elderly people) that it was delivering to advertisers and, along with darts, snooker disappeared from that station's portfolio. It made a brief reappearance on this channel early in 1999, with coverage of a newly revamped world team tournament. However, it remains very much at the margins of the ITV network's sports programming.

While the BBC retains and promotes the World Championship and snooker still has a profile on the sports satellite channels, the case of snooker demonstrates the extent to which television exposure can transform a sport, from a pastime into a global sports business, making millionaires of the game's top players along the way.

However, the relationship is never equal and ultimately it is television that remains the dominant partner (Rowe, 1996); what television gives it can take way, as fashions shift, leaving a sport dependent on corporate sponsorship dangerously exposed with a limited spectator fan base.

Screening sport: terrestrial and satellite versions

It's down to men, machines and teamwork.

Jim Rosenthal, commenting on the build-up to Formula One motor-racing coverage on ITV, 1 November 1998

Between them Goldlust (1987), Whannel (1992) and Blain *et al.* (1993) offer comprehensive overviews of the techniques used by television to transform sporting events into television programmes. What we want to do here is to examine briefly the extent to which changes in the sports broadcasting environment looked at in the previous chapter and the growth in satellite coverage of sport in the UK in particular have altered the principles outlined in these books.

Formula One

Watching television sport in the UK at the end of the 1990s one is struck by the extent to which the divisions between the traditional PSB – BBC/ITV – style of presentation and the more staccato paced editing and televisual style of US televised sport have blurred considerably. Aspects of BSkyB's entertainment-driven style of rapid pace, music and action which characterizes much of its sports coverage and trailers has been borrowed by terrestrial broadcasters, in particular the increasingly commercial ITV network.

In their analysis of the impact that satellite coverage has had in transforming both the structure and televisual image of Rugby League, Arundel and Roche (1998, p. 80) note how people within the game generally viewed BSkyB's coverage, backed by a considerable financial investment, as having improved the televisual coverage of the game. In turn, this coverage, involving at times up to 17 cameras at a match, has forced the BBC to rethink and adopt some of the production techniques employed by the satellite broadcaster. This has also been true of other sports.

ITV's live coverage of the 1998 Japanese Grand Prix from Suzuka clearly demonstrates the continuities of television coverage as well as the developments. Formula One motor-racing became a key part of the ITV sports portfolio when it secured the rights from the BBC in 1997. While physically a difficult television sport to cover – the cars on the television screen never appear to be travelling at their actual speed and it can become difficult to distinguish one from another – all the core elements of television sport are there in the coverage.

Telling the story

The slick title shots of a racing car, emblazoned with the programme sponsor's name, owe much in their look and feel to BSkyB's treatment of sport. The studio anchor Jim Rosenthal makes sense of the event by a build-up to the race in which he reminds us of the many twists and turns there have been so far in the race to become the 1998 world champion. Then the experts Tony Martin and Martin Brundle inform us about the battle today between the two contenders for the title, the Finn Mikka Hakkinen and the German Michael Schumacher.

Both experts bring us 'up close and personal' to the pre-race action, passing on rumours and gossip from the pit lanes and the teams, enthusing about the atmosphere and tension, with ex-driver Brundle taking us down on to the track among the posse of drivers, technicians and media to secure an interview with Hakkinen – who he assures us never gives interviews – fifteen minutes before the race. In the track-side studio, the anchor, Jim Rosenthal can't resist telling us that these few banal questions and answers, constituted 'the interview everyone wanted, and you heard it first on ITV'.

Central in sports coverage is personalization and story-telling. In his book on Grand Prix, Richard Williams (1998, p. 2) argues that:

> When television turned motor racing into mass entertainment,
> information became currency. Nowadays the course of rumour is
> pursued as avidly as the story of the race. While television coverage
> provides the bare bones of the narrative structure the newspaper
> journalists, led by the representatives of the tabloids will add layers of
> dramatic meaning by telling you exactly how much the two drivers
> concerned hate each other because one of them stole the other's
> girlfriend or, of even greater emotional impact, stole his seat in the best
> car in the field.

We would add to this relationship outlined by Williams and suggest that, increasingly, those tabloid stories also filter back into the television coverage of the race, both in setting the agenda during the extensive pre-race scene-setting, and in the actual coverage itself. At one point in this race Martin Brundle informed us how Damon Hill would be particularly keen not to let Schumacher pass him, given their previous rivalry both on and off the track.

While cameras are carried in the cars, the basic visual style of motor-racing has actually changed little over recent years with perhaps more visual information being displayed on the screen as the viewer attempts to keep track of who is positioned where in the race. What has changed is the focus on the battle between personalities and the construction teams, added to with cut-away reaction shots of the teams in their pits (all watching television screens!) during the race.

The key to the coverage, however, remains the commentary, with ITV securing the high-octane Murray Walker from the BBC as its main commentator, with summarizer and former driver Martin Brundle providing more information on the technical and strategic aspects of the race. We examine the role of the commentator in more detail below, suffice to say here that the commentator is central, even on the visual medium of television, in imposing a narrative structure on events, and is particularly crucial in such a potentially visually confusing television sport as motor-racing in both informing the viewer as to what is happening and connecting together the story lines highlighted in the pre-race scene-setting.

The view from the Sky

While Sky Sports, part of the BSkyB network of satellite channels, has altered the television sports landscape during the 1990s with its introduction of competition into the sports rights marketplace, stylistically it owes a considerable debt to established patterns of terrestrial television sports coverage. Sky has both adapted these and also innovated, drawing heavily on a US model of sports broadcasting.

Thus its cricket coverage of the 1998/99 Ashes series between Australia and England mixed well-known faces such as former England players Bob Willis and Ian Botham while adding to the established pace and pattern of terrestrial test-match coverage. A multiplicity of camera angles, side on to the wicket, behind the batsman, behind the bowler's arm, in the stumps, all allowed the viewer to keep close to the action.

In addition, extensive use of reaction shots and medium close-ups of the batsman, bowler and fielders and slow-motion replays of every ball bowled, all add to the intimacy of the sporting contest for the viewer. However, Sky appears to have toned down the overly intrusive use of graphics that it applied to earlier coverage of cricket and, while both pacy and tighter in focus, the coverage retains aspects of the more traditional coverage, in particular through its relatively hyperbole-free commentary.

Selling the game

One noticeable difference in looking at Sky Sports in 1999, as opposed to 1992 (Blain *et al.*, 1993), is the increase in the quality of the sports now offered on satellite. These have been cleverly packaged into three channels which means that, while 'fillers' still exist, more hours are devoted to key sports which are attractive to subscribers. Sky Sports still aggressively markets its sports coverage better than the other channels, although both Channel 4 and more recently Channel 5 have realized the importance in both trailing sports coverage and in attractively packaging the event itself.

It would be wrong to suggest that packaging sport is what Sky does best, it is also attempting to change what we understand and expect from television sport. For example, in its coverage of rugby league it attempts both to draw on the traditional audience for the sport, while attracting a newer viewer to the sport.

Arundel and Roche (1998, p. 81) suggest that often this has been at the expense of emphasizing the hard masculine physicality of the sport, over the more cerebral and technical elements of the game. This aggressive, staccato editing style is evident in much of BSkyB's treatment of sport, both in its actual coverage and its trailing of future events. In addition, this is often accompanied by extensive hyperbole, as the promise of excitement, drama, action (and, in the case of international events, the settling of old scores) is sold to the viewer.

The opening titles to its coverage of the 1998/99 Allied Dunbar Premiership rugby coverage perfectly illustrate the key influences shaping modern sport. Opening with a bank of television screens and cutting between fans entering and filling up the stadium and television OB units and cameras setting up to cover the match, we move to players kicking and running with a Ford-sponsored rugby ball before we cut between close-ups of passionate supporters and committed players involved in try-scoring action. The sequence finishes with a big close-up of a Ford-sponsored rugby ball. The voice-over, just about audible against a backdrop of dramatic operatic music, tells us 'Everyone unites with a single common goal. In a game to which they give their soul. This is the land were the legends are made.'

Significantly, in 1999 BSkyB feels confident enough in its own position within sport to suggest, apparently without irony, that sport actually means television, fans and players working together in a mutually beneficial relationship. While some fear that sport has sold its soul to television, Sky views itself as delivering the new field of dreams for the next generation of rugby and sports fans and correctly identifies that, far from stealing the soul of sport, sports have been only too keen to pass it to television for financial gain.

Sports commentary: codes and conventions

In 1995 BBC Television began a new comedy–sports–quiz programme entitled *They Think It's All Over*, hosted by the English actor and comedian Nick Hancock, with two team captains recently retired from their respective sports of football and cricket, Gary Lineker and David Gower. The programme is a hybrid of sports trivia and satirical comment, where the manner and style in which the game is played is more important than the final score.

The title of the programme is of interest as an example of the familiarity of televised sports discourse, its transcendence into mythologized, structured narratives of sport as popular culture and the way in which it serves as an excellent reference 'to the ideological character of images and stories which naturalise and disguise the reality of the historical and the man–made' (Silverstone, 1994, p. 22).

The title of the programme is taken, of course, from Kenneth Wolstenholme's running commentary of the 1966 World Cup Final at Wembley (the complete phrase: 'Some people are on the pitch, they think it's all over [Geoff Hurst scores for England] it is now, it's four' is probably the most frequently repeated sports commentary in British broadcasting history). Wolstenholme's commentary has gained mythological status as it is the key signifying element of England's World Cup victory of 1966; specifically, it denotes England's fourth and final goal against West Germany at the end of extra time, and the moment when Geoff Hurst scored the only hat trick in the history of the World Cup final. As Whannel (1992, p. 148) suggests, television, consumed by millions, aids 'this instant production of myth'.

According to the BBC's Audience Research Unit approximately 27 million viewers watched the 1966 final on BBC Television; several millions more have seen the image of Hurst's final raid and shot from the edge of the German penalty area, complemented by Wolstenholme's commentary.

Sporting drama

The moment is not only replayed as a significant part of English sports history (often to the annoyance of Scottish viewers), but often presented as a central element of British television's history (the broadening of the national nomenclature is also of significance here). In many respects, the event represents a transformative period in British television, both in its social and cultural importance and, more pertinent to what we argue here, in the codes and conventions of the communicative process of televised sport.

As we argue in Chapter 8, the coverage of such large sporting occasions connects with and inscribes a range of social relations and cultural meanings, which are both general and specific in any given time and space. Therefore, it is the biography of such television texts – their production, distribution and reception – which is central to an understanding of the relationship between the technology of television and its mediation of sport. Similarly, in creating these links between mediated form and social process, television also produces a double movement of mediation by ingestion and projection: what Corner (1995, p. 5) has characterized as 'centripetal interplay' and 'centrifugal interplay'.

By centripetal interplay, Corner suggests that television has a powerful capacity to draw towards itself and incorporate wider elements of society and culture. This leans heavily on the idea of Williams (1974) who talked of 'Drama in a Dramatised Society', where much in culture bears a resemblance or relation to what is 'on the box'. Clearly, televised sport with its rhetoric of realism, very much fits into this typology, with the key transformations centring upon a mix of commentary, edited highlights and action replays.

By centrifugal interplay, Corner is alluding to the process whereby television projects its images, characters and catch phrases into broader aspects of the culture. Once again, Wolstenholme's commentary from the 1966 World Cup is an evident case in point, and is now verging on pastiche and satire, as illustrated by its use in the title of the aforementioned comedy–sports–quiz programme.

The use of such 'golden moments' in television, therefore, becomes a contested site of a struggle for control over meaning and potency – the significance of Wolstenholme's commentary is clearly different for supporters of English football from the fans of Scottish, Welsh or Irish football.

There is a third dynamic to which Corner alludes which is important in understanding the mediation of sport by television; it is also a dynamic integral to the popularity of the game *per se*. This is the need to understand the contingency of sport and television: their uncertain variables, their conditional elements and incidental moments which, within televised sport, create narrative pleasures. In the early years of television there would have been doubts as to whether a television picture could be produced at all, which, as we suggested in Chapter 2, produced an institutional and promotional discourse (specifically within the *Radio Times*) preoccupied with the technology of the medium: the wonder of television.

As we have already seen with radio broadcasts from sport, once the techniques, codes and conventions were established, this unpredictability changed, and discourses preoccupied with the aesthetics of television and modes of address became more dominant. Therefore, the expectations of the audience with regard to televised sport have changed with the development of new technologies.

The relatively sophisticated institutional discourse of Wolstenholme, and the way in which it combines with the camera image of Hurst as he attacks the German goal (which is also institutionalized), refer not only to that moment in the game, but also take on their own significance, through the unpredictability of what happens next, and create their own powerful communicative poetics.

The codes and conventions of sports commentary are social processes that have developed over time. In various ways, commentary as an institutional discourse of television has become the context for thinking, talking and writing about sport: in other words, television becomes central to our perceptual field of what sport actually means.

Presence at the microphone

There can be no doubt that the television coverage of the football World Cup, the summer and winter Olympic Games, world heavyweight boxing, the Super Bowl, the US Masters golf, Wimbledon and the Grand National has produced some of the most enduring images within twentieth-century popular culture. However, it is not merely the visual mediation of the athletic ability of Pele, Carl Lewis, Franz Klammer, Mohammad Ali, Joe Montana, Tiger Woods, Bjorn Borg or Red Rum that is recalled in popular memory, but also the descriptive narratives of the commentator which provide the bases of such communication.

As we outlined in Chapter 2 with regard to radio commentary on sport, this particular form of sports discourse had to be invented, through trial and error and, as Whannel (1992, p. 26) has highlighted, by overcoming 'the conflicting aims of naturalism and construction'. This tension alludes to the fact that sports commentary is, as part of television technology, a social process, and employs specific techniques as a roundabout way of achieving a desired effect: that of realism and entertainment.

The Sound of Summer – Cricket commentator and journalist John Arlott during the 'golden age' of BBC Radio sport in 1949. *© Hulton Getty*

The conventions for delivering a coded narrative of a sporting event with an economy of words was a process well underway within BBC radio commentary by the mid-1930s, under the guidance of de Lotbiniere. The level of economy of speech required by radio and television were, however, different, and were recognized as such by de Lotbiniere as he anticipated the arrival of television in 1937:

> The art of the 'sound' commentator is scarcely ten years old and it still has a long way to go. But there may not be much time left for its normal development, as television will soon be making a different demand on the commentator, and, I believe, a lighter one. (*Radio Times*, 4 June 1937)

The necessity for a mellifluous quality within sound broadcasting – painting a picture with words – seemed unnecessary and almost intrusive with the medium of television, and the notion of using the same commentary for radio and television was soon discarded after the 1938 Cup Final when the radio commentary was used for both broadcasts.

With radio there was room for error. If there occurred 'a slip 'twixt eye and lip', the radio commentator could use little 'white lies' to get him out of a sticky situation. For instance, one BBC producer advised radio commentators: 'if you make a mistake in identifying players, don't leave the audience in any doubt, don't let on that you're not infallible, make him pass it' (from an interview with Kenneth Wolstenholme, July 1995).

However, television revealed – although selectively – the actual sporting performance and, therefore, continually opened up the possibility that viewers could recognize mistakes in the narrative and be reminded of the transformative nature of television, despite all the rhetoric to the contrary.

Creating the sports commentator

Another comparison is of interest at this point, that of the recruitment of new commentators by the BBC in the late 1940s and 1950s. Within radio, prospective candidates had been asked to perform under broadcasting conditions by providing a closed-circuit commentary to a 'blind' listener who would adjudicate his talent (or lack of it).

According to de Lotbiniere the number of what he considered to be 'good commentators' was scarce, and anyone taking the test would have a difficult task in displacing the now familiar voices of George Allison, Teddy Wakelam and Fred Grisewood (all of whom shared a similar upper-middle-class status to that of BBC producers and directors). In the shadow of radio, recruitment into television sports commentary appears even more *ad hoc* and circumstantial. Take, for instance, the movement into television by the BBC's first recognized football commentator Kenneth Wolstenholme.

In an interview with the authors, Wolstenholme recounted how he had always possessed a desire to be a sports writer, and had been fortunate enough to meet the editor of a Sunday newspaper, Harold Mays, while on active service during the Second World War. Immediately after the war he met Mays once more at the FA Cup semi-final between Charlton Athletic and his home-town side of Bolton Wanderers in 1946, whereupon Wolstenholme was asked to write a small feature on cricket in Lancashire.

At the same time he had written to the BBC informally applying for work, and was subsequently asked, upon the strength of his article, to provide an eye-witness account from a cricket match. He was then asked to do a full radio commentary on an amateur international trial match between Northern Counties and Southern Counties. As Wolstenholme describes:

> So that was sheer luck. Which I suppose is the short answer to how you become a football commentator. If you're cheeky enough to ask for a job, you're lucky enough for someone to ask you to do it. (Interview with one of the authors, July 1995)

Wolstenholme's move into television was due to a similar happenstance. Jimmy Jewell, who had refereed the first televised Cup Final of 1938, had taken over the role of football commentator for television immediately after the War.

Wolstenholme had moved from BBC Radio in the North West to become Jewell's understudy when the ex-referee suddenly died of a heart attack, leaving Wolstenholme as BBC Television's principal football commentator.

Even as television began to cover sport in a more comprehensive fashion in the 1960s, personnel appeared to drift into working within the medium, for example Scottish football commentator Archie MacPherson. A school teacher by profession, MacPherson had written a series of short stories, a selection of which he had been asked to read for broadcast by BBC Scotland.

Upon hearing the distinctive grain of voice and with the knowledge that MacPherson had previously had a brief spell with the Glasgow club Partick Thistle, the sports producer Peter Thompson asked the teacher if he was interested in giving eye-witness accounts of Scottish League matches for BBC Radio Scotland. MacPherson soon found himself promoted to BBC Television in Scotland after turning down a commentary post in London on the advice of another young BBC radio commentator, Brian Moore. MacPherson continued to teach throughout his early years of commentary until he realized in 1965 that a full-time career could be made in broadcasting.

The biographical backgrounds of Wolstenholme and MacPherson reflect wider connections of sport with both the military and education, rooted in a historical concern for disciplining and schooling the body (Hargreaves, 1986). The assumption that sport was morally and socially a 'good thing' lurked beneath the discourses of both commentators, as it had done for those early producers of televised sport.

'They think it's all over' – the 1966 World Cup came during an era of innovation in televised sport, epitomised by the use of action replay during the finals.   © *Hulton Getty*

Established voices of sport

Another route of entry into the role of sports commentary was sports journalism, traditionally a cloistered profession, which was given a new lease of life by television. For instance, David Coleman joined the BBC in 1954 after an apprenticeship with the *Cheshire County Express* and several years as a freelance radio contributor; Barry Davies joined ABC TV in 1966 before moving to the BBC in 1969 after beginning his career with the British Forces radio in Cologne, and a spell as a sports correspondent with *The Times*; John Motson worked for the *Barnett Press*

Weekly Newspaper and the *Morning Telegraph* in Sheffield before joining BBC Radio in 1969, and making his debut for television in 1971; and Martin Tyler, now BSkyB's principal commentator, began as a staff-writer and sub-editor for a publisher, before becoming an editorial assistant on LWT's *On The Ball* with Brian Moore, and moved to commentating for Southern TV in 1974.

These career profiles sketch a more familiar pattern of entry into 'factual' broadcasting: from print, to radio and then television. In this respect, these commentators share similar career patterns with sports producers and editors.

However, as Wolstenholme and MacPherson testify, there is no clear-cut or straight-forward 'career-ladder' upon which the budding football commentator may climb. One thing is certain, it remains an exclusively male preserve, despite the few women sports journalists who have managed to cross over into broadcasting to stake a claim in an otherwise ubiquitously masculine domain (the presenter Hazel Irvine of BBC Scotland is a rare case in point – see Chapter 7).

It is also worth noting the longevity within broadcasting of all the above practitioners. For the BBC Wolstenholme provided the commentary for twenty-three FA Cup finals before being replaced by Coleman in 1972, then Motson in 1977 and more recently by Davies in 1995; and for ITV the recently retired Brian Moore had been the principal commentator since 1968 and was preceded by less familiar men at the microphone like Peter Lloyd and Ken Walton (once an actor) who had provided some of the earliest ITV commentaries, and a host of regional commentators, most notably, perhaps, Hugh Johns (of ATV in the Midlands region) who provided ITV's commentary for the 1966 World Cup final.

Other sports reflect similar patterns: Murray Walker commentated on motor sports for over forty years with the BBC before joining ITV Sport in 1997; Dan Maskell was for many viewers the essence of watching Wimbledon from the 1940s through to the early 1990s; Peter O'Sullivan, another recently retired BBC commentator had been reaching that familiar crescendo of description and excitement towards the end of a horse race since the 1950s; and Peter Alliss continues to be the calming and humorous voice behind the BBC's coverage of golf.

The commentator's address

One reason for such longevity is the need for familiarity by broadcasters to obtain and maintain an audience for their sports programmes. When a new commentator is introduced one can sense that a 'bedding-in' period is required for acceptability by the audience. As we have seen with radio, this requires a conversational style, building up sentences with a familiar lexicon of sporting phrases and idioms and weaving a continuous narrative without losing shape. Here we see the congruence between radio and television commentary.

The mode of address of the commentator is governed by the general mood of the programme and the professional ideology of the producers, directors and editors who structure it. In our interviews with sports commentators, professionalism and teamwork were heavily emphasized: from the background researchers who feed an endless supply of biographical and statistical data on sports women and men, managers, coaches and clubs, to the production engineers who enable the commentators' performance with television monitors, microphone equipment, and 'lazy talkback' (which allows communication with the final team members), the producers, directors and editors who orchestrate the whole broadcast with their control of sound and cameras (again, operated almost ubiquitously by men).

Although the tight production teams which used to operate within the pioneering years of BBC sport have disintegrated to a certain extent, partially due to advances in technology and a level of homogeneity of practices in outside broadcasting (many sporting federations now set strict guidelines on camera positions and editing) Wolstenholme's adage that 'any broadcast with commentary needs as much teamwork as on the field' would appear to substantiate claims to slickness and professionalism in production.

Whannel (1992, p. 60) illustrates how the professional ideologies of sports broadcasting are a fusion of journalistic practices of objectivity, entertainment practices grounded in the principles of 'good television' and dramatic practices which involve the audience in a narrative.

These ideologies can be seen to govern the principles of football commentary and were clearly evident when the BBC began its first regular football highlights programme *Sports Special* in 1955, the residual effects of which can be seen throughout contemporary television coverage of football in Britain. Wolstenholme recalled how he utilized the general guidelines of de Lotbiniere: 'you've got to think of the audience as a pyramid' from the small cross-section of specialists at the top to the broad audience made up of occasional viewers at the bottom.

The tensions between realism and entertainment are evident once more. The commentator has to explain why a player is offside without regurgitating the laws of the game. Technical or 'in' expressions need to be avoided but the commentary must be well informed and put over the significance of the event.

The description of play is required to be faithful to what is happening on the field, but must also avoid being overly objective and has to introduce human interest and suspense. Associative material in the form of pre-researched notes are frequently utilized, but the commentary needs to avoid the appearance of being scripted and requires a level of fluency and informality of address.

Sports commentary is very much part of a social process. It is also a crucial means by which television attempts to convey the dramatic form of expression which is intrinsic within sport. Television commentary both ingests from and projects into a public discourse on sport. As John Hargreaves (1986, p. 12) has suggested, these forms of public discourse on sport constitute 'some of the basic themes of social life – success and failure, good and bad behaviour, ambition and achievement, discipline and effort'.

What television had to develop was a convenient discourse which addressed the need to inform and entertain both the fan and the family audience. Many of the techniques of addressing this tension had been carried over from radio, which has ensured that televised football retains a high level of talk-based communication.

To our knowledge, sport in Britain has never been televised without commentary. Many fans criticize the often inane comments of the football commentator – seen most vociferously in the irreverence of many football fanzine skits on televised football (Haynes, 1995) – but, in order to escape this sports chatter, are left with the inferior alternative of turning the sound down. Digital television may change the possibilities available to the 'armchair supporter' in this respect (see Chapter 11).

Sport may still be mediated, but with more control as to what the viewer sees and, more importantly in this discussion, what they hear. Digital television may make it possible for viewers to individualize their consumption to the extent that choosing from an array of commentaries on any one particular sporting event may provide the ultimate means of identification with such a discourse: each competitor, team or nation involved could have a commentary biased in its favour, and a third could attempt to be impartial in the classic tradition.

Movements in this direction have already occurred within football with the rise in pre-recorded video, which maps the performance of individual clubs through a season from a partisan perspective.

Conclusion

We have argued in this chapter that there are a number of reasons, economic, cultural and social, that explain why sport matters to television and broadcasters. This involves a constant evolution of the transformation of sport into television sport, or sports adapted for television.

While this evolution has been driven in the past largely by an institutional and technological impetus informed by notions of public service, this is no longer the case. Commercial and technological imperatives now drive this process of transformation and, when allied with the erosion of public-service broadcasting in a multi-media environment, have led to a blurring of the codes and conventions of terrestrial and satellite coverage of sport. There remain differences, but both increasingly borrow and innovate from each other in attempts to secure audiences, advertisers and increasingly subscribers.

The ideological aspect of this process of transformation is examined in more detail in Chapters 6, 7 and 8 of the book; however, the next chapter sees us turn our attention to one of the core functions of the media's coverage of sport: the creation of the sports star.

CHAPTER 5

Who Wants to be a Millionaire?

Media Sport and Stardom

It is now possible not only to play your golf with Palmer clubs while dressed from cleat to umbrella tip in Palmer clothes (made in the US, Canada, New Zealand, Australia, Hong Kong, Japan, France or South Africa), but to have the Palmer image at your elbow in countless other ways.

You can buy your insurance from a Palmer agency, stay in a Palmer-owned motel, buy a Palmer lot to build your home on, push a Palmer-approved lawnmower, read a Palmer book, newspaper column or pamphlet, be catered to by a Palmer maid, listen to Palmer music and send your suit to a Palmer dry cleaner.

You can shave with his lather, spray on his deodorant, drink his favourite soft drink, fly his preferred airline, buy his approved corporate jet, eat his candy bar, order your certificates through him and cut up with his power tools.

Mark McCormack (1967), sports manager and agent writing about client and golfer Arnold Palmer in 1967, p. 112

People don't concentrate their emotional energy on products in the way fans abandon themselves to the heroes of their games.

Donald Katz (1994), on Phil Knight's philosophy of selling Nike sports shoes through stars like Michael Jordan, p. 6

Introduction

If the media, and television in particular, have transformed the organization and economic importance of sport in the twentieth century, they have also dramatically transformed the relationship between sports performers and the public they entertain. Perhaps the most important aspect of media sport is the centrality of the star and the cult of celebrity that generates the contemporary fascination with the men and women who reach the pinnacle of their sport. This chapter reveals the processes that create sports stars and analyses some of the economic, social and ethical consequences such processes have for sport as popular culture.

We begin with an investigation of how new sports stars are constructed by the media, taking up some of Garry Whannel's (1992) points on the interrelationship between stars and narratives. Secondly, we investigate the origins of sports celebrity and the rise of the sports agent, perhaps one of the most influential additions to the business of sport. Thirdly, we draw on a case study of the new model of sports stardom represented by the synergy of media, popular culture and merchandizing witnessed in the National Basketball Association (NBA) in the USA. Fourthly, and related to the case of the NBA, we analyse some of the key transformations in sports labour markets created by sports stardom. In conclusion, we raise questions about the ethical problems posed by sports stardom, focusing on the mavericks of the world of sport who undermine the conventions of media celebrity.

A star is born

The rags to riches story is a familiar motif in the narratives society tells itself about sport. During the final round of the 1998 British Open Golf Championship a seventeen-year-old amateur, Justin Rose, finished his fourth round with a pitch shot from forty-five yards for a birdie three and a round of sixty-nine. This sealed his position as the highest placed amateur, as well as joint fourth in the overall Championship.

Unfortunately, for Rose, he would not collect a single penny of his £69,875 prize money because of his designated amateur status. However, as the youngest, and highest placed, English player in the tournament he was soon propelled into the media spotlight as Britain's answer to the World's leading golfer Tiger Woods. Unlike Woods, who held off turning professional until his twentieth birthday, Rose shed his amateur status immediately after receiving the Silver Medal for the Open Championship, one week before turning eighteen.

His 'star status' now guaranteed, thanks to the dramatic entry onto the global sports stage, Rose also signed with the sports management group Carnegie to oversee his affairs. In a profile of the 'Young Master' the *Daily Telegraph* (20 July 1998) suggested: 'Rose has the perfect temperament for a champion. He can walk with princes and not lose the common touch.'

The language commonly used by the media to describe such moments and the sudden 'rise to fame' of individuals is intrinsically tied to the fact that 'star performers are characters within a set of narratives' (Whannel, 1992, p. 121). In other words, the televisual and back-page blitz that greeted Rose as he walked off the eighteenth green was symptomatic of the media elevation of sporting achievement as part of a wider story, connecting the individual with society. As Whannel has commented, sports performers hold a 'threefold function' for broadcasters and the press:

> [A]s stars they are the bearers of the entertainment value of performance; as personalities they provide the individualisation and personalisation through which audiences are won and held; and as characters they are the bearers of the sporting narratives. (Whannel, 199, p. 122)

Rose had provided a stream of newsworthy moments for the television cameras, not least his final shot of the Championship.

Both television and press coverage of Rose laid emphasis on his incredible temperament throughout his four rounds of golf. His effervescence on the course became an important trait of his emerging personality, and commentators continually remarked on his remarkably calm presence for one so young. His meteoric rise was meticulously (re)told for the television audience, constructed in such a fashion that the audience was carried along with his story, sharing the highs and lows of a previously 'unseen' sporting hero.

Whannel (1992) also argues that there is an inherent tension in the star-system of mediated sport caused by the increasing commercialization of the individual that eclipses any attempt to place sports stars in the national ideologies of representative sport. Again, in the case of Rose, four months after his entry into the professional ranks he failed to qualify for the European PGA Tour. The BBC's *Nine O'clock News* lamented Rose's failure and, in its moment of national grief, failed to mention that 'journeyman' Ross Drummond had won the 'qualifying school' at San Roque, Spain, much to the chagrin of Drummond's caddie, the writer Lawrence Donegan (*Scotsman*, 28 November 1998).

In contrast to the furore, Rose himself remained optimistic, viewing his failure as a mere 'blip' in what he envisaged would be a long and financially rewarding career in professional sport. Such a calculated response from a relatively inexperienced sportsman highlighted the financial motivation that now underwrites contemporary sporting achievement. Clearly, Rose had witnessed the financial reward and carefully managed career enjoyed by Tiger Woods, a 'model professional' and according to the media a 'nice guy' to boot!

Heroes and villains

A further tension in the social and mediated construction of sports stars stems from the various idiosyncrasies of sporting characters (Rowe, 1995, pp. 115–18). As with any cast of characters, the sport star-system sets up a range of 'heroes' and 'villains' in order to play out sporting narratives. Either through design or default the private lives of sports performers converge with their public personas to reveal sports celebrities as model citizens and family members or fallen idols and 'flawed' individuals.

Where the details of sordid private lives invade the public domain of sports performance, the favours enjoyed under the media spotlight can quickly disappear as the media, and the press in particular, take great pleasure in morally denigrating the crimes and misdemeanours of past favourites. Indeed, within the UK, and the English-based press in particular, the back-page 'gossip' and 'sleaze' of the sports press mirrors the political 'mud' used to undermine the political aspirations of MPs on the front pages of national newspapers (Leigh and Vulliamy, 1997).

Moreover, the status of sports stars in society frequently means that 'sleaze' from the realms of sport can enter a wider public domain, creating headline news, displacing regular 'hard news' items on war, politics, the economy, disasters and law and order. When sport 'hits the front page' it is invariably related to celebrity: from footballer Paul Gascoigne's marital problems and alcoholism to the salacious details of rugby player Will Carling's alleged affair with the Princess of Wales. As the above examples also illustrate, the reportage of sports stars revolves around a predominantly masculine and masculinized set of frames.

Women do not feature prominently as sporting heroes or villains, and are marginalized as cultural icons. This is reflected in the imbalance of reward between male and female sports (see Chapter 7). For example, in 1994 Britain had two outstanding performers in athletics: Linford Christie and Sally Gunnell. Both were world champions, both had received wide television exposure at numerous meetings, but, in terms of prize-money and endorsements, Christie earned more than three times the income of Gunnell (*Guinness Sports Yearbook*, 1994).

Making a name for oneself is a double-edged sword in the hypnotic contemporary media-saturated 'world of sport'. These stars, such as Manchester United footballer David Beckham, exist outside their sporting domain, appearing in non-sporting magazines, newspaper gossip columns and in print and television advertising campaigns related both to sporting and non-sporting products. It gives contemporary sports performers a wider visibility in the public domain and can lead to extraordinary wealth for many sportspeople. For critics of modern sport, it was not always this way, and the origins of this process can be traced to America in the 1960s.

The origins of the sports celebrity and the sports agent

The first quote at the beginning of this chapter is taken from a biography of the golfer Arnold Palmer by his friend, lawyer and business partner Mark McCormack, head of one of the largest sports–media management organizations in the world, International Management Group (IMG). It is a snapshot of the Palmer business empire that used golf as a launch pad for a fantastic array of enterprises. Golf was the medium through which Arnold Palmer became a global brand-name known far beyond the field of sport.

The trailblazer

The 'brand-name principle' through which Palmer and McCormack approached the business of sport was, in the early 1960s when they first teamed up together, the first attempt to transform the business activities of leading sports personalities. As noted in Chapter 3, it was not that sport and business were not previously related, nor that an individual sportsman or woman had not cashed in on his or her fame through endorsements and promotional activity, it was more the scale of the enterprise, the level of horizontal and vertical integration that made McCormack's promotion of Palmer unique for its time.

According to Stephen Aris (1990), McCormack invented what he terms 'Sportsbiz'. Where golfers like Sam Snead had used agents to handle endorsements and appearances, with Palmer, McCormack took this relationship further, overseeing contract negotiations, proactively seeking business opportunities and planning the sale of the Palmer brand on a long-term basis rather than the *ad hoc* promotion of earlier sports stars. McCormack set a precedent for selling people as marketable commodities.

Furthermore, in the game of golf the professional sport had a direct link to corporate America as the preferred pastime of the American middle class. Selling the Palmer brand to this audience made the transition from the business of sport, to sport as a business remarkably

The Trailblazer – American golfer Arnold Palmer one of the first sporting superstars of the modern era.   © *Hulton Getty*

smooth. Within two years Palmer's earnings had risen from $59,000 to more than $500,000 a year. By 1962 IMG was also the agent for Gary Player and Jack Nicklaus, presenting McCormack with a triumvirate of the best golfers in the world.

The demands of maintaining 'celebrity status' in order to fuel the sports stars' media ubiquity and mystique requires a constant vigil. Again, Palmer led the way in America, making numerous appearances on television shows, advertisements, celebrity golf tournaments and business events. While many of these activities are for direct payment, they also facilitated the promotion of both Arnold Palmer Enterprises specifically and the sport of golf more generally. However, such evangelical patronage of golf comes at a price when figures like Palmer are concerned.

With his every move on a golf course potentially captured by television, Palmer, and those that have since followed him, realized that they are human advertisements. So when completing a round of golf a fresh bottle of Coca-Cola neatly placed in Palmer's hand would evade the expense of ad-spend on air-time, displacing a fraction of that money instead to the pocket of the golfer.

Spreading the gospel of golf

Palmer, along with his contemporaries Player and Nicklaus, have done more to spread the culture of golf on a global scale than any other professionals. The extent to which new golf courses are designed and built has dramatically accelerated since the 1960s, where supply has struggled to keep pace with demand. As well as having severe environmental impact, the process of star-led initiatives creates a further supply of both ready-made golf venues and events made for television.

Of all the sports which respond to the demands made by television's insatiable appetite for sports 'product', golf is surely the master. In the contemporary world of televised golf, summer is perpetual, as the professional tours move from continent to continent to satisfy demand from global sponsors, advertisers and audiences.

Pro-Celebrity tours and programmes (a long-running feature of golf programming on the BBC during the 1970s and 1980s hosted by commentator Peter Alliss), add to the patina of superstardom many of the top golfers now enjoy. Breaking down barriers between sport and the entertainment industries has become a key feature sustaining the sports-star system. While written over thirty years ago, the wider meaning of the contemporary sports-star as performer is explicitly related in Palmer's biography by McCormack:

> At heart . . . Arnold is an actor. When he walks down a fairway, he
> seems to want everybody's eyes on him. There is something in the way
> he moves that almost says, 'Look, look, I'm Arnold Palmer, and aren't
> we having fun.' McCormack (1967, p. 184)

Sports-stars, then, must perform in all manner of capacities, as skilled athletes and practitioners, interviewees and sometimes interviewers, ambassadors for sport and sports sponsors, and celebrities in and of themselves. This last point alludes to the fact that celebrity is a self-fulfilling process, where stars become famous for being famous. This enables stars whose moment in any given sport has passed to maintain a public presence.

Sport can also attempt to extend the longevity of a generation of stars through secondary tournaments and events. Golf's Senior Tour (currently screened on CBS) provides an opportunity for professional golfers to play on a competitive basis for the television cameras with all the peripheral promotional activity such a venture incorporates. The idea of 'Senior' sport is also maintained within other sports including tennis and football. While such events do not challenge the status of top professional sport, they do provide vehicles for further promotional activity that can be tied into the sponsorship activities of 'first-class' sport.

Michael Jordan and the NBA brand

> Basketball isn't my job. For me, my job begins the moment I walk off the floor. It's everything that surrounds the actual playing of the games. My job is being a product endorser, an employee of the Chicago Bulls, trying to live up to the expectations of others, dealing with the media. That's my job.
>
> Michael Jordan (1994) *Rare Air: Michael on Michael,* p. 43

Basketball has become one of the prime examples of the interweaving of media–sport production and marketing interests that have transformed sports performers into global stars. Over the years the game has undergone numerous mutations to arrive at its current venerable status: the introduction of time-outs for television ad breaks; the twenty-four second rule to speed up the action; the three-point rule to increase the level of scoring; overtime to ensure a result when the scores are tied; and the erosion of the sovereign governing body of the sport to allow television a free reign in the choice of live broadcasts.

These changes have also had a profound effect on the performance of basketball players. After a slump in the popularity in the game during the 1970s a re-emphasis on the heroic nature of the sport, in the manner in which it was promoted, augured a new era of basketball superstars in the mid-1980s. Characters like Larry Bird and Magic Johnson epitomized the introduction of a new set of entertainment values that laid emphasis on display and glitz.

However, both Bird and Johnson would be eclipsed by the most prolific basketball player the game has ever seen, Michael Jordan. Jordan, apocryphal son of the modern NBA, has come to be viewed as 'Michael the Marketed' or a 'post-modern sports commodity of truly heroic proportions' (Vande-Berg, 1998, p. 146). Jordan's commodification of sport is integrally related to his African-American origin tangibly linked to broader elements of black popular culture. His symbolic worth, as a highly successful black sportsman, has been transformed from cultural to monetary capital.

Be like Mike?

Through his agency Pro-Serv, Jordan capitalized on the 'sneaker' as an essential element of black urban street style through his promotion of Nike footwear under the signature of 'Air Jordans'. The 'sneaker' or 'trainer' universally represents youth, hedonism and the individualization of consumption. Indeed, in many respects, the style wars of the 1990s have been fought on the feet of millions of people, for whom the trainer represents the ultimate in 'hip', 'cool' and 'chic'.

How does Jordan fit into this process? And why has he emerged as the 'crown prince of Nike'? As Dyson (1993) has suggested, one element to Jordan's wide appeal is his ability with a basketball: his style and craft. Sport, for Jordan, has become a marker of his self-expression. Many quotes from Jordan on the playing of basketball eschew any mention of money and his monetary worth as a performer. As the above quote indicates, that part of his life, 'his job', is dealt with off the court. Rather, his status as a sporting hero, stems from his basketball craft.

Dyson (1993) argues there are three elements to this. First, a will to spontaneity, expanding the 'vocabulary' of athletic ability and spectacle through innovative manoeuvres and plays. Second, a stylization of the performed self allows Jordan an aura and persona on the basketball court that sets him apart from other players.

For example, his ability to hang in the air, in a specific manner, that ultimately led to the moniker 'Air Jordan'. Finally, allied to this last point, is Jordan's edifying deception, his ability to subvert the common perception of what is culturally or physically possible. All these elements combine to make Jordan an exceptional athlete and heroic figure.

This exposition of the relationship between the sporting body and culture has been criticized by Hoberman (1997) who argues that Dyson presents an essentialist view of African-American sports performance, conveniently forgetting the lack of political empathy Jordan has often showed to the politics of race in the United States.

However, the discourse of African-American popular culture has generated some resonance with new audiences for the NBA. Here, black basketball stars are paraded as the epitome of street credibility. The sports media and promotional activity that surround the game play heavily on such black cultural style, fusing elements of popular music (rap and hip-hop) and fashion (from sneakers to tattoos) with a guarded sense of racial politics.

US stars in the UK

In the UK, an example of this 'street' mode of address can be seen in Channel 4's coverage of the NBA. Here, the programmes that support the live action are framed by Channels 4's unilateral presentation from 'courtside' with young presenters from both sides of the Atlantic. Furthermore, a special magazine programme entitled *NBA 24/7* blends edited highlights from the NBA with behind-the-scenes interviews, travelogues from key host cities of the NBA, short features on the rules and skills of the sport ('Mad Skillz'), reviews of the latest rap, soul and R&B releases and any other points of interest from US popular culture.

This form of sports programming, therefore, places sport firmly in the popular culture in which it is consumed. The emphasis on 'black' popular culture, utilizing specialized language and paralanguage, presents a 'way in' for a young, white audience who engage the style-led sub-culture of basketball through a form of trans-Atlantic gaze (Melechi and Hearn, 1992).

The positioning of celebrity black athletes as the endorsers of various brands and the sport itself is central to this process. Michael Jordan provides the most obvious example of this ambassadorial role individual stars now occupy. With US merchandizing revenues from the NBA reaching a plateau in the mid-1990s the need to expand the NBA product in other parts of the world became imperative. The marketing plan of the NBA's president David Stern has sought to gain leverage from the superstardom of key individuals and the brands they all sponsor.

At one and the same time Jordan carries heroic status and, on the eve of his retirement from the sport in January 1999, a report on the website of *CNN/Sports Illustrated* (1999) suggested: 'He's the one player that the TV networks and corporations looking to push product won't shy away from.' Amazingly, as we have stated above, Jordan's star status manages to reconcile the paradoxical marriage between the traditional virtues of heroic sport and the contemporary demands of large-scale corporate business and global capital.

The resolution of the traditional with the modern stems from basketball's roots in popular culture that maintains the iconic hipness of the stars to a predominantly white audience, as well as securing the health of the sport in general. As Whitson (1998, p. 67) has pointed out:

> What this illustrates is that in 'circuits of promotion' there are no obvious starting points and endpoints, but rather recursive and mutually reinforcing public texts that generate more visibility and more business for all concerned.

This process is marvellously revealed in an advertisement for Nike in the immediate aftermath of Jordan's retirement.

In a low-angle photograph taken from underneath a basket, revealing a backdrop of a packed Chicago Stadium, a white silhouette of a basketball player in mid-flight, arm bent in preparation of a 'slam dunk', dominates the frame. Instinctively we know who this figure represents, the signature shaved head and the athletic but relaxed body posture, tellingly reveal Jordan in action, doing what we know he did better than anyone who has ever played the game. However, the cleverness of this ad is not in the recognition of who this is, it is in the revelation that Jordan will never competitively grace a court again and that Nike are sharing in the basketball fans' sense of loss.

The only concrete sign that this is an ad for Nike for those who know, is a small red symbol in the top right-hand corner of the page: the brand logo for 'Air Jordans'. The meaning of this ad is, therefore, multi-layered and multi-faceted, and epitomizes the degree to which sport, promotional media and popular culture are embodied in the contemporary mega-star.

Although we can recognize Jordan's astonishing achievements as a sportsman and, as one American journalist put it, 'the greatest corporate pitchman of all time' (quoted in Deford, 1999, p. 6), it is fair to question the extent to which the extensive media exposure of a series of African-American sports celebrities has fed back into the grass-roots of the game.

From a particularly cynical perspective on the position of black athletes in American sports, Hoberman (1997, pp. 34–5) has argued that the 'mythifying, deracializing strategy transforms black athletic superiority into "magical" entertainment' and that 'racial identity goes onto the market as a commodity available to any particular purchaser of rap music or athletic apparel or a black hairstyle'.

Sports stars, then, are central to the political economy of media sport. In the next section we explore how the exploitation of sports talent and labour is related to media interests. In particular, our concern is with the industrial relations of sport and its relationship with the needs of television to provide a constant stream of stars and narratives.

Stars and transformations in sports labour

Some time earlier I saw another star performer borne by a chauffeur-driven car to his place of employment. This was at Yankee stadium, during a long night of baseball.

Trevor Fishlock (1986) *The State of America*, p. 138

A combination of factors have led to key transformations in the sports labour markets: the media focus on stars and the rise of sports agents; the increasing mobility of individual sports performers between teams, leagues and nations; and legal challenges mounted against antiquated administrative systems of sport.

Running the show

We have covered the rise of stars and their agents in more detail above; however, in terms of industrial relations, it is quite clear that these developments have undermined the ability of sport administrators and organizations to govern the destiny and careers of leading sports men and women. This is chiefly due to the increased symbolic power sports stars now enjoy in comparison to their sporting ancestors.

As with the case of Arnold Palmer, sports stars are now marketable commodities and, like any product, they require legal support to maintain their value and protect their interests. As Steve Redhead has noted in the field of sports jurisprudence, the heightened intrusion of market forces in sport 'is posing all kinds of questions about legal rights and duties which have rarely been subjected so strongly to the judicial gaze' (Redhead, 1997, p. 27).

The negotiation of transfer fees and employment contracts has become an important domain where sport and the law have become synonymous. In an era of 'hyperlegality' (Redhead, 1997) we would not expect any élite sports man or woman to sign along the dotted line without first consulting their lawyer to fine comb the small print. In football, and increasingly in other élite sports, the price, worth and wages of top players provides a staple diet of speculation and gossip for daily and Sunday newspapers, which have a salacious appetite for revealing the latest record-breaking fees.

Reviewing the transformations of domestic football in England during the 1990s, David Conn astutely captured the new era of industrial relations in sport to assess critically the impact the massive injection of money from television has brought to the game:

> Football in 1992 was thrown utterly to the winds of market forces. The
> players, advised by their agents, now do their deals to a backdrop of
> anonymous stands, corporate sponsorships, knowing that flotation is
> making fortunes for the clubs' owners. The money has flooded in and
> much of the soul has been squeezed out, but the argument is hollow.
> The clubs have put no framework in place to show the players a more
> rounded way to think about football. They have led by mercenary
> example. (Conn, 1997, p. 225)

Given the 'mercenary' context sport now occupies, exactly what the
'rounded way to think about football' entails is not absolutely clear.

The confusion is born of the constant tension set up by the industrialization of sport between the socio–cultural meaning of sport and
sport as business. As we argued in Chapter 3, the two have never been
mutually exclusive, but sports business is no ordinary business.

Doing the business

In negotiating a new contract for a club, tour or federation, or in making the decision to join another, we can readily surmise that contemporary sports stars will consider the financial options before any other.
This is not wholly surprising, but it is quite a departure from the origins
of payment for play where one could equally argue that issues of locality and loyalty figured far more strongly. Even post-war football heroes
Stanley Matthews and Billy Wright have given testimony in their biographical accounts of how wider recognition brought illicit financial
reward, but more importantly, status and pride among their families,
peers and communities.

This is not to suggest that emotional sentiment or the desire to win
championships or titles do not play their part in motivating contemporary élite sports men and women, rather, we are merely pointing out
that the financial capitalization of an athlete's star potential and worth
are foremost in the development of their professional careers.

In England, for example, organizations like the Professional
Footballers Association (PFA) have lobbied long and hard to ensure that
those from the professional ranks of sport receive fair reward for their
talents and security once their careers in the top flight are over. The
PFA, in particular, has maintained a strong media presence whenever
the livelihood of its members or the sport itself are threatened.

Transformations in the legal status of sports professionals can, however, produce conflict in the aims of such organizations. The most
important case in this respect has been that of Jean-Marc Bosman,
where the European Court of Justice ruled in 1995 that the operation of

the transfer system and the 'three foreigners rule' amounted to an infringement of European Law under the Treaty of Rome.

One of the ramifications of the Bosman ruling is that players are now free agents once their contract with a particular club has ended. This had severe ramifications for the old system of transfer fees because instead of money circulating between clubs (maintaining a flow of income within the game) cash windfalls moved directly to players on signing for their new club (rather than the money returning to the game).

A further consequence is that players who originate from the EU can move freely between the various leagues of EU member states without the need for work permits. Hence, the contradiction for the PFA is that, while some domestic players are reaping the financial rewards of their new-found mobility, there is also a growing fear among the members of the players' union that 'foreign' players are saturating the market by openly plying their trade in the lucrative context of the English Premier League.

This process has recently been compounded by a further court case taken up in 1999 by a Polish basketball player, Lilia Malaja, who successfully challenged EU work-permit restrictions on Eastern European athletes in a French court on the premise that Poland had an open trade agreement with the EU. On hearing reports of the case the PFA chairman, Gordan Taylor, announced:

> This could have serious repercussions. We could become a dumping ground for world football, since this is one of the game's honeypots.
> (Cited in Butcher, 1999)

And it is a honeypot created by television's money.

The boy done good

The impact of BSkyB's involvement in English football, allied with the Bosman ruling, has completely transformed the earning power of young football stars in that country. In a game relentlessly hyped by all sections of the media, each with their vested interest in attracting readers, advertisers, viewers or subscribers, the football industry has powered individual players into the first division of sports earners.

While in 1999 the top ten richest sports stars in Britain featured only two football players, it was significant that the golfers, boxers, racing drivers and snooker player all made their earnings from sports which operate in global competitions. By contrast, the footballers Shearer and Gascoigne make their money almost exclusively within Britain. However, perhaps more significant, given the relatively short time in which football has boomed, is the extent to which young players in their twenties, and even younger are making their financial mark.

In a survey of the richest 30-year-old or younger entertainers in Britain published the same year, no less than 19 of the top 40 places were occupied by sportspeople (all male), of which 10 were footballers playing in the English Premiership (The Young Rich, *The Observer Magazine*, 11 April 1999).

Young players such as Robbie Fowler of Liverpool are earning in the region of £32,000 a week. This type of figure doesn't take into account the lucrative media-related deals which are today part of the overall marketing mix in the selling of sports stardom. In the week that Fowler was being fined two weeks' wages for poor on-the-field conduct, his team mate Michael Owen, still only 19, was signing a three-book deal with HarperCollins worth almost £2 million. This would fit nicely with the growing portfolio of endorsement deals which his extensive media exposure gained while playing for England in the France 98 World Cup had helped generate.

Others such as 23-year-old David Beckham of Manchester United adds to his £25,000 a week with endorsement deals with Adidas, Pepsi and Brylcreem, the last worth about £1 million a year. Symbolically, Beckham's relationship with Victoria Adams of the pop group The Spice Girls (between them they are worth about £29 million) consummates the linkage between sport – football in particular – and the popular music and entertainment industries in the UK of the late 1990s. British football and its stars have become an integral part of the landscape of the media entertainment industry, where everyone wants a part of you.

Stars in control: the battle in American sport

In a wider context, what these case studies represent is a transformation in the level of power exerted by individual athletes over the control of their performance, both in the sports arena and its representation through the media. This mirrors the performing rights of other individuals and groups in other realms of the entertainment industries: from pop stars to Hollywood actors, everyone has their price.

The power of some sports stars can seriously undermine the authority of the organizations they work for, and the gain or loss of a sporting hero can dramatically affect the share price of a sporting plc.

The governing bodies of the four main North American team sports, the NFL (American football), Major League Baseball, the NHL (ice hockey) and the NBA (basketball), have attempted to allay some of these financial and legislative threats to their administration of sport through the collegiate draft and some element of wage capping. The philosophy behind such collective bargaining between the player unions and the Leagues is to maintain competitiveness through the distribution of talent. This ensures that no one team can dominate the entry of new sports talent by buying up all the best players.

The draft enables competitive equality and impedes aggressive bidding for amateur players, thus keeping a check on the cost of sports labour. It also places great importance on the selection process, and the ability to spot future potential becomes acute. For example, in the NBA draft of 1984 the Chicago Bulls were given the third pick in the first-round draft of rookie pros after a disastrous performance in the previous season. Luckily, for The Bulls, Jordan had been passed over by the Houston Rockets and the Portland Trailblazers leaving the road free for them to negotiate a deal for the NCAA player of the year. The rest is history as far as the Chicago franchise is concerned, which, propelled by the leadership of Jordan, went on to win six NBA titles during the 1990s.

The draft system is indicative of the extraordinary business of sport, where a tension arises between the need for team success and meaningful competition. This state of monopsony in North American sport (Scully, 1995) allows teams to perpetuate 'their special need to be rivals and partners simultaneously, since they must act as partners to carry out the conditions that make rivalry possible' (Koppett, 1994, p. 284).

However, in order to maintain a worthy product, Leagues, operating collectively on behalf of the franchises, must negotiate with players who collectively bargain the parameters of their salaries through player unions. One major problem with this collective bargaining is that the transformations in the sport–media nexus mean that salaries may not be proportionate with the rapid rise in television rights' fees filling the coffers of the clubs and the governing bodies of sport.

During the 1990s this has become a familiar scenario for North American professional sports markets. Player lockouts, or strikes, driven by breakdowns in contractual negotiations between Leagues and player unions have seriously disrupted the seasons of Major League Baseball in 1994 and the NBA at the start of the 1998/99 season. Long spells of inaction have significant consequences for the ancillary businesses of professional sport, in particular, television and sponsorship. NBC and Turner had signed a $2.6 billion deal over four years for the combined television rights to the NBA and the lockout was a clear threat to their advertising revenues as basketball was 'off the box'.

The NBA star players, who had headlined the push to increase player salaries, had also threatened the excellent public relations they had built up during the reign of Magic Johnson, Larry Bird and Michael Jordan, at a period where sports merchandise was experiencing a grave downturn in sales (*Sports Business*, February 1999). Disputes of this kind can seriously undermine the status of stars who run the threat of betraying the trust of the sports fan and the television audience. This fine line between hero and villain is the subject of our final section on sports stars that investigates instances where sport stardom can be as much of a burden as it is a boon.

The trouble with fame

The use of sports stars to promote various products and services of sponsors, advertisers and communities can be a potentially risky business. Media sport frequently has the ability to reveal the human nature of the heroes it produces. That sports men and women are open to the vagaries of everyday life is hardly surprising; however, as the financial stakes in sport spiral to unprecedented levels, the cost of a fall from grace becomes more pronounced.

Gazza

The media spotlight shines the brightest on the rich and famous in sport and, because of this, the parameters of acceptable public behaviour narrow in a reciprocal relationship to their notoriety. The loss of privacy is often viewed as the 'price of fame' and many young star performers are now coached in how to deal with the media exposure, with some players reluctant to speak to the press without their own press secretary in tow.

However, it is clear that the pressures of celebrity can impinge on the performance of top sports stars as their private lives are ritually scrutinized by newspapers and magazines.

A footballer such as Paul Gascoigne has lived most of his footballing career in the media spotlight. We have followed him from his tears in Italia '90, through his battle with injury following the 1991 FA Cup final, on his high-profile journeys to Rome (playing with Lazio) and Glasgow (playing with Rangers), before his return to his native north-east of England with Middlesborough.

Along the way, through the media, we have watched his life spiral in and out of control, his marriage, his divorce, his battles with drink and depression, his clowning and poor behaviour both on and off the pitch. At times he has been happy to use the media, at others he complains of its intrusive nature and the loss of privacy.

In many ways Gazza, the media construction of Paul Gascoigne, typifies many of the aspects of sports stardom in the 1990s. For all the pressures that he has both self inflicted and had placed upon him, he has emerged a very wealthy young man, despite fulfilling only part of his early sporting promise. In the 1990s it appears that Gazza, the media star, is more famous than Paul Gascoigne the professional football player.

Sports scandal

Very little research has been done on the what we would call 'sports sleaze': the public scrutiny of sports celebrity and morality. The exception to this is David Rowe's (1997) review of the 'anatomy of a sports scandal' where he reflects critically on three case studies: the drugs scandal of the Canadian sprinter Ben Johnson; the 'bad boy' image of the American basketball player Magic Johnson; and the murder trial of American footballer and actor, O.J. Simpson.

All three cases, Rowe argues (1997, p. 219), reveal how the 'media are key conduits in the communication of the meaning of the sports scandal', setting the parameters of acceptable behaviour by 'switching between official and popular discourses and private and public domains in a relentless quest for the "truth" of the day'. These are extreme cases where sport grabs the headlines of newspapers, radio and television news. On such occasions sport jumps from the news enclave of the 'sports page' into a wider public domain, carrying a wider resonance with societal concerns and general interest.

In Britain during the 1994/95 season, two key cases involving two star footballers, Bruce Grobbelaar and Eric Cantona, fixed attention on the place of sport in society and the place of the media in the coverage and reporting of the game.

Allegations of attempted match fixing for a betting syndicate in the 'Far East' were raised against Grobbelaar by the *Sun* newspaper. Two specific games were highlighted: Newcastle United against Liverpool in November 1993, and Coventry City against Southampton in October 1994. Allegations were built on video evidence that revealed Grobbelaar willingly receiving money for a fake bribe set up by the *Sun*. In a staged publicity stunt, footage of the transaction was publicly delivered to FA Headquarters by the *Sun*'s two investigative journalists to reveal the newspapers' role in 'cleaning up the game'. A police investigation followed and two further players, John Fashanu and Hans Segars, were questioned with Grobbelaar about the allegations.

The issue of bribery strikes at the heart of sporting ethics, and in football has a history as old as the sport itself (Inglis, 1987). The question of fairness and the notion of a 'level playing field' underwrite all competitive sport. Moreover, the ideals and moral rhetoric of sport have a wider resonance with moral codes in many Western cultures, based on various notions of social democracy.

It is the transgression of these codes that propelled the match-fixing allegations into a wider public domain. For Grobbelaar, his media-constructed persona as the lovable 'clown prince of football', due to his often extrovert antics on the field, became a point of scrutiny as his character was brought into question.

However, the distinct realms of 'hard news' and 'sports news' did begin to approach the issue of corruption in sport in quite different ways. This was most pronounced in television sport programmes, where a tension arose between the sports pundits' peripheral role of passing comment on the violation of the sporting order and their promotion of the sport as a televisual spectacle.

Television sport strives to maintain its distanced sense of objectivity in the coverage of scandalous events. Rarely is sport itself brought into question, rather, ex-stars of the game, in their role as pundits, pass judgement on transgressive behaviour in sport by ultimately 'closing ranks' on the sport that feeds their careers. Television's protection of the culture of sport serves to maintain the hegemonic position it enjoys with sport, for it knows that it must not kill the goose that lays the golden eggs.

King Eric and that kick

When in January 1995 Manchester United's star Frenchman Eric Cantona lunged kung-fu style at a Crystal Palace fan, having just been sent from the field of play, it produced a slightly different scenario of how the media treat illegal behaviour in sport. The case is interesting from a media perspective as it illustrates the often fickle and contradictory nature of press reporting of sports stars. The immediate aftermath of the event saw the demonization of the player in both broadcasting and newspaper reports.

The largest-selling newspaper in Scotland the *Daily Record* (27 January 1995) printed a blown-up picture of a Nike football boot, Cantona's sponsored footwear, with the headline LETHAL WEAPON, a particularly sensational pun on the flying kick that led to the player being convicted of common assault. The knee-jerk judgemental reaction to Cantona's violence also fell back on stereotyped language based on the Frenchman's history of transgressive behaviour on the pitch.

For example, the BBC 2 programme *Sport on Friday* (27 January 1995) carried a feature introduced by former professional Garth Crooks

King Eric? – Dramatic headlines frequently follow the vagaries of sports stardom, including the highs and the lows. © *The Daily Record, Glasgow*

that used an extended montage of Cantona's past misdemeanours as evidence of his uncontrollable Gallic temperament. As an extensive review of the 'Cantona Affair' by Simon Gardiner (1998) has illustrated, much of the media rhetoric that poured scorn on the player was premised on a wider cultural animosity of the English for the French.

As with the demonization of other sports 'anti-heroes', such as Mike Tyson, the media reporting of the Cantona incident produced a set of essentialist discourses that conflated narratives of race and ethnicity with deviant or criminal behaviour (Sloop, 1997).

The paradoxical twist in the iconic status of Cantona was the about-face in the treatment of the player on his return to the game in September 1995 after an eight-month suspension from the sport. Prior to the event in 1995, Cantona had been perceived as a mercurial talent, the epitome of the European 'flair' player, who twinned his creativeness on the field with a self-fashioned, pseudo-intellectual persona in his private life.

The maverick portrayal of the player was recast on his return to the game, although added to his armoury was a sense of reflection and wisdom in both his play and public pronouncements. Cantona had never lost his support from the Manchester United supporters, and fears that he had decided to quit the game were laid to rest when he played a central role in one of the clubs' most successful periods from September 1995 to May 1997 when he eventually retired from football to focus on a career in film.

In spite of an initial media backlash, Cantona reinvented himself, ironically capitalizing on the event, where he was viewed as a victim of abuse rather than a perpetrator of violence. Most notably, in three advertisements for Nike, Cantona's complex persona was articulated both politically and symbolically to advocate the products of the global sportswear company.

In the first advert Cantona reflected on his image as the 'enfant terrible' of sport; in the second, the player challenged those who denied his right as an individual to play football in an ethnically and racially divided society; and in the third, he exorcized his demonic alter ego by shattering the image of the devil by driving a ferocious shot towards goal causing the devil to implode. The dialogue and the images of the adverts clearly draw on the paradigmatic elements that combine to construct Cantona's media persona, as well as drawing on the mythological status of the sporting hero.

Conclusion

Cantona's complex characterization in the media illustrates some of the problems contemporary sports stars now face when they are elevated to iconic status and lauded as role models. However, the stereotypical roles prescribed to stars are rarely lived up to.

While the sports star dates from the earliest commercial moments in sporting history, few generations have had to deal with the level of interest which the media, now the main sponsors of sport, currently focus on the stars of the contemporary sporting stage.

The pressures that star status bestows on any athlete (who is often inexperienced in dealing with matters of business, law and public relations) ensure that the nuances of everyday life and private inter-relationships are in tension with the fictionalized persona constructed by the media. It appears that fame does come at a price.

CHAPTER 6

The Race Game

Media Sport, Race and Ethnicity

There are teams where you have got players who, from a distance, look almost identical. And, of course, with more black players coming into the game, they would not mind me saying, that can be very confusing.

John Motson, BBC Television football commentator, Radio 5 Live interview, January 1998

Introduction

As a central component in popular culture, sport and its mediated versions operate within a terrain heavily laden with symbolism and metaphor. As we have argued earlier in the book, the issue of representation remains central to any study of media sport. Mediated sport is saturated with ideas, values, images and discourses which at times reflect, construct, naturalize, legitimize, challenge and even reconstitute attitudes which permeate wider society. It should come as no surprise that a cultural form which has narrative and mythology at its core can also become a vehicle for what Cohen (1988) calls 'rituals of misrecognition'. What these next three chapters examine is the extent to which mediated versions of sport play a role in the larger process of identity-formations of race, ethnicity, gender and national identity.

While we focus our attention on a specific area in each chapter, we are aware that often these strands interact. So that at a key moment issues of race will apparently be subsumed within the larger framework of national identity (such as when black athletes are representing Britain), while at other times the differing fault lines which run through society are also clearly evident within a sporting context (when Celtic play Rangers in football). However, we make the separation over the next three chapters to allow us to focus on some of the specific issues involved with each area.

In this chapter we look at the media's treatment of black (using the political term here to refer to those of African, Caribbean and southern Asian origin) and Asian (those of Indian sub-continent descent) sportspeople. Later we also briefly highlight the issue of ethnicity as it relates to sectarianism and media sport in both Scotland and Northern Ireland.

Sporting and media representations of race

Issues around media representations are fundamentally about power and status in society. A community's or individual's ability to feel themselves represented accurately in media discourse is in part related to assumptions about the power of the media to shape and change public opinion. In the areas of television comedy or drama this can often be about using stereotypes and stereotyping as a type of cultural shorthand for comedic or dramatic purposes.

This often reduces diffuse and complex groups into simple and straightforward characters with distinctive characteristics. Jarvie (1991, p. 2) notes also that discussions of issues relating to race and sport have in the past ignored the diversity and differing experiences of various ethnic groupings and also largely removed gender difference from the discussion.

In their overview of media coverage of African-American athletes in the US, Davis and Harris (1998) note how particular stereotypes of the 'natural' black athlete have been used to explain the apparent over-representation of black people in sports. This explanation, rather than the more materially rooted one which links it to class and deprivation, has also been prevalent in discussions relating to British black sportspeople during the 1970s and 1980s (Cashmore, 1996). While Wilson (1997) has also demonstrated how media images of black athletes in the US are also replicated, with some variation, in the Canada experience.

Martin Polley (1998, p. 158), writing about the interface between race and sport in post-war Britain, argues that racism has been a large part of sporting culture in this country. He notes that racist abuse suffered by black and Asian sportspeople has often gone uncommented upon by the media. He argues that

> For black Britons, sport has remained a double-edged sword in post-war society, offering both advancement and obstacle, acceptance and crude stereotype. That many individuals have excelled must be read both as a sign of a growing tolerance – particularly when national representation is at stake – and as a sign of perceived limited opportunities in other walks of life.

While, as we see below, there is an argument which suggests that the changing media profile of black people in general and their centrality within the realms of mainstream popular culture has diminished or undercut negative racist stereotyping in the late 1990s, Holland (1997) clearly shows how racism still fundamentally affects professional black football players within the English game.

Jarvie and Reid (1997, pp. 218–19) alert us to the need to be wary of applying universal theories of sport, ethnicity and racism. They argue that this 'is not to deny different theories of race relations but to caution against their universality as ways of explaining different situations throughout the globe'. This could be extended when media coverage is added to the equation, in other words the particular social, cultural and historical context becomes important when examining the production and consumption of media representations of sport, race and ethnicity.

Sporting mediascapes

One of the striking features of the British televisual sporting landscape in 1999 is the almost complete absence of black and Asian sports presenters and commentators working within the mainstream. This is particularly noticeable given the advances made in other areas of television, in particular news and current affairs. Part of the reason is the lack of movement in much of television sports commentating personnel (discussed in Chapter 2), with individuals, such as John Motson quoted above, being associated with particular sports and channels for decades.

However, even the more recent terrestrial and satellite channels still have their mainstream popular sports programmes largely fronted by white presenters. This is at a time when the visibility and profile of black sportspeople within Britain has never been greater.

This profile also exists outside the confines of the sporting arena. As Linda Grant has argued, within a British context:

> Where blacks once complained about their invisibility, now black
> footballers and black musicians and black supermodels define the word
> cool for us. Even the middle class have found their own way of
> accessing black culture – an authentic, African culture, of course,
> combined of an equal mix of World Music, Live Aid and holidays in
> post-apartheid South Africa. (*The Guardian*, 15 April 1997)

However, as Grant and others such as Gilroy (1993) have noted this doesn't mean that racism or other forms of political and economic discrimination have disappeared or been eradicated. Grant's article centred around claims made by supermodel Naomi Campbell that the fashion industry was racist.

In the arena of sport there has been a number of cases of black and Asian players claiming they have suffered racist abuse from other players; these include, during 1998, Stan Collymore of Aston Villa in England and Dave Barnett of Dunfermline in Scotland. The latter resulted in the player leaving the club and prompted one journalist, Jonathan Northcroft (*Scotland on Sunday*, 23 March 1998) to suggest that within the British game, and to a large extent within the mainstream football media, there exists a culture – despite footballing initiatives to 'Show Racism the Red Card' – of 'Let's Sweep Racism under the Carpet'.

What is clear is that, while the range of media images associated with black and Asian sportsmen and women has expanded, and is often more positive than it may have been previously, this is not necessarily an indication of a less racist and more tolerant society. The complexities and contradictions of the multiple identities people have are often brought into focus only in specific contexts. Thus it is not uncommon at football matches in Scotland or England for fans to abuse a black or Asian player on the opposing team in a racist manner, while praising a black or Asian player who is playing for their team.

Prince Naz: 'For Britain, the Arab world and Adidas, wicked sponsor!'

When the boxer Prince Naseem Hamed ceremoniously courted the crowd in the Nynex Arena Manchester, viewed by a further 1 million viewers of Sky Sports 2, after his second round KO of Mexican boxer Remigio Molina, the boxer's thoughts turned to his complex, yet tangible, identity that reflected his birthplace in Sheffield, his ethno–religious origin in the Yemen, and his global presence as a sports star. Following the mercenary approach to boxing advocated by the black British middleweight boxer, Chris Eubank, Hamed's bravura both in and out of the ring has been viewed as either youthful arrogance or a symbolic representation of his pride in, and confident celebration of, his own identity.

As Sugden (1997), in his cross-cultural analysis of boxing in Ireland, the United States and Cuba, has noted, the sport has historically been used to promote and maintain various ideological notions of racial, ethnic and national superiority in Western societies. Paradoxically, Sugden suggests, institutional racism and discrimination against particular ethnic groups in society has ultimately drawn black men into boxing out of economic necessity (Sugden, 1997, pp.33–4).

The American ghetto, the concept that describes the lived experience of poverty in large urban centres and acts as the generator of varied, exciting forms of popular culture, has achieved a wider resonance with the origins of boxing talent in Britain. For Hamed, the setting for his career in pugilism began in the post-industrial city of Sheffield, with all the tensions caused by the marriage of traditional South Yorkshire conservatism and a cultural mix of various immigrant groups.

The origins of one of Britain's brightest sports stars is evocatively captured by Geoffrey Beattie whose top-selling sports book, *On The Ropes: boxing as a way of life*, focused on the St Thomas gym in Sheffield, run by Hamed's trainer Brendan Ingle:

> The gym was always packed – a bustling, vibrant, multi-ethnic
> community training, working, dreaming. Somebody had scrawled
> 'National Front' on the wall of the garage that runs alongside the gym.
> It didn't stop them coming here. Nothing would. They came here to
> dream. (Beattie, 1997, p. 17)

Again, as both Beattie's and Sugden's studies illustrate, Hamed's experience epitomizes the 'farm system' of professional boxing, where a mix of dependency and dedication combines to produce the occasional success story amid an array of mediocrity and unfulfilled expectations.

For Hamed, his discipline to his craft is seen to be framed by his Muslim background, and the boxer has frequently proclaimed his abstention from alcohol, tobacco and recreational drugs as being a central feature of his sporting success. This ethno–religious pride is combined with a youth cultural style that draws as much influence from black subcultures of New York or Chicago as it does from Hamed's particular experience in the Muslim community of Sheffield. All these ingredients are fused in Hamed's performance in the ring and the wider media persona that has emerged through his alliance with Sky Sports during the mid-to-late 1990s.

Men viewing Naz

In a focus-group study of men viewing violence, conducted by the authors among English and Scottish men (in Schlesinger *et al.*, 1998), respondents were invited to express their views on boxing as a form of aggressive masculinity. In particular, they were asked to comment on the 'glitz and glamour that satellite television coverage has brought to boxing', epitomized by the coverage of Prince Naseem Hamed on Sky Sport.

Key to the investigation was the level of identification different groups of men held for Hamed, in terms of the boxer's identities as a sportsman, an Anglo-Arab Muslim and a wealthy, often arrogant global television celebrity. When asked their thoughts on the boxer's ethnicity it became clear that for some men, in particular young Pakistani men in both England and Scotland, Hamed represented an important role model and Muslim icon in British popular culture. However, their reverence for the boxer was not only based on his ethno–religious background, but also on the unconventional style of his fighting and his apparent financial success outside of the ring.

By contrast, young white working-class men took a more contradictory stance on the position of Hamed in the media. Negative attitudes emerged where group members lived in close proximity to sizeable ethnic minority communities and, in one exchange, working-class men in Rochdale expressed their dislike for the boxer, as follows:

> Speaker 1: I don't like him, he's a Paki.
> Speaker 2: I'd like to see him get a good kicking.

The responses show a confused reaction to Asian, or in this case Arab, sportsmen in Britain where all are labelled 'Pakis' and their success in a sport is viewed as threatening, alien or in contradiction to the stereotypical image of their position in society.

The contradictory processes of sport, ethnicity and national identity were expressed by a member of a group of gay white men aged 30–39 from Manchester, who noted that boxers were predominantly black and working-class, performing for a predominantly white audience:

> I think people feel it's socially acceptable for a black man to fight for
> his country but it isn't socially acceptable in some circles to have a
> black man sit next to you having a drink. They would cheer Naseem on
> TV because he is fighting for Britain, but they wouldn't sit next to him.

In such cases, the issue of race and ethnicity gets discounted from the importance of representing the nation, whether it be in boxing, cricket, football or athletics, the four main fields of black sporting excellence in modern British sport.

The media coverage of élite sports men and women with ethnic minority backgrounds in Britain is rarely framed as a success story for any particular ethnic minority group. Moreover, issues of race or ethnicity are rarely discussed overtly in the media (Davis and Harris, 1998), with more emphasis placed on other aspects of an individual's career, such as their celebrity status in the world of sport or even their wider commercial interests.

Again, the success stories of black British boxers during the 1990s, such as Frank Bruno, Nigel Benn, Chris Eubank and Lennox Lewis, reflect the invisibility of race and ethnic issues in the media coverage of sport. Where the issue of skin colour or ethnic difference does surface in a more overt sense, it occurs in a process of negative stereotyping that obscures the varied lifestyles of minority groups in society.

In a discussion of the British boxer Nigel Benn, in the aforementioned study, young white Scottish men drew on a set of racial epithets to characterize their image of the boxer to argue:

> He must have been involved in drugs. So he must be a gangster . . .
> must run a bouncing business or something.

The statement reveals the use of racial stereotyping where myths of black men are equated with criminal activity, and may be given as evidence of the ways in which the media representation of black communities can negatively feed into wider perceptions of black sporting figures who do not conform to more conventional stereotypes of sporting prowess.

Through their knowledge of a series of brutal fights involving Benn, and revelations of an occasional violent episode in his private life by the tabloid press, Benn was categorized by some men as a dangerous figure, reflected in his media moniker as the 'Dark Destroyer'.

In focusing on boxing, we have attempted to illustrate some of the ways in which skin colour and ethnic difference can produce inaccurate and contradictory representations of Arab, Asian and black sports stars. Boxing, in particular, is open to a range of negative stereotypes because of its political economy which exploits disadvantaged groups in society that is premised on issues of class or socio–economic difference as much as issues of race or ethnicity.

Studies by Wacquant (1995) and Sugden (1997) reveal that achievement in the boxing world is due to a complex web of circumstance, structural inequalities, and individual courage and dedication. Wider socio–economic and cultural processes, therefore, need to be understood when attempting to unravel both the media celebration of, and the racist attitudes to, boxers or other sports stars from ethnic minority backgrounds.

Context remains all important. When *Guardian* journalist Jim White travelled to America to cover the return of Mike Tyson to the boxing ring he observed:

> At the casino's gold plated main entrance, security guards, backed up
> by brown shirted Las Vegas cops, stopped anyone black from coming
> in. The tension and mutual distrust was palpable. As they say in these
> parts, this was fear and loathing. And when you see it in action – this

assumption that anyone who is black is a riot about to happen – you begin to understand why these guys identify with Tyson when he complains about white America, and to appreciate why they admire him for refusing to behave to its standards. You can see why they love someone whose power and physique sets off the alarm bells buried deep in the white gene pool. (White, 1999)

Here we gain another perspective on the Tyson phenomenon, one that is largely absent from the television coverage

Below we explore further the varied contexts in which racism in sport exists, in an attempt to reveal a wider frame for thinking about identity and prejudice in sport and popular culture.

Sectarianism, sport and popular culture

John Brewer (1992, p. 353) has noted the parallels and differences between sectarianism and racism. He argues that, unlike racism, sectarianism remains a relatively undertheorized area of study, partly because of the supposedly declining importance of religion in Western societies.

Instances where religion remains a potent social marker are usually marginalised by being seen as a third world problem (India) or as an aberration of modernity (the Lebanon, Northern Ireland).

He goes on to argue that sectarianism, like racism, operates at three interrelated levels: in the domain of ideas, in individual behaviour and when its values become embedded in the social structure of any society. There is obviously a linkage between these levels. For example, in a country where there are discriminatory laws this is liable to both reinforce and legitimize individual personal prejudices.

What team do you support?

The symbolic and material support for either Rangers or Celtic offers the possibility of sectarianism operating at all three levels described by Brewer above (the domain of ideas, behaviour and a set of values which have become naturalized in social structures).

Sectarianism then can be viewed as a system of beliefs through which a social group differentiates itself from a perceived other, primarily through religious difference. In their study of the role of sport in a divided Ireland, Sugden and Bairner (1993) argue that:

sectarianism can be best understood in two overlapping ways: first as symbolic labelling process through which community divisions are defined and maintained, and second, as an ideological justification for

discrimination, community conflict and political violence. (Sugden and
Bairner, 1993, p. 15)

They argue persuasively that religious labelling becomes part of a wider
semiotic system through which, in revealing one's sporting preferences,
at the same moment one marks out a position for oneself on the complex terrain of political/cultural/religious affiliation in Northern Ireland.

Being labelled Catholic or Protestant also identifies one with a range
of political and cultural positions which are triggered by having a religious label attached to oneself or one's support for a particular sport or
football club highlighted. For example, for someone from Northern
Ireland to show support for the games of the GAA (Gaelic Athletic
Association), immediately identifies them as having nationalist and possibly republican sympathies.

To play cricket in Northern Ireland would place one as a middle-
class Unionist, to support Linfield FC, as a working-class loyalist and so
on and so forth. Cronin (1997) has argued that even in a sport such as
boxing, which at first glance may appear to straddle both communities,
the wider political and cultural conflict ultimately impinges also.

In addition, the centrality of religious labelling in collective identity
formation, and its attendant connection with support for either Celtic
or Rangers, is still very much a part of everyday experience for many
people. To know which team (Celtic or Rangers) a person supports
becomes 'an oblique mechanism for determining a person's religious
persuasion' (Sugden and Bairner, 1993, p. 16).

Sporting and social identities

Brewer (1992, p. 360) suggests that in Northern Ireland your religious
persuasion is also triggered by, among other things, the name of the
school you have attended, your place of residence and even your name.
While Scotland is obviously not Northern Ireland and has suffered none
of the violence and political upheaval associated with that part of the
world, a combination of the proximity of the north of Ireland to
Scotland and the close historical and cultural links between them – not
least in terms of shifts in population which have occurred across the
Irish Sea – have resulted in religious labelling and aspects of sectarianism (both at the symbolic and material level) having an impact on
Scottish society and sport.

The residual legacy of this relationship provides a specific sport–
media environment which doesn't exist anywhere else in Britain. It is
simply unimaginable that England's largest selling newspaper would
lead with a story about the alleged extreme Loyalist paramilitary links

of an international football player. However, as we see below, this was the type of material making the media headlines in Scotland during early 1999.

Bradley (1994, p. 432) has argued that: 'Many Catholics in Scotland have an identity in relation to both Ireland and Scotland which varies in intensity and emphasis depending on circumstance and environment.' He suggests that the close interplay between a religious identity (Catholic) and a cultural identity (Irish) mark out this group as being a distinct ethnic community in Scotland. It could be argued that this ethnicity finds one arena of public expression in its support of Celtic FC.

In this sense the linkage between football support, religious and ethnic identities differs from other football clubs in Britain where support for a football club, with its emphasis on collective symbolic displays of loyalty and ritual, lends itself to being a very public marker of identity among groups.

That sectarianism has shaped the culture of Scottish society is not disputed by social commentators (although there is a marked dearth of material on the subject). However, there is disagreement as to the extent of this influence, and its presence in contemporary Scottish society. In Scotland, and in particular in the west of the country, the continued influence of sectarianism in contemporary society is disputed. It appears that, if the issue of sectarianism is not spoken about, in some sense it is a phenomenon which no longer exerts any influence on patterns of social and cultural behaviour in sections of contemporary Scottish society.

However, some writers do comment on the issue. The Irish writer Colm Toibin visited Scotland in 1993 while researching a book about the influence of Catholicism in contemporary Europe (Toibin, 1994). He arrived from Northern Ireland, where he was warned that Scotland was 'a deeply sectarian and divided society'. In his review of the book journalist Ian Bell comments:

> Toibin ferrets out facts that Scotland prefers to ignore. Name me, he asks of several people, a Scottish Catholic writer. When a 'distinguished poet' remarks that these are the wrong questions and Scotland isn't as it seems, Toibin replies that the country reminds him of Alabama in 1954, and wonders how the poet would reply if there were in 'another society where blacks represented 30 per cent of the population (as Catholics do in Scotland), no black writers.' (*The Herald*, 22 October 1994)

While Calum Brown, commenting on the close proximity of Northern Ireland to Scotland, states that in his opinion:

Sectarianism still does not have anything like the relevance it has in
Ulster or in parts of Europe, but the links with the Irish troubles ensure
that the issue remains on the agenda of Scottish popular culture.
(Brown, 1993, p. 37)

He notes that Scotland in the 1990s has 80,000 members of the avidly
anti-Catholic Orange Order. It can also be noted that nowhere outside
of Northern Ireland are Orange parades and marches more frequent
and prominent than in Glasgow during the summer months.

Bairner (1994) is aware of the extent to which football can reinforce
social divisions as well as acting as a focal point for collective identities.
He views religious difference and sectarianism as still powerful social
forces in modern Scotland, and argues that both find an expression
through fans actively supporting particular football teams. He notes:

sectarianism continues to influence football support in Scotland.
Supporters do not leave the small towns, far less the cities, to watch the
Old Firm simply because they want to associate themselves with
success, although this is a partial explanation. The choice of club is
what really matters. That choice is directly related to the histories of
Celtic and Rangers and to the persistence of religious division in
Scotland to which those histories are part. (Bairner, 1994, p. 18)

It appears that religious labelling or affiliations associated with these
clubs play a key role in attracting a specific kind of support, while at the
same time this process reinforces a distinctive identity between supporters and their club.

Sport, ethnicity and media bias

The extent to which the media play a role in their treatment of sport in
either reinforcing, challenging and perhaps at times even illuminating
the issues around sporting identity and conflict is in fact quite underdeveloped in studies of sport. Research carried out by one of the authors
in Glasgow and Liverpool found a wide perception of bias, among supporters of Celtic, against the club and its supporters among sections of
the media, the press in particular. The issue of media bias was also an
issue widely commented upon by the interview groups in Glasgow.

What was significant, however, was that, while in Liverpool there
was a perception of bias against the city from the English national and
regional press, in Glasgow (the main centre of the Scottish media)
nuances of bias were perceived to be aimed not at the city as a whole,
but at specific clubs and, by association, their supporters. This is an

important point in that it suggests a degree of sophistication of reading among many fans. In other words, it calls into question the extent to which the output of many mainstream media organizations (especially the national press) is trusted by sections of supporters whose attitudes are shaped by knowledge gained in other social contexts.

Among Celtic supporters, media bias against the club forms part of a wider perception of discrimination in general against Catholics from within some sections of Scottish society. Typical replies among Celtic supporters included:

> Let's not forget that, at the end of the day, Scotland is basically a Protestant country, and the media broadly reflect that. Yes, it's not as bad as twenty years ago, but the idea that discrimination, the nods and wink culture, has disappeared completely simply isn't true.
>
> It's not long ago that the Scottish media didn't even mention Rangers all-Protestant signing policy, and let's be honest it was actually an anti-Catholic institution. It was natural in Scotland, wasn't it! It was the biggest secret in the media. That is only twenty years ago.
>
> You need to read everything, because otherwise you don't know what people are thinking about you and Celtic. We take an accumulation of everything, and select from it.

With regard to the Scottish press, across the five groups of Celtic supporters interviewed, it was the same papers, the Scottish *Sun* and the *Daily Record*, which were highlighted as being either anti-Celtic, or pro-Rangers*. There is, of course, an economic reason for the quantity, if not the quality, of Celtic and Rangers stories in the press. Put simply, stories relating to Glasgow's two major clubs sell newspapers.

This is also the case in the city of Liverpool, but both the *Liverpool Echo* and the *Post* are not dealing with the same kind of internal city rivalry between Liverpool and Everton that exists in Glasgow where the religious and cultural labels associated with the Glasgow clubs remain strong.

Part of the Scottish *Sun*'s strategy in its circulation battle with the *Daily Record* has been to devote more attention to its sports coverage and forge closer links with particular clubs. During Graeme Souness's reign at Rangers, for example, relations between the manager and the *Sun* newspaper resulted in a number of exclusives for the paper, the

---

* Scottish-based newspapers comfortably outsell the London-based nationals in the Scottish market. The *Daily Record* is Scotland's largest selling newspaper with a circulation in 1999 of over 680,000. During this same period its main rival in the popular market, the Scottish edition of the *Sun* had a circulation of 390,000.

most notable being the signing of the Catholic, and former Celtic player, Maurice Johnston for the club in 1989.

Souness's close relationship with that newspaper when he returned to Liverpool as manager (with his agreement they carried exclusive pictures of him recovering after major heart surgery) did little to endear him to supporters at that club who still viewed the *Sun* as an anti-Liverpool paper, following the lies it published about the city and its football fans in the aftermath of Hillsborough.

The 'Old Firm' link with sports journalism in Scotland is interesting and highlights some of the geographical problems faced by journalists working within a relatively small sporting environment (see Chapter 9). The degree of attention devoted in the press and broadcasting to the 'Old Firm' is a source of constant irritation to football supporters outside the west of Scotland.

This is related to the importance of sources in aiding journalists. In such a relatively small marketplace, it sometimes appears that journalists are not keen to upset some of their key sources. Indeed, it could be argued that there appears at times to be a relatively stable consensus among various sections of the Scottish media regarding sporting issues.

Stuart Cosgrove, Director of Nations and Regions at Channel 4, sports columnist and writer on Scottish football, has noted how that, as neither a Celtic nor Rangers fan, it appears to him that Rangers, and its chairman David Murray in particular, get treated differently from their Glasgow rivals Celtic. He suggests:

> It is ironic that Rangers fans are often more inquisitive and critical of their club than the Press. Some are tired of the perpetual diet of 'good news' and feel that it would actually help the club in the future if David Murray's regime was put under more scrutiny.
>
> If everyday decisions at Rangers were put under the same scrutiny and cynical criticism that Celtic seem to attract it would be interesting to see how the club would fair. (*Daily Record*, 22 January 1999)

Of course, this does not necessarily mean that a wider systematic bias based on a wider discrimination against Catholics exists. However, it does point up how perceptions and issues of sporting and ethnic identities (Catholic/Irish–Protestant/Scottish), often assumed unimportant elsewhere in Britain, are played out in part through the interaction of media discourses and individual and collective experiences.

The goalie and the UVF

For example, in early 1999 Scotland's largest selling newspaper, the *Daily Record* (8 February 1999) splashed a story, initially broken by its

Sunday sister paper the *Sunday Mail*, which featured the former Rangers and Scotland footballer, and current goalkeeper at Scottish premier League side Motherwell, Andy Goram, on both the front and back pages. While this may have been unsurprising at a time when the English papers were doing the same in covering the dismissal of the England national football coach Glen Hoddle after remarks made in a newspaper article (see Chapter 9), the Goram story centred on alleged links between the player and the Northern Ireland Loyalist paramilitary organization the UVF.

It would be difficult to imagine an English newspaper carrying a story relating to alleged links between English footballers and terrorist organizations. Catholic/Protestant religious markers of identity simply do not play out in England in the way they might in Scotland, which in turn differs significantly from how they are mobilized in Northern Ireland (see Cronin, 1997 and Bairner, 1999). On its inside pages, the *Daily Record* story, GORAM'S DANGER GAME, continued:

> Whatever the source of it, The Goalie's apparent support for the loyalists has inflamed the religious bigotry that scars communities across the west of Scotland.
>
> The strife is not limited to Glasgow and the industrial belt, many rural communities are overwhelmingly Protestant and rumours of violence, intimidation and discrimination against Catholics abound.
> (8 February 1999)

This is significant, as it appears to mark a shift in the newspaper's recognition that, in certain parts of Scotland, the issue of religious discrimination and bigotry may exist against Catholics – something not always openly put forward and discussed by the media. It is also worth noting that something which most Celtic fans have always suspected rightly or wrongly about Andy Goram (and which, of course, dates back to when he was a Rangers player, but was not 'exposed' during this stage of his career by the media) is unlikely to come as any great surprise or even less likely to fan any flames of bigotry, other than among rival media organizations all keen to follow up the story.

Moorhouse (1991) has argued that the media portrayal of Glasgow as a tribal city, with two 'warring' communities (Catholic and Protestant), is reproduced by both the UK national and Scottish media. This image, he claims, is popular in Scotland:

> and possibly more so in England where it exudes that enticing whiff of primitive savagery which it is one of the cultural roles of the fringe 'nations' of the UK to provide . . . it is often not realised outside how

> proud the Scottish football culture is of the clash of Rangers versus
> Celtic – 'the greatest club game in the world' as it is routinely referred
> to – as something the English have not got and cannot match.
> (Moorhouse, 1991, pp. 204–5)

While agreeing that the media play a key role in constructing a particular version of the 'Old Firm', which helps not only to sustain interest in the clubs and the fixture, but has the important economic element of selling newspapers and attracting viewers to television, this rivalry should not be mistaken as some simple media construct.

While it could be argued that the rivalry between Celtic and Rangers represents one of the last vestiges of religious intergroup conflict in Glasgow (although one would have to add to any list the Orange Order marches which still take place every summer in the city), to ignore or dismiss the feelings and passions invested in the clubs by their supporters is to be guilty of both misreading and underestimating the symbolic allegiances individuals still have with particular forms of collective identities.

Conclusion

As we have mentioned earlier, the separation of issues of race, ethnicity and national identities is one we have made here for the purpose of focusing on specific issues. They are, of course, deeply interwoven, at some times and in specific contexts more so than at others.

For example, when Cronin (1997, p. 144) argues that the more general principle that sport can bring people together is only useful when placed within the specific wider political and cultural context. Thus in a politically and culturally divided Northern Ireland, we see a wider sectarian culture impact on the image of even such a sport as boxing.

> Until there is a strategy that addresses and resolves the competing
> traditions of Loyalism and Nationalism, sport generally, and sportsmen
> and women specifically will always have a confused and problematic
> identity thrust upon them.

This wider argument for structural change also finds an echo in some commentators looking at the media profile of black and Asian sportspeople: that, while positive images are better than either being ignored or treated negatively, they do not guarantee deeper or more structural shifts which would facilitate a less racist society.

However, the situation is both complex and fluid. Bairner (1999, p. 14), in his work on the relationship between the media and sport in

Northern Ireland since the Good Friday Peace Agreement (1998), suggests that the changing print media treatment of sports, historically divided along sectarian lines, 'far from being ephemeral in terms of the politics of the north of Ireland reflects, contributes to and . . . at times challenges influential social and political trends'.

What is being suggested here is the role that the media can play in creating climates of opinion, within which wider and more deeply rooted political and structural change may occur, or at least suffer from less opposition. We suggest that this is one possibility held out by a more accurate and sensitive treatment by the media of the issues centred around race and ethnicity in sport. This may remain difficult to achieve given the at times too cosy relationship between the media and sporting industries.

In the past the media's treatment of black and Asian sports people in various contexts has been either absent, or stereotypical. As John Hoberman has argued:

> Such ideas about the 'natural' physical talents of dark-skinned peoples, and the media-generated images that sustain them, probably do more than anything else in our public life to encourage the idea that blacks and whites are biologically different in a meaningful way . . . The world of sport has thus become an image factory that disseminates and even intensifies our racial preoccupations. (Hoberman, 1997, p. xxiii)

As a starting point a greater scrutiny by the media of areas of discrimination in sporting culture and a willingness to connect this with society at large would be useful. Media should also expose the reluctance with which some sports governing bodies appear to display in either acknowledging or dealing with any problem they may have.

However, as Emma Lindsay, writing about the UK Government Football Task Force's *Eliminating Racism from Football* document in the sports pages of *The Observer* (29 March 1998) notes, these issues will remain endemic in sports as long as 'the issue of racism . . . doesn't appear to concern enough of the right people, with power to effect radical change, in the "mainstream" itself. And radical change, not worthy words, are what's urgently needed.'

CHAPTER 7

For Men Who Play to Win

Media Sport and Gender

It was 5am and there was Jimmy McGovern, one of our foremost dramatists, admitting that never in a million years did he expect a football wife to be on the writing course on which he was still holding court after his guest lecture the evening before.

Well, who could blame him. After all, our particular species has been well and truly pigeon-holed into the 'dim bird' category. What's more, we're Malibu-drinking bimbos who live in tacky houses . . .

Shelley Webb, writer, broadcaster and author of *Footballers' Wives Tell Their Tales*, London, Yellow Jersey Press 1998

Introduction

Sport has always been a sexual battlefield. The issue of gender, and the representation of biological difference between the sexes, has long been central to our perceptions of sport in society. The media representation of sport is no different and, as this chapter sets out to argue, no analysis of media sport would be complete without an understanding of how patriarchal structures are constructed through media institutions and their coverage of sport.

Equally, no understanding of how patriarchy is reinforced in capitalist societies can ignore the importance of sport in communicating familiar stereotypes of men and women and their physical abilities. Indeed, the tendency towards the invisibility of women in media sport suggests a whole field of public life in which women are marginalized.

Playing the game

Women's participation in sport has been blocked on several levels throughout the history of modern sporting practice. Whether as athletes, coaches, administrators or sports journalists, women have found it difficult to establish the right and recognition of their place in the sporting world. The notion that there are favoured or permitted sports for women to participate in has been well documented by feminist sociologists and historians of sport (see Williams *et al.*, 1985; and Hargreaves, 1997).

Political struggles to gain equality in sport have been fought and won since the turn of the nineteenth century, most visibly seen in the painstakingly gradual gains women have made in the Olympic movement. The social movement for gender equality in sport has proved a valuable terrain for liberal feminist activity and reform throughout the twentieth century. However, serious feminist critiques of sport did not gain any momentum until the 1970s and 1980s, when challenges to the hegemonic dominance of men's sporting structures and cultural practices emerged from feminist critiques of Marxist sociology (Hall, 1985) and Cultural Studies (Willis, 1982; and Hargreaves, 1986).

What the various contemporary feminist studies of sport reveal is that sport remains an incredibly conservative domain for the representation of men and women. Moreover, feminist scholars of sport have repeatedly confirmed that differences in sporting chances are a matter of power, not only across genders but within them. It has been argued that the sex/gender system as it is reproduced in sport is one site where patriarchal cultural hegemony can be challenged and that it is important to address the possibility that transforming sport may help to break down stereotypical representations of the sexes as they are framed by the media.

The key to the political challenge to male dominance and female subordination in sport has been the deconstruction of biological values and principles formulated and articulated in sport. The Victorian legacy of modern sport has ensured that concerns about women's medical vulnerability, emotional nature and social limitations have endured at a very banal level. Essentialist notions of men and women are manifested more frequently through sport than in any other public domain and this differentiation of physical prowess is confirmed by the disproportionate media treatment of men's sport over women's sport (Creedon, ed., 1994).

This chapter sets out to examine the role of women in media sports' institutions and the representations of women in sport. We are also interested in integrating the study of male patriarchy in media sport, and in particular the importance of violence in male sport cultures and the media celebration of masculinity and manliness.

Representing female sports and sportspeople

Women who wish to stake out a career in professional sport often face more obstacles than their male colleagues. The idea of women being actively involved in sport, either as participants or spectators, appears to remain unacceptable for sections of the male-dominated sports industry.

In his examination of sport in post-war Britain Martin Polley has noted how this period:

> has seen sport continue to act as a location for the display and negotiation of gender politics. In line with changes in the political and economic spheres, sport as a physical activity has provided women in search of equality and recognition a cultural sphere in which to test traditional assumptions based on physical difference, and the popularity . . . of women's rugby, football, cricket, athletics and even boxing demonstrates a change in the wider discourse of gender relations. (Polley, 1998, p. 109)

While there have been broader social shifts in gender relations, resistance to women's sport is still evident, and as often as not it takes place off the actual field of play and is embedded in the mostly male subculture which still surrounds many aspects of the sporting industry.

It is also not only athletes who can suffer discrimination. In 1998 for example Rachel Anderson, the only female football agent working in the English game, was banned from attending the Professional Football Association's award ceremony in London after being invited by a number of the players she represents. The PFA stated that for 25 years the ceremony had been a men-only evening!

Despite the advances made over the years, it is still routine in 1999 to find women golfers having difficulty in being granted the facilities and rights offered to male colleagues. This was also the year in which that bastion of English middle-class male identity the MCC (cricket club) finally voted to allow women members to be admitted.

Despite negative attitudes from some quarters, significant changes are taking place. Backed by a FIFA initiative in 1995 to both recognize and encourage the development of women's football, participation rates in the game have grown dramatically. In 1991 there were 23 female football coaches in Scotland, by 1997 this had grown to almost 3000, with 45,000 women playing the game across the UK (*Glasgow Herald*, 24 February 1998).

More women are also watching sport on television, with the dedicated subscriber sports channel Sky Sport 1 recording a 30 per cent female viewership in 1998 (BSkyB Annual Report, 1998, p. 29). This is not, however, as many as some television sports would like. Both Rugby Super League and the Cricket World Cup were being promoted in early 1999 to a female spectating and viewing audience by focusing on the sex appeal of the players involved and some not very subtle word play. A woman rugby league fan tells us in a Super League cinema advert that 'I like it hard and fast and straight up the middle' (*Financial Times*, 20 February 1999).

These women who are watching sport on television are significantly watching male sport, as female sport remains dramatically under-represented on television in the UK. As Pam Creedon (1994, p. 172) has noted:

> In sports, more often than not, underlying the 'importance' of an event and its audience 'interest' is how much money the sport earns for the athlete or team and the media institution itself. The more revenue the sport and sporting event produces, the more likely it is to receive more significant coverage.

This appears to be increasingly the case in American television.

In the States there is a developing awareness among television sports executives of the potential advertising revenue to be gained in targeting a female sports audience. Val Ackerman is president of the Women's National Basketball Association (WNBC) and has been at the forefront in driving the television profile of that sport in the US. Building on the success in television rating terms of the women's game in the 1996 Atlanta Olympics, they rescheduled their season for television and in the process gaining good rating figures which in turn have attracted major sponsors keen to access an audience which accounts for 50 per cent of the retail sports dollars spent in the US market (*Sports Business*, February 1999, p. 10).

It is important to recognize the differing roots of the game in the US and the UK, with the game being deeply embedded in the American college system. However, other sports such as women's golf are also enjoying a higher profile in the US, again in part driven by the economics of the sports business with sponsors keen to gain access to a potentially underdeveloped female market.

In the recent build-up to the Women's football World Cup in the summer of 1999, Lifetime TV (Television for Women) in the US, with access to 73 million households, became a media partner with the organizing committee and began to promote the tournament heavily. Lifetime TV is becoming an increasingly important player in women's sport in America. The female tournament has already secured corporate sponsorship from, among others, Adidas, Coca-Cola and MasterCard.

In addition, since 1997 in America there has existed a professional women's football league, while almost 40 per cent of the 8.5 million Americans playing football are women (*The Guardian*, 10 December 1998). As a result, a growing number of women who wish to play the game professionally are being lured to the US on scholarship schemes.

There is also the issue of the financial rewards which flow from sporting success. Even in sports such as athletics which allow a substantial degree of media exposure for female performers, it appears that male sportstars are better rewarded than their female counterparts. In part this becomes part of a circuit of promotion which we outlined in Chapter 3, where sports which fail to attract television exposure find difficulty in getting sponsors on board, which in turn make it less likely that 'stars' will be created and given the media exposure which generates the accompanying lucrative endorsement portfolio (see Chapter 5).

In 1999 the 40 top-earning UK entertainers aged 30 or less included eight women, mostly pop stars or models (*The Observer Magazine*, 11 April 1999). Despite the fact that almost half the people on the list were drawn from the world of sport, none of them was female. A month later a row flared when the Lawn Tennis Association, organizer of the Wimbledon tournament announced that once again the prize money earned by the Men's Champion would be greater than his female counterpart. A clear indication that in 1990s Britain the lucrative media-driven sports industries still position sports men in the premier division of financial earners.

Gendered accounts of sport

In the UK the explosion in print media coverage of sport during the 1990s (examined in Chapter 9) has not resulted in a growing profile for female sport on the back pages. The cultural capital (Bourdieu, 1988) of women sports performers is considerably less than that of men on the back pages of daily newspapers. In research carried out in 1995, Samantha Smith (1995) demonstrated that on average about 3 per cent of the space devoted to sport in both national and Sunday newspapers during November of that year was given over to sport involving women. While this is likely to increase during the track and field athletics season, or the Wimbledon tennis fortnight in July each year, it remains an extremely low figure.

This trend was also commented on by Biscomb *et al.* (1998), who examined the differing trends in treatment by the print media of women in sport between 1984 and 1994. They identified an increase in print-media coverage of sport, but an actual decrease in the percentage coverage devoted to women's sport. They did, however, note that 'the type of description [given to female athletes] was directed away from appearance [and] towards [their] performance' (Biscomb *et al.*, 1998, p. 145). They also noted the ways in which men's and women's sport are treated differently in terms of the language used to describe and make sense of them. While they also argue that the language used in coverage of men's sport has also changed since 1984, the notion of a gendered treatment of sports coverage remains valid.

We would concur that there is a highly gendered treatment given to female athletes – and, as we see below, sometimes even by female journalists – when they do appear in print. While this appears to be improving, the overarching maleness of sporting culture in Britain still clearly comes through in a number of ways.

Examples are not difficult to find. When Britain's European and Commonwealth heptathlete Denise Lewis was interviewed by the broadsheet *Daily Telegraph* (5 April 1999), we were told much about her physical appearance with her having 'looks that Aphrodite would have killed for'. She was asked about whether she had ever modelled and we were informed that the photographer felt she reminded him of supermodel Naomi Campbell.

Tennis has also been a field of sport where the attractiveness or 'ladylike' temperament of women players is central to media narratives. From Chris Evert Lloyd to Martina Hingis, grace and finesse in the women's game have been courted with more praise and deemed more feminine than the power games of Martina Navratilova or Venus Williams. The emphasis on women's bodies is also used to question the legitimacy of muscle tone and evidence of classically 'masculine' body traits, such as big shoulders and biceps. An example of the unreceptiveness to women changing their bodies is given by *The Times* sports feature writer Simon Barnes in this review of Mary Pierce after the French tennis star transformed her physical appearance:

> Now she has changed tack. She has grown a set of quite terrifying masculine appendages. Phwoar, look at those muscles! Suddenly, bursting out of her skimpy tennis tops, we have a pair of arms like Boris Becker's thighs. It is like the Incredible Hulk in drag and slow motion. (*The Times*, 5 May 1999)

The point being that often female athletes find the frame of reference within which they are positioned relates to their sexuality and their appearance in a way male sportspeople are rarely defined. Another trait is to relate women athletes to their domestic/family environment; while this may be important in some cases, it clearly represents a gendered approach in the treatment of male and female sportspeople.

Women taking control

There are changes taking place, however, in what is perhaps the key battleground in the struggle over representation and role models: the news room. The 1990s has seen the welcome growth in female sports journalists in both the print and broadcast media, although it is generally accepted by female journalists that the former remains a more difficult arena for women to establish themselves in.

BBC Scotland has been at the forefront in promoting female sports journalists and presenters and in 1999 has four high-profile women working across its key radio and television sports output. In April of that year Channel 4 also announced that for the first time on British television a woman, Sybil Ruscoe, would front its coverage of both Test match and English domestic cricket on that channel. This was a recognition by Channel 4, who had recently secured the rights to cricket, of the extent to which the traditional BBC coverage of the sport on television had tended to exclude a female audience.

In part this also signifies a change in attitude among both male television executives and also the audience who appear happy to accept female sports presenters. It was not always so, and even ten years ago the dominant consensus among the men who ran BBC and ITV television sport was that the audience would never accept a woman presenting a football programme despite this being relatively common practice elsewhere in Europe.

BBC Radio 5 Live, the news and sports station, has also proved to be an important media outlet in promoting female journalists who deal directly with sports coverage. There is a certain irony here, given that the station has acquired a reputation as 'radio bloke' with its sports – overwhelmingly football – coverage and its male-dominated radio phone-ins. However, by 1999 the ratio between male and female listeners appeared to have shifted from 75:25 to 60:40 (*Broadcast*, 19 March 1999) – perhaps indicative of the overall increase in popularity of male football among both female fans and listeners.

Journalist Eleanor Oldroyd suggests that there remains a substantial difference between women working in broadcasting and the more closed world of male sports journalism. While there is a growing number of female journalists working on sport in both broadsheet and popular newspapers, competition for women remains particularly fierce at the tabloid end of the market, where sport has traditionally been characterized as being a male preserve, covered by men, talking to a male audience.

In her 1995 survey Smith (1995, p. 37) suggested that 'it would appear that the acceptance into the male-dominated field of sports journalism largely depends on the type of newspaper the female reporter works for'. It is also clear that, as the number of female sports journalists grows, however slowly, they in turn will act as role models for a new generation of female journalists who previously may have viewed sports journalism as out of bounds.

Women journalists in this section of the industry are aware that any mistakes, which may be allowed to pass for a male colleague, will be seized upon by others. There is also a strong recognition that, as long as female sports do not gain more television exposure, they will remain under-reported by the print media, which assume that there is not a readership for them.

Ironically, this gendered treatment can also be evident when a female journalist writes about a female sports presenter. In 1997 the *Sunday Times* (23 November) ran a feature on the first female presenter of a television rugby programme on British television, BBC Scotland's Rugby Special host Jill Douglas. Despite emphasizing the undoubted skills and knowledge of the game that Douglas brings to her job, Shields also focused on the 'good-looking woman with an attractive too-many-cigarettes huskiness to her voice'.

Under the headline, JILL TACKLES THE MEN AT THEIR OWN GAME, the article looked at the difficulties women face in overcoming male prejudice within the sport; however, it also simply reproduced some of the most obvious aspects of this in the feature itself. There was a strong focus on Douglas's appearance and a framing of the subject by her domestic environment even referring to Douglas as a 'girl', rather than a woman, something no male journalist would be allowed to get away with. The article ended with questions relating to whether she will marry her long-term partner who happens to be a rugby player. What this feature demonstrates is that, until we can treat female presenters of sports programmes as simply television presenters and journalists, then much work – despite the advances being made – remains to be done.

Masculinity and sport

During the 1990s there has been a concerted effort among researchers of sport to draw on critical feminist analysis in order to understand the position and representation of men in sport and the media. Attention has been placed on both the construction of male hierarchies in sport and media institutions and on the dominant discourses of men and masculinities in media representations of sporting achievement.

The focus on men has not only maintained an interest in the various disadvantages faced by women as athletes and media professionals, but also looked more closely at the structural contexts in which 'hegemonic masculinity' (Connell, 1987) is constructed and maintained. In particular, work in Messner and Sabo (eds.) (1990) and Messner (1992) provides historical and empirical examples of how cultural and symbolic power in sport has been used to define and substantiate wider beliefs about manliness. Moreover, following Connell (1987), such studies have shown that any particular definition of masculinity in sport exists in relation to other masculinities and notions of femininity. The problematizing of male identity, then, has the potential to produce new avenues of research for sport–media studies that bring together interdisciplinary concerns for the production, distribution and consumption of sporting texts and wider issues of power in popular culture.

As we have noted above, media sport is a powerful context for the representation of gender identities, and men's place in the world is often framed, one way or another, by their interest or lack of interest in sport. As this binary social code suggests, sport is heavily laden with values of maleness. Men who abstain from male sporting subcultures can be stereotyped as being effeminate in character, in a context where a feminine trait is viewed as a negative, less empowering, attribute. Male sporting subcultures, therefore, operate twin dynamics of misogynist and homophobic behaviour.

As discussed in Chapter 5, the concentrated media attention on male sport stars does much to consolidate the belief that men's physical prowess in sport has a positive and worthy function in society. Lack of ability in sport can, where male familial and peer pressure exists, lead to low self-esteem and a sense of failure. Similarly, if determination to succeed in sport is found wanting, athletes may be criticized in the media for not showing enough grit and courage to achieve their goal.

Masculine traits, such as strength and toughness, are celebrated in the media coverage of sport and operate to reaffirm the myths of male prowess. Where a sportsman's masculinity is brought into question, as by the heterosexist gesture by the Liverpool footballer Robbie Fowler towards the Chelsea defender Graham Le Saux in March 1999, the abuse gains its power from society's wider prejudice of gay and lesbian groups.

Le Saux is not gay, but was viewed as being effeminate because of his middle-class origin and, what some might call, more refined cultural tastes than the average footballer from a working-class background. In this instance, the complex relations between gender, sexuality and class were revealed to exemplify how masculinity is perceived differently by different socio–economic groups. Le Saux may conform more closely with the gentility of the marketing industry's middle-class 'new man', whereas Fowler, whose bravura could be said to have been born of the similarly media-constructed 'new laddism', was clearly displaying the homosexual fears of traditional male working-class culture.

The meaning of masculinity is also fought over in the spectating of sport. Men's conspicuous consumption of sport, in particular of football in Britain, has gone hand in hand with more varied images of men and masculinities. This can be seen during the 1980s and 1990s by the proliferation of men's 'style' magazines (Nixon, 1996) and some specific transformations in football as popular culture (Redhead, 1987 and 1991).

Young male fans are not merely continuing the male secular ritual of supporting a particular football club, as their fathers and grand-fathers had before them, but bring to this profane culture more promis-cuous, consumerist lifestyles, where preoccupation with fashion goes hand-in-hand with passion for the sport. The development of 'style wars' at football grounds had their roots in the crossover between football and popular music in the late 1970s and early 1980s, but have more recently drawn on a wider male popular cultural desire for designer clothing.

The shifting patterns of young men's consumption, with heavy emphasis placed on 'the look' and style of appearance may not, however, suggest a wider transformation in sexual politics. Sport, again, plays a key role in controlling masculine relations. While fashion at the football ground may provide status and recognition among peers, it is still the assertion of hegemonic male relations through pride, honour and a sense of superiority that binds men to their particular community.

Sport and violent masculinity

Football fandom lies at the heart of the historical fear of sport-related violence (Dunning et al., 1988). Any resurgence of spectator violence in sport is often viewed through the eyes of a media moral panic. However, violence in the playing of sport is an important carrier of wider mean-ings of violent masculinity. Many sports are predicated on aggressive values, where competition demands violent physical contact and often the deliberate infliction of harm or injury.

The display of violence in sport is further legitimized by the voy-euristic gaze of the television camera. As Sabo and Curry Jansen (1998, p. 209) have observed:

> Within the commercial imperatives of television, the blood sacrifice of the athlete performs the same function that it does in dramatised violence.

The ritualized expression and linkages of sport, masculinity and men's violence are most startlingly realized in the television coverage of box-ing. Emphasis on male physical power and strength are frequent motifs of media narratives on male sport. As Connell (1997, p. 52) states:

> In our culture, at least, the physical sense of maleness and femaleness is central to the cultural interpretation of gender.

The legitimacy of violence in sport, therefore, balances upon the axis of power in the gender order, where physical combat, blood and bruises are considered 'natural' for men, and alien to women. As Connell and others have further concluded, the media accounts of 'natural mascu-linity' based on biological determinants are scientifically unfounded and fictional.

Boxing and being a man

Nowhere is the metaphor of the male body as weapon or fighting machine more evident than in the sport of boxing. Boxing has received a new level of critical analysis during the 1990s, with interest from soci-ology (Wacquant, 1995; Sugden, 1996), psychology (Oates, 1994; and Beattie, 1997), cultural studies (Sloop, 1997; Baker, 1997; and Jefferson, 1998), feminist analysis (Hargreaves, 1997) and new sports journalism (MacRae, 1997). A theme that runs through all of these studies is the centrality of masculine identity as it is embodied through boxing.

Any critical study of boxing, then, demands an analysis of the con-struction of gender difference and development through sport. Boxing as an 'iconic embodiment of masculinity' can tell us much about the 'representations of the masculine body *and* their psychic underpinnings' (Jefferson, 1997, pp. 78–9). Jefferson also notes that boxers, in particular Mike Tyson, come to be identified with a level of 'hardness', in terms of both 'mental' and 'physical toughness'.

This characterization of boxing, as an exclusive, essentialist mascu-line domain, is dominated by metaphors of power, strength, ferocity of the competitive spirit, and courage. These discourses are retrieved, cir-culated and reinforced in the media coverage of boxing. In February

1995 one of the most brutal fights to be screened on British television was fought between Nigel Benn (UK) and Gerald McLellan (USA) for the World Boxing Council (WBC) version of the 'Super-Middleweight' Championship of the World.

In the week before the fight Benn was considered the underdog, his challenger, McLellan, a man *The Observer* (19 February 1995) sports writer Kevin Mitchell proclaimed to be 'a fighter of distinctly pit-bull tendencies'. However, it was further observed that 'Benn is at his most dangerous when in trouble'. The British boxer, known as the 'Dark Destroyer', conjuring up images of 'blackness' and 'hardness', was well known for his ability to come back from the brim of defeat, having previously had well-publicized and bloody battles with the other British Super-Middleweight champion Chris Eubank. It also illustrates the complex interplay between discourses of masculinity, race and nationality. The media epithets that are frequently used to promote boxers before big fights set the scene in a gladiatorial fashion, laying emphasis on the destructive capabilities of the men involved.

In the event, Benn suffered a series of heavy blows that knocked him out of the ring in the opening round. The British boxer was continually buffeted about the ring, only denying defeat by literally scrapping for his life. McLellan appeared to be moving towards an inevitable victory until a clash of heads in the ninth round clearly distressed the American, turning the advantage to Benn. Spurred on by the partisan crowd and the injury to his opponent, Benn delivered some crunching blows that overwhelmed McLellan, causing him to drop to his knees and accept defeat by a technical knockout. As Benn celebrated his victory with the crowd, McLellan slipped into unconsciousness, ultimately to be left in a coma from which he later suffered brain damage.

Nearly 13 million viewers watched the fight live on British television on ITV, witnessing the destruction of two men – Benn was also hospitalized for observation suffering from exhaustion. The atmosphere in the arena was intense and the commentary by Reg Gutteridge and ex-professional boxer Jim Watt was equally charged with emotion after an incredible turnabout in Benn's fortunes. The fight was subsequently celebrated in the sporting press as one of the most exciting fights of the modern era. Some journalists did reflect on the brutality of the fight and struggled to equate their dependence and engagement with the sport as 'the manly art' with the concern that the horrific consequences of boxing could not be justified or legitimated.

Reflecting on the fight a year and half later, in a postscript to Benn's last fight and defeat by Steve Collins, *The Independent* boxing correspondent Harry Mullan (11 November 1996) admitted that the fight with McClellan was 'the most savage 10 rounds I have ever seen'. When Benn prematurely admitted defeat against Collins, the reaction from the crowd in the Nynex Arena in Manchester, was to boo what they saw as an uncharacteristically 'unheroic' performance.

The media hype that framed the contest clearly prescribed a set of inflated expectations for the audience. The 'blood lust' that often generates the excitement of the crowd can at times be seen to be more harmful and destructive to the boxer than the fighter's own wilful intent to injure and be injured.

Wacquant (1995) and Sugden (1996) have illustrated in their ethnographic studies of boxers and the culture of boxing, that many pugilists are fully aware of the damage they can cause their bodies, and continue with the 'fight game' because it socially and psychologically 'inhabits' them. The sense that boxing is 'in your blood' is a common descriptor by boxing pundits to explain the self-destructive urge that appears to motivate them – self-evident in the media characterization and narratives that celebrated a 'scrapper' like Nigel Benn.

Masculine bravura and entertainment

A more cynical outlook on the profession would view it as a means to a financial end, a way out of poverty, an opportunity to enter the media spotlight. Similarly, as long as boxing entices large enough audiences, it will continue to enjoy the televisual spectacle it currently enjoys on satellite and cable networks around the world. As Bryant *et al.*, (1998, p. 253) have observed with regard to world heavyweight boxing: 'violence in sports "sells"'.

Benn's fight with Collins was part of a ten-hour feast of televised boxing orchestrated on both sides of the Atlantic by the promoters Frank Warren and Don King. Promoted as 'Judgement Night', the evening comprised six world title fights, three in Manchester and three in Las Vegas. The three British fights were available to Sky Sports subscription holders. The three American fights were available on pay-per-view (ppv) on Sky Box Office for a standard price of £9.95 (rising to £14.95 on the day). An estimated 420,000 ppv customers watched the event, bringing BSkyB's 50 per cent share in the revenue to more than £25 million.

'Judgement Night' augured a new experience for fans of boxing, packaged and glossily delivered by television. The hype that surrounded the event had more in common with World Federation Wrestling, with its hybrid of showmanship and sport, than the era when boxing was soberly screened by the BBC. The 'master' showman of contemporary boxing is World featherweight champion Prince Naseem Hamed. Hamed ritually enters the boxing arena in an extravagant manner: lasers, lights, dry ice and thumping dance music lead to his 'trademark' somersault over the ropes to the ring. This show of bravura is for the crowd and the cameras, and signal what *The Guardian* sports writer Gavin Evans (8 November 1996) has called 'the trappings of the ersatz gladiatorial arena of modern boxing'.

In the run-up to 'Judgement Night' Evans argued that Hamed thrives on the adrenaline rush of 'putting on a show' as much as he appears to relish 'the pleasurable anticipation' of knocking out his opponent. As we revealed in Chapter 6, Hamed is acutely aware of his own identity, and this does not only apply to him being a British Arab Muslim. His physical ability and exhibitionist performance are also part and parcel of the relationship boxing fans carry with the man. As Hamed put it in a pre-fight interview before 'Judgement Night':

> It's not about boxing is it? It's about watching this little guy on the telly tonight. He's so flash, so cocky that you want him to take a right lesson but somehow he always wins. A lot of people tell me that. (Interviewed in the *Financial Times*, 9 November 1996)

But boxing is not just about the characters and star performances. Evans's considered feature article in *The Guardian*, revealing a more reflexive attitude of the 'dirty reality' of boxing than is familiarly raised in the banal reports of tabloid newspapers, picked up on the immediate, tangible experience of boxing 'behind the glittering façade':

> Boxing has a smell coming off it, and a feel, that the camera is not designed to detect. Unless you have boxed, or at least watched from ringside, it is hard to glean a true picture of what happens in there: the taste and sometimes the stink of sweat, snot and blood as bodies clash and clinch; the surprise of how small most boxers are and just how hard they hit; the excruciating thud of a hook to liver, the sharper shock of a fist or head in the mouth or nose, the momentary haze from being caught on the side of the jaw, the exhaustion, the concentration and the exhilaration of getting it all to flow just right. There's nothing more intense for the participants in the mainstream sporting world. (Evans, 1996)

What the juxtaposition of hype and glamour on television and the 'reality' of the sport described above illustrates is that the processes of mediation, from ring to screen, detracts from the brutality of the sport, celebrating instead the manly endeavour and bravura of the stars involved.

The ritual of the pre-fight weigh-in, the menacing eye-to-eye stares, the courage and competitive spirit that winners and losers display are the dramatic elements that constitute the sporting narratives of boxing. The pain, destructiveness and occasional death from boxing are glossed over to preserve the civility of the sport. Emphasis is placed on manliness and machismo and not violence in its rawest sense.

Conclusion

Women's role in boxing has stereotypically been consigned to scantily clad models strolling around the ring holding up number cards that precede the next round. However, in a review of women's association with boxing at various levels, Jennifer Hargreaves (1997) has observed that women's boxing has prospered against strong opposition throughout the twentieth century.

In 1995 a sanctioned bout for the Women's World Championship was promoted in the US, inevitably, by the boxing impresario Don King. In the UK intransigence towards recognizing the official status of women's boxing has led to court action as part of a concerted effort to establish the sport. Jane Couch, the women's world welterweight champion, had been refused a licence to box in the UK by the British Boxing Board of Control (BBBC). Couch had won the title in 1996, boxing under licence in the US.

However, she had never been able to defend her title legitimately on home soil. After repeated refusals from the BBBC, Couch took the governing body to an industrial tribunal on the grounds of sexual discrimination. In 1998 the court decided in favour of the boxer, dismissing the BBBC's claim that boxing was not a suitable sport for women because they suffer from pre-menstrual tension. Couch received £20,000 compensation allowing for her 'hurt feelings' and gained more media coverage for women's boxing than it had ever enjoyed before.

The marginalization of women's boxing is perhaps the clearest manifestation of patriarchal ideologies in sport. The gendered values of sport are acutely realized when the physical capital ascribed to men and women's bodies differs so greatly. Female muscularity is viewed as distasteful and inhumane. Masculine strength and bravura are celebrated and viewed as heroic.

Success and power in sport come to represent the iconic symbol of manhood. Women's boxing clearly disrupts and challenges such stereotypes, attempting to co-opt the quintessential male sport for its own celebration of women's power and physical ability. However, after a century of women's prize fighting, the professional sport remains a long way from attaining wider recognition. Until women's boxing is courted by television it will continue to be viewed as a minority sport, and the dominant image of women and boxing will be one of titillation, from the 'Playboy girls' in the ring to the occasional boxing symbolism of topless Page 3 models in the *Sun* newspaper.

CHAPTER 8

Games Across Frontiers

Mediated Sport and National Identity

Nationalism is one of the basic principles which is used by media and 'advertisers' to attract the viewers' attention towards international sport events.

Television 98: European Key Facts

Congratulations also to France. She has discovered, during these last few weeks, that football can be a unique opportunity for everyone to get together, wherever you were born, whatever the colour of your skin, whatever your ideas, in order to party.

***L'Équipe*, 9 July 1998 commenting on the football World Cup**

Football and crude nationalism aren't distant cousins. They are brothers under the same T-shirt.

Peter Preston, *The Guardian*, 22 June 1998

Introduction

With its visibility and focus on symbols, winning, competition, partisan fans – and in team games the necessity of collective struggle – few other cultural forms lend themselves as easily as sport to being used as an indicator of certain national characteristics and, by extension, of being representative of a national identity. Whether it is the gaelic games of hurling or football typifying Irish character (Humphries, 1996), the integral position of football in Scottish culture (Cosgrove, 1998) or the extent to which cricket has come to symbolize a particular aspect of Englishness (Paxman, 1998), the ritual and ceremony of sport – particularly national and international sport – carry with them a symbolic significance which far outweigh sport's importance as organized play.

Much of that symbolic importance is inherently attached to sport and its subcultures; however, as noted in Chapters 4 and 5, crucial ideological work is also carried out in the way that sport is both represented, constructed and transformed through its contact with the various forms of media.

Newspapers, magazines and books, in conjunction with the visual media help define the social and political position of sport in society. They also act as the interface between sporting, political and ideological discourses of identity and meaning. Examples of this are not hard to find. The success or failure of the British Olympic team appears, according to sections of the media, as a direct barometer of the position and state of Britain in the world. A sporting crisis for national teams is often linked and connected with wider political or cultural shifts, so the abject failure of the Scottish national team at the football World Cup in 1978 is used to help account for the failure of nerve among the electorate in the subsequent devolution referendum a year later. In Britain, sports coverage with a national dimension appears often not to be about sport. As Blain and O'Donnell (1998, p. 41) suggest, often it 'seems rather to be an obsession with corporate national self, to which sport is virtually incidental'.

However, before we begin to read sporting character and success or failure simply as attributes which can be easily influenced by, or indeed can determine wider political and cultural characteristics, we need to examine the relationship between sport, media and national identity and outline and highlight some of the central issues. We then look at two case studies which bring into focus some of these issues, before finally broadening out the debate to examine the relationship between global trends in media sport and collective identities, an issue developed in more detail in the final chapter of the book.

Media, discourse and identity

Organized sport has been viewed by governments of all political persuasions as an important sphere in the forging of 'national character', with this project often serving specific political ends (Cashmore, 1996, pp. 235–57). This particular point is well made in the work of Houlihan (1994), which examines the relationship between sport, politics and international relations. He notes:

> sport has always been a resource within the international system
> available primarily to governments, but also to other non-governmental

political interests and, while it has, on occasion, been the primary tool
of diplomacy and policy implementation, it has more often been an
element of a broader and more comprehensive political strategy.
(Houlihan, 1994, p. 209)

Examples are readily available. Duke and Crolley (1996, pp. 24–49)
document the politicization of football in Francoist Spain during the
period between 1939 and 1975. Franco was not alone in attempting to
align sport and, due to its universal popularity, football in particular,
with specific political regimes (Hoberman, 1984). This process takes
place most notably at the level of international sport, and worldwide sporting competitions such as the Olympic Games or the football
World Cup.

Sport, politics and hegemony

In the past countries such as the former Soviet Union and the German
Democratic Republic have directly linked the health of the state to its
ability to perform successfully in the international sporting arena
(Houlihan, 1997). This linkage of political discourse with that of
sport is still evident throughout contemporary Europe and beyond
(O'Donnell, 1994).

To view this use of sport as some form of simple political manipulation by powerful interest groups in society, to which people readily
succumb, is both simplistic and patronizing, and ignores the contradictions, tensions and struggles that exist within all supposedly national
cultures.

Sports can be an arena of cultural struggle, in which oppressed
groups use it as a form of symbolic resistance. The turning of that most
imperial of English games, cricket, by the West Indies (and other former
British colonies) into an expression and celebration of indigenous culture is one such example (Malac, 1995).

Political scientists such as Hoberman (1984) argue that sporting
activity in itself is not intrinsically ideological. However, sport as a
cultural form based on competition is uniquely open to political and
ideological manipulation.

The work by Sugden and Bairner examining *Sport, Sectarianism and
Society in a Divided Ireland* (1993) is an excellent example of a study of
sport from within the political sciences. In this work they demonstrate
how sporting culture in Ireland is closely shaped and informed by the
political crisis that exists in Northern Ireland. They argue that in the
north of Ireland sectarianism becomes:

> a symbolic labelling process through which community divisions are
> defined and maintained, and . . . an ideological justification for
> discrimination, community conflict and political violence. (Sugden and
> Bairner, 1993, p. 15)

By tracing the symbolic linking of certain sports to specific political and
cultural groupings, they show how sport, and the culture surrounding
this activity, becomes an important part of this process of labelling and
differentiating various groups in society.

Sugden and Bairner reject the criticism that Gramsci's concept of
hegemony is too focused on class as the primary determining factor in
social relations and argue that:

> Gramsci's approach is admirably suited to explaining divisions which
> spring from non-economic sources such as national identity, ethnicity
> and religion. (Sugden and Bairner, 1993, p. 14)

However they do not play down the economic in their analysis, and
demonstrate, for example, how the British state, for ideological reasons,
has played a key role in the funding of the leisure/sports infrastructure
of Northern Ireland (to an extent that is disproportionate to the size of
its population within the UK). It appears that there is a belief that, if
young people are involved in sport, they are less likely to get involved in
political and paramilitary activity.

One criticism which can perhaps be made of their work is the extent
to which the role of the media in the process of identity formation
is largely ignored. However, their material is characterized by a clear
understanding of the integral relationship that exists between the
domains of sport, politics and identity in Ireland.

Also, as we have seen in Chapter 6, the more recent ongoing work of
Bairner (1999) has begun to focus on the interplay between the sports
media and identity in Northern Ireland. While it may appear obvious
that in a crisis-ridden Northern Ireland the symbolic importance of
sport will have a heightened political significance, it also draws attention to the extent to which many of the academic encounters with sport
have been English-centred and have placed social class as the primary
definer of different patterns of sporting behaviour.

Sugden and Bairner's work is a useful reminder of the theoretical
difficulties that exist when social class is cut across by other factors
such as ethnicity and national identity, something that is often missing
in English society based accounts.

An important addition to this body of work located outside England
has been the collection of essays edited by Jarvie and Walker, *Sport in*

the Making of the Scottish Nation: Ninety-minute patriots? (1994), which examines the complex relationship between sport and identity in Scotland and emphasizes how specific political, economic and cultural factors have all shaped the nature and position of sport in Scottish culture. Interestingly, one of the features of this work was the multi-disciplinary approach taken by the editors in their drawing of contributions from a range of disciplines such as history, sociology and media studies.

Media sport and national identity

The media's relationship with modern sport has helped transform our understanding of this particular area of popular culture. Mediated sport can be an important cultural arena in which ideas about various aspects of social relations can become naturalized. Today most sporting cultures are to some extent mediated through television, radio or the print media. As has been argued elsewhere, in this process of transformation not only are discourses of identity mediated or simply transmitted, but in many instances they can be constructed or even at times invented, if the political or economic climate is suitable (Whannel, 1992, Blain *et al.*, 1993, Blain and Boyle, 1998).

This is particularly true in the field of international sporting competition, where sport can become a symbolic extension of various collective identities. In some instances this can be positive, for example the success of the Republic of Ireland football team since the mid to late 1980s has helped to promote a particularly positive image of that country and its fans abroad. Moreover, the success of a sport which has been historically viewed as 'foreign' in that country has been an important part of a wider process of rethinking about what constitutes the defining cultural characteristics of Irishness. In addition, it has helped in the two-way process of reconnection between people living in Ireland and those who form part of the Irish diaspora (especially young people).

At other times, international media sport becomes an arena in which the supposed superiority of one country, or ethnic group over another is celebrated. As Hugh O'Donnell has noted in his study of the construction of international sporting stereotypes:

> [Sport can] function on an international level as a site in which advanced countries can and must act out their preferred myths through self – and other – stereotypes, and celebrate those qualities which, in their own eyes, make them more modern, more advanced, in short superior . . . This process routinely involves downgrading other national groups. (O'Donnell, 1994, p. 353)

While much of this process of myth reinforcement is conducted in the media's transformation of sport, a note of caution regarding the origins of many of these discourses needs to be introduced.

Firstly, media institutions are themselves subject to a range of economic, cultural and political pressures which in turn heavily influence how they choose to frame or make sense of events. For example, the *Sun* newspaper in England may report a riot involving England supporters differently than the edition of the same paper aimed at a Scottish readership, as they address different culturally defined markets (Blain and Boyle, 1994).

The popular press's at times overtly racist treatment of a German motor-racing driver may differ from that found even on a commercial broadcasting channel such as ITV (where any racist overtones will be much more subtle). In other words, the mobilization of particular discourses of identity is partly determined by a range of factors such as the audience being targeted, the specific media institution and how it is funded, as well as current political and social attitudes.

Secondly, it is worth emphasizing the point made by Philip Schlesinger when he argued:

> not to start with communication and its supposed effects on collective identity and culture, but rather to begin by posing the problem of collective identity itself, to ask how it might be analysed and what importance communicative practices may play in its constitution. (Schlesinger, 1991, p. 150)

It can be misleading to place the media at the centre of the process of identity-formation. While they may be a key site in constituting and reconstituting various discourses (and indeed in many instances both legitimizing and marginalizing ideas and value systems), they are not necessarily the primary definers of either discourse or aspects of identity.

Adrian Mellor has warned against what he views as an increasing tendency within the academy either to view the media as the definer of individual and collective identities, or, at the other end of the scale, the tendency within some postmodernist writing to suggest that people are in some sense completely autonomous from social structures. He argues that the:

> alternative is to treat people as active agents interacting with real structures. People make their own cultures, albeit not in circumstances of their own choosing. Amongst these circumstances – within and towards which their activity is directed – are structures of

Celtic Connections – Sport and national identity can often be front page news, as when Wales triumphed over England to hand the Five Nations Championship to Scotland in 1999. © *The Daily Record, Glasgow*

representation; but so too are structures of class, ethnicity and gender, along with deliberate economic and political strategies that bear upon these. These things are real. They do not merely exist in discourse. Their reality and their consequences exceed their representation. But people are not merely constructed by them. (Mellor, 1991, p, 114)

What is argued is that it is important to situate media coverage in detailed contexts of interpretation. This does not negate the power, importance and role that the media can play in helping to make sense of a group's collective identity (usually by a process of boundary marking), but simply alerts us to the fact that this influence will vary depending on the specific influence of a range of other factors at particular moments in specific social circumstances.

All together now

An example of the overt linking of sporting activity to political rhetoric was evident with the re-entry of South Africa into the world sporting community, and in particular its successful staging of the 1995 Rugby World Cup. President Nelson Mandela explicitly associated himself with the Springboks team, projecting it as a symbol of the 'new' multi-racial democratic South Africa (this despite the fact that there was only one black player in the team).

> 'One team, one country,' is the adopted motif of the Springboks' World Cup campaign. For once it seems to be more than just a PR gimmick. President Mandela spent three hours with the squad on the eve of the match and delayed his intended departure from the match yesterday so that he could be sure that 'his boys', as he calls the team, hung on for victory. 'Our loyalties have completely changed,' said the president. 'We have adopted these young men.' (*The Guardian*, 26 May 1995)

Throughout the tournament, which South Africa would win, Mandela lost no opportunity to use the team's success both as an indicator of the positive and dynamic political changes taking place in that country and as a vehicle with which to project a positive image of the country to the world through the international media coverage of the event.

However, Steenveld and Strelitz (1998, p. 625) in their examination of this media event caution against ascribing too much long-term power to the images of unity generated by the success of South Africa. Echoing the point made earlier by Mellor (1991), they suggest, 'if there was a coming together during the tournament, it was a temporary phenomenon and in no way laid the foundation – as the media and the government politicians would have us believe – for the creation of a collective self identity'.

You could also make a similar argument about the long-term impact of the *Forza Italia* movement in Italy during the 1990s. Here Silvio Berlusconi, media–sports owner, used the popularity of football in that country to help realize his own political ambitions; however, after initial success, both Berlusconi's Prime Ministership and the fortunes of his club AC Milan suffered severe reversals of fortune (Frei, 1997, pp. 213–45).

UK sporting tensions

Within the UK's sporting environment, there exists the problem of mediating the complicated political and cultural relationship between the different component parts of the UK (for example Scotland and England) – a situation which is already becoming more acute in the late 1990s with the devolved Parliament in Scotland and Assemblies in Wales and Northern Ireland beginning to reconfigure the political relationships which exist within and beyond the Union.

Due in part to the universality of sporting activity, sport has been an important cultural arena through which various collective identities have been articulated. Richard Holt (1990) has documented how the political history and economic relationship of Scotland and Wales with England has been mediated through sporting occasions:

> Sport acted as a vitally important channel for this sense of collective resentment . . . Football gave the Scots a way of fighting the 'old enemy', whilst addiction to rugby came to be one of the major ways in which the English defined the Welsh and the Welsh came to see themselves. Cultural identity was a two-way process. (Holt, 1990, p. 237)

This viewing of cultural identity as a continuous process that is subject to political, economic and cultural constraints and pressures is important. It also emphasizes how the concept of localism is relative. Within Scotland, for example, the national press can mean the Scottish, not the UK press, and the idea that the British media's coverage of sport unproblematically reproduces the British 'nation' is dependent on how that nation is defined and from what cultural and class position the viewer/reader is engaging with this discourse (see the next chapter).

This is not to argue that television's transformation of sport as a cultural form does not have a role to play in cultural identity-formation. What is being suggested here is that to view this process as unidirectional is to underestimate the other factors that shape collective identities and the degree of resistance that may exist among certain groups to any 'official' discourse.

While discourses of sporting national identity do differ across sports, depending on whether they are individual or team games, what class connotations are attached to individual sports, and their profile within the media arena, the contradictions and tensions that exist in any 'national culture' are rarely articulated at the international sporting level. As Schlesinger comments:

> National cultures are not simple repositories of shared symbols to which the entire population stands in identical relation. Rather, they are to be approached as sites of contestation in which competition over definitions takes place . . . It may also reproduce distinctions between 'us' and 'them' at the intra-national level, in line with the internal structure of social divisions and relations of power and domination.
> (Schlesinger, 1991, p. 174)

Thus it appears useful to view the media as one important part of the process of identity formation, but not to start from a media-centred view of society.

Scottishness/Englishness

Hargreaves (1986) rightly asserts that the televisual constructions of Englishness/Britishness through sport are important in legitimizing particular articulations of such identities at the expense of alternative viewpoints. However, we also need to be alert to the opposition that may exist among certain groups to these dominant discourses. Hargreaves acknowledges this problematic when he comments:

> The paucity of firm, well-grounded conclusions in research on the effects of mass communication so far dictates caution when interpreting the relation between media sport and working-class culture and the likely effects of media sport on the working-class audience.
> (Hargreaves, 1986, p. 160)

For example, the portrayal in both the Scottish and European media of the supporters of the Scottish national football who travel abroad as 'The Tartan Army' is not simply a media construct, but highlights the complex relationship between media discourses and audiences.

The Scottish national team supporter who travels abroad constitutes part of perhaps the most image-conscious footballing group in Europe. Many of the images of the 'fun-loving' internationalist Scottish supporter are juxtaposed by the media with the dour aggressive xenophobic English supporter. This is a point which is not lost when Scottish supporters travel abroad and are faced with reporters and television cameras and realize that, by adopting particular dress codes (the kilt, tartan and such like) and cultivating a friendly attitude towards the local population, they clearly differentiate themselves in the eyes of the media as being Scottish and not English (Giulianotti, 1991, 1994).

We would argue that the mediation of national and international sport can only be understood by locating it within the specific economic, political and historical contours which shape societies. Often mediated sport will reproduce, reinforce and even normalize attitudes and values which exist in other spheres of political or cultural life. Blain and O'Donnell (1998, pp. 51–3) have argued that football, as mediated by the press, has three kinds of relationship with society.

Football is a sign of society: in other words footballing success or failure is one part of a country's overall sense of identity. It can also be an extension of society: here sporting failure is viewed as a wider failure of society as a whole. And finally football may be a simulacrum of society: where, for example, the Scottish national team is 'at least partly presented as referring only to itself' (1998, p. 53).

They argue that these categories of coverage reflect to varying degrees the level of political and economic modernity in each country, so that a country such as Spain or Germany treats football as one part of its overall identity, while in less well developed countries (in terms of modernity) such as England/Britain, English sporting failure is mediated as an indicator of national decline.

We would agree that these categories are useful when examining media (the press in particular) treatment of international sport. However, one has to take into account the complexities of the media industries, all mobilizing sporting discourses for differing commercial and/or ideological reasons aimed at a range of audiences/readerships/viewerships. In other words, we would suggest that the boundaries between these categories are perhaps less rigid and well defined as they initially appear.

At any one time aspects of all three categories may be used in differing sections of the press or media. While we would argue strongly for the important link between a country's political and economic development and its cultural confidence and sense of judgement, often this can also be quite specifically linked to economic booms or downturns in the economy.

This certainly becomes the case in this argument if football is replaced by sport (in all its variations) and the press by the broader media. Thus, while the relative success of the Republic of Ireland football team during the 1980s and 1990s was often portrayed as another positive aspect of a more confident post-nationalist country, earlier footballing failures (of which there were many) were not viewed as national disasters. In this instance attention was simply turned to other individual sporting successes involving Irish athletes such as Eamon

Coghlan and John Tracey – while its football fans often appeared, like the Scots, to have a heightened awareness of their own self image in the media. A recent downturn in the Irish team's fortunes has been treated, not as a national disaster, but as a minor setback at a time when the economy is booming and Irish political confidence in European developments buoyant. However, elsewhere on the Irish sporting landscape, any crisis in the overtly nationalist and still very popular gaelic games is treated as a national scandal and an example of decline in standards of public culture.

Thus images and imaginings of a country's past, present and projections of its future, come together to underpin the mediation of sporting discourses. Put simply, at certain specific political, economic and cultural moments these can come together around one sport or sporting event and be evident across both sports and media institutions (such as the South African Rugby World Cup discussed earlier). At other times they may be more diverse and even contradictory, but are always rooted in the tensions between change and continuity which characterize societies. In some instances sport will carry the burden of national expectation, at other times, depending on the political and economic climate, it won't.

Political football: Euro 96 and the Auld Enemy

QUESTION: What is the difference between English fans and Scottish fans?
ANSWER: The rest of the world likes Scottish fans!
QUESTION: Why?
ANSWER: Scottish fans don't FIGHT with opposing fans. All right, they can be a bit – okay very – noisy and I'll even concede annoying. But except for a tiny minority, they are never violent, whereas the boys from Blighty are gaining a reputation that Gengis Khan's mob could only look at in envy.

We'll Take Blighty by Storm, *Scottish Sunday Express*, 2 June 1996

Our first case study examines Scottish newspaper coverage of the England/Scotland football match which took place at Wembley as part of the Euro 96 tournament held in England. We want to look briefly at a number of themes which emerged from the coverage of this match, one given a heightened edge by the growing political demands of Scotland for a distinctive parliament, the other being how infrequently this once annual fixture is now played.

History on the march with the Tartan Army

One of the most striking aspects of the coverage of Scotland and its supporters in the build up to Euro 96 in general and the clash with England in particular was the unproblematic usage of the term 'the Tartan Army' to describe the followers of the national team. This term is used across both the tabloid and broadsheet press leading to a plethora of military references and analogies. It should also be noted that this term is also not confined to the sports pages but routinely used in news and feature articles which talk about Scottish supporters.

In the run up to the World Cup in France, for example, Stuart Cosgrove documented for *The Observer* (7 June 1998), under The heading THE TARTAN ARMY, the history of away days involving the Army as it followed the Scottish national team around the globe. In much of the media coverage the fans come to personify the character of the country, and of course are defined against their English counterparts.

This marks an important aspect of Scottish reporting of the national team, that is the extent to which journalists become fans. The burden of national identity appears for many to outweigh their responsibilities as journalists. Graham Spiers of *Scotland on Sunday* sums up this attitude and also offers alternative images of Englishness:

> . . . finals being played on English soil, which makes the Scottish blood gurgle a little stronger. Our footballing man doesn't think of England as [the] Tower of London . . . St Paul's . . . he thinks of a myriad of snapshot images, a toothless Nobby Stiles, a gleaming FA Cup, a green Wembley sward peppered in cavorting tartan hordes, a collapsing crossbar, a hammered Scot, a Jimmy Hill or a Joe Jordan . . . I will be at Wembley on June 15 . . . nervously prowling the press area and trying to be as adult and as mature as I can be. I'm a fraud. Inside, my little boy's voice will be shrieking: sock it to them Scotland! (*Scotland on Sunday*, 9 June 1996)

Part of the Tartan Army theme is that of the footsoldier, with a newspaper tracking one fan throughout the Euro 96 'campaign' as he follows Scotland.

The Scottish *Sun* (7 June) in its 8-page pull out has WE'RE GOING TARTAN BARMY:

> SunSport's No 1 Scotland fan GARY KEOWN has unfurled his saltire and is joining the charge across the border in support of Craig Brown and his troops. He'll be reporting in every day from the front line with a fan's eye view of the battles facing Scotland against Holland, the Auld Enemy and Switzerland.

We find Gary suitably attired in *Braveheart* warrior dress of course the fan turns out to be one of the *Sun*'s football journalists and indeed a lapsed member of the Tartan Army, admitting he hasn't been part of the travelling support for three years. While reservations had been made in some quarters of the press about the self-parodying Scottish fan, the overwhelming image of the Scottish fans in the tabloid press is broadly positive.

While this is also the case in much of the broadsheet press, the clear connection between fandom and political and national identity is also drawn. The day before the opening Scottish match of Euro 96, a *Scotland on Sunday* editorial (9 June 1996) places the Scottish campaign within a broader political context: SCOTLAND CAN WIN GRACEFULLY: 'we hope that the Tartan Army returns from England with its reputation unblemished'. It even suggests that this outweighs the importance of any footballing success:

> With Europhobia filling the political debate day after day, it is crucial that Scotland emerges from the championship without damage to its credentials for internationalism. It is better by far to lose a football match than to gain a reputation on the continent for thuggery and xenophobia. Ask England. There is little shame in a small nation losing a football match; there is in street-battles and hooliganism.

This projection of a rational and mature Scotland was not much in evidence among the tabloids, where the clichéd use of the *Braveheart* theme was played to death as a signifier of a more emotional warrior Scotland.

Examples included Ally McCoist appearing in *News of the World* magazine dressed as Wallace, with obligatory face paint – ALLY MCCOIST: WHY I'M SCOTLAND'S BRAVEHEART (2 June 1996). On the day of the match the Scottish *Sun* had an actual scene from the *Braveheart* film reproduced on its wrap-round front cover with the heads of the Scottish team airbrushed onto the shoulders of the warriors.

Sporting nations

Kevin McCarra writing in the *Sunday Times Scotland* (9 June), noted how:

> There are nations who arrive like colonisers at a major tournament. Italy and Germany, for example, always seem bent on putting down roots and taking up residence. Others, however, can only envy their assertiveness. At these events Scotland behave as if they are on a weekend break, snatching a look at a couple of the sights before dashing home to pore over the holiday snaps.

He mobilizes a range of images, ostensibly football-related, but to grasp his meaning fully we need a passing acquaintance with recent European history. As with so much reporting of international sport, the language and images used to make sense of the event are steeped in wider cultural and political references (O'Donnell, 1994; Blain and O'Donnell, 1998).

A reading of the Scottish press during the summer of 1996 would have assumed the country was awash with people obsessed with events and battles centuries old, rather than a country which stood on the brink of a new political era. However, throughout the coverage there were more thoughtful pieces which attempted to analyse the mediated outpouring of national feeling both south and north of the border.

James McKillop in the broadsheet *Glasgow Herald* (1 June 1996) examined how a xenophobic attitude in the south is affecting the whole of Britain, in particular the English newspaper coverage of the beef crisis and their attitude in particular to the Germans.

Amid the pages and pages of hype another more critical and wary voice was that of Ian McGarry in the Glasgow *Evening Times* of 13 June: PATRIOT GAME IS A REAL LOSER. He notes the fun had by Scottish and Dutch supporters in Birmingham. Turning to the England game he laments the continual references to Bannockburn and asks: 'Is our sense of national identity so perverted that the single most important source of reference is the bludgeoning of human life on a muddy field outside Stirling? The sad reply is yes.'

Other more reflective pieces included the feature article in the *Scotsman* Weekend magazine on the day of the match, 15 June, by Tom Lappin, entitled ENGERLAAAND ENGERLAND. Lappin argues that the hatred of the English shows up the Scots' own prejudices and that the 'real English' have more in common with the Scots than they care to admit. He finds the 'real English' in Ilford, Gateshead and Bootle, they are inner-city and working-class: 'The Scouse lads on Hertford Road think England will beat Scotland, but apart from that, feel a closer affinity to Glasgow than London. "You know in Glasgow , they are pretty much the same as us, like," yells one. "There are only two things that matter, football and getting bevvied."'

In the *Glasgow Herald* (17 June 1996) J.P. Leach, monitoring the Scottish television coverage of the match, watched Scottish Television's live pictures of a 'riot' in Trafalgar square after the match. When the anchorman in the studio asked if the troublemakers were English, he was told 'Well Jim, they're Scottish, they're English, but worse than that they're mental'. Leach noted: 'It may have been intended to be pithy, but instead came over as the next recruiting slogan for British casuals. Despite the press hysteria, it's notable that the "riots" were rather unremarkable, lacking the mayhem and injury to the English that was suggested.'

It's all over

England beat Scotland 2–0, and the Scots exited the tournament in their traditional manner of heroic failure. The Scottish media coverage took pride in the overall good behaviour of the fans and lamented a cultural sense of *déjà vu*. While Scotland's footballing fate is viewed as important, previous defeats have taught the Scots to enjoy the party, and the low expectations of the team before the tournament added to this.

Throughout there was an overwhelming positive media focus on the fans; the anti-English rhetoric was broadly lighthearted, although a nasty exchange between Scotland's largest selling tabloid the *Daily Record* and its rival the Scottish *Sun*, with claims by the former that the latter was really an English newspaper, simply served to highlight how important certain signifiers of Scottishness are for newspapers as they attempt to sell themselves into a specific Scottish marketplace.

For the English media, of course, Scotland and the Scots were not the real enemy (see Blain and O'Donnell, 1998; Blain and Boyle, 1998). The extensive space and energy devoted to the English by the Scottish media would be reserved for the Germans and Spanish south of the border. Small countries are always concerned with putting one over a larger, more powerful neighbour, a feeling which is usually not reciprocated. However, the extent to which this will remain the case, given the pace of political and constitutional change in the UK, is much less clear.

As England, and the English media, finally begin to take on board some of the implication for them of a Scottish Parliament, Scotland is moving quickly up the media coverage treatment league table normally reserved for the Germans and the French and other European partners.

Richard Weight (1999) has argued that the proliferation of St George's Cross flags among English supporters at Euro 96 and at France 98, coupled with the equally marked decline in fans carrying the Union flag, is another significant indicator of a shifting awareness among the English about changes in their cultural identity and political position within Britain (the English having assumed that British meant English!). One can expect the strains of anti-Englishness, which run through sections of the sports reporting in the Scottish media, beginning to be reflected back by colleagues south of the border. That mediated sport should become another arena in which a growing English resentment of Scottish political influence should be displayed would be regrettable, but, given what we have argued above, not surprising.

France 98: a nation once again?

Could something as ephemeral as football change the affairs of a nation?

Nick Fraser, Cup of Joy, The Guardian, 15 July 1998

FROM WORLD CUP HIGH TO DEPTHS OF DESPAIR

Dominic O'Reilly on the Tour de France, *The European*, 3–9 August 1998

For much of the summer of 1998 the sporting eyes of the world focused on France. When we say eyes, we of course mean the media who relayed, transformed and interpreted events at the World Cup finals for their own indigenous audiences. For, while the football World Cup and the Olympics are truly global spectacles, how they are framed and made sense of is often much more parochial in nature (Blain *et al.*, 1993: O'Donnell, 1994).

The event which inspired the largest street party in Paris since the city's liberation over 50 years previously was the national team's success in winning the World Cup hosted in their country. It wasn't football which brought these people out into the streets, of course, it was national pride and a sense of collective identity which major sporting success can help to focus and lend expression to.

However, what was particularly commented on was the extent to which the multi-ethnic French team, with over half the squad drawn from players of African extraction, came to symbolize for some a new, more inclusive definition of Frenchness.

Multi-ethnic France

In a country where the National Front, which blames the immigrant population for most of the economic and social ills of France, gets 15 per cent of the vote, the universal support for a team underpinned by players of Arabic origin was symbolic. It didn't go unnoticed by commentators in Britain. Darcus Howe compared the inclusive approach of French football with the insular world of English cricket where he suggested Asian cricketers are not encouraged to develop after the age of 18 by the county sides (*New Statesman*, 17 July 1998).

Hugh O'Donnell (1999, p. 6) monitored the French media coverage of the event and suggests it was only as French success in the tournament began to look more likely that 'more high-level interventions attempted to appropriate . . . how France saw itself as a society more in political and economic terms'. He notes how newspapers such as *L'Équipe* drew on the symbolic composition of the national team to reflect on how this reminded the country of the positive things it could achieve.

Ironically the fragile – and at times transitory – nature of sporting imagery was further demonstrated a mere three weeks later with the almost total collapse of the Tour de France due to allegations of cheating and systematic drug abuse by teams involved in the cycle race. The Tour, which passes through both rural and urban France has come to symbolize a specifically French national and international event.

The famous yellow jersey of the race leader, while originally created as part of a rivalry between French newspapers, has come to be viewed as part of the cultural landscape of French identity. The sullying of the race by drugs and corruption has come to symbolize the dangers of investing too much national pride in an event underpinned by commercial rivalries and governed by an association unwilling to grasp the realities associated with modern high-performance sport.

If the success of the multi-ethnic French football team put the issue of citizenship on the agenda, for however short a time, and the scandal of drug-taking on the Tour de France shattered the carefully nurtured television image of that sporting event, in England during that summer there were more traditional concerns.

Kevin Mitchell, writing in *The Observer* (7 June) about the possible meeting with Germany in the World Cup noted:

> Few opponents in this tournament will be more acutely aware of the historical and emotional baggage they bring with them every time they meet . . . in a context beyond sport, it is a mixture of respect, cultural commonality and resentment that joins England and Germany.

As it transpired it would be that other ideological enemy – Argentina – who would eliminate England from the tournament. Throughout the coverage of the World Cup, England's team was continually reminded that it carried the expectations of the nation on its shoulders.

Due to the timing of the tournament, it occurs when there appears to be little else on television and political news is scarce, and there is a more cynical commercial realization that hyping aspects of what Billig (1995) calls 'banal nationalism', which invariably surround an international sporting contest in which England, and indeed Scotland, are involved, helps to boost television audiences and newspaper circulation.

The England v Argentina match attracted 23.78 million television viewers, the largest sporting audience of 1998, and one of the largest television audiences of the year.

All of which prompted a *Guardian* (2 July 1998) editorial to ask:

> Are the English so insecure these days that they need to read great tropes of national identity and fortune into the accidents of a single sporting contest?

While the answer may in fact be yes, that remains a debate for another day. We agree with the underlying assumption that ultimately symbolic sporting moments may not necessarily change the social and political world into which sport is interlocked. Sections of the French press expressed the same opinion even in the afterglow of France 98. *France-Soir* of 11 July 1998 argued:

> People are describing this remarkable tricolour team as a remarkable example of integration through sport. This mosaic of twenty-two black-white-*beur*. . . . Agreed, but for every Zidane or Thurman how many immigrant kids are there who will never get out of the ghetto? A lot more is needed, dear rulers who are covering themselves in praise, to solve the problems of the suburbs.

However, it can also be argued that to deny the *possibility* that the achievements of Zinedine Zidane and his colleagues in France 98 may, in some contexts, both shape and reflect broader shifts in the related social, political and economic arenas is also wrong and is to underestimate the power of the symbolic in a material world.

At the very least, in specific contexts they may contribute to creating, what we have called in an earlier chapter a climate of opinion, within which more deeply rooted structural changes can more readily occur.

Globalization and the local

Finally in this chapter, it is worth briefly making a number of points regarding the relationship between the forces of globalization and how they are impacting on sport and identity. The extent to which sport is being increasingly reshaped by forces of globalization, by which time–space relationships are being altered with political and cultural implications, has been addressed directly elsewhere (Jarvie and Maguire, 1994, pp. 230–62). As we have argued, while football World Cups and Olympic Games appear to offer examples of global cultural events, the impact these may have on national and cultural identities is complex (Blain *et al.*, 1993).

Ultimately any impact on the process of identity-formation of such events is determined by the specific historical, economic and political circumstances within which they are made sense of. As Houlihan (1997, p. 135) notes:

> the picture painted of sport and its relationship with global culture and with ethnic and state notions of identity creates an impression of a highly malleable source of cultural symbolism.

He argues that the impact of a sport, or an event may be intense and powerful, but have a relatively short shelf life.

Caught in the middle . . .

While much has been made of the process of globalization standardizing cultural habits and eroding others, this presents a partial picture. In a small country such as Scotland what you see are external European and global pressures impacting on both the football and media industries in that country, but this has not necessarily led to some sort of cultural erosion or standardization in Scottish sport (Boyle and Haynes, 1996). What has happened has been a resurgence of interest in what might be called the local or regional; however, this is often taking place within boundaries which are determined by global media interests.

Arundel and Roche (1998) in their detailed examination of British (actually English) rugby league convincingly argue that the interplay between global media and the sport is changing the localized traditions of the game. What is being suggested is not on one hand the overly optimistic resurgence of local traditions and difference, but neither is it 'some kind [of] simplistic cultural homogenisation (p. 84)' driven by global media forces.

In Scotland, this process or interplay between the global and more rooted forms of sporting culture is being driven in part by a realization of the economic benefits that media organizations can accrue from focusing on issues specific to Scotland which are not covered in other media. Both BBC Scotland and its main commercial rival in the Scottish market, Scottish Television, have been keen to promote themselves as being distinctly Scottish in their output, with sport, and football in particular, a crucial part of their portfolio.

Some of the writing about the media/sport/identity nexus appears at times to have fallen into this over-deterministic approach. Despite drawing on the flexible Gramscian approach to the study of sport in society, Hargreaves (1986) places great emphasis on the media's ability to construct the 'imaginary' nation through television coverage of sport. He notes how mediated international sporting events:

> constitute conventional reference points signifying membership of a unique community, sharing a common, valued and specific way of life, which supersedes or takes precedence over all other loyalties and identities. (Hargreaves, 1986, p. 154)

Hargreaves is correct to highlight the key role that sport plays in modern society as a form of symbolic ritual. There is little doubt that international sport, with its attendant media coverage, can become ideologically loaded with political and cultural significance like few other areas of popular culture.

However, it is important to appreciate that, even at global international events such as the Olympic Games or football's World Cup, it is how these events are made sense of at the local level that is important (in this instance the local may mean an entire country). It may be useful to treat with caution some of the claims being made about the role of the media in eroding distinctive cultural characteristics at some transnational level.

As Blain *et al.* comment:

> in fact sports journalism, albeit very unevenly, is as likely to produce a turning inward towards national concerns, and a buttressing of a sense of difference, as it is to operate ideologically on behalf of a harmonious world, even, as we have seen, at that mythic habitat of the familial, the Olympics. (Blain *et al.*, 1993, p. 196)

In addition, as Schlesinger points out when discussing national culture:

> It is more accurate (but less provocative) to suggest that it is a site of contestation and inherently an object of transformative practices. In any case, to assert that national cultures might, indeed, do, exist does not by any means exclude the reality of there being a transnational or global culture as well . . . To insist upon 'either . . . or' makes for good polemics or political sloganeering, but poor analysis. (Schlesinger, 1991, p. 305)

The Scottish media's interest in, say for example, the Celtic/Rangers rivalry, is as pronounced as ever, emphasizing that, while media and sporting organizations are subject to global economic pressures, this is in some instances accompanied by a resurgence in the local. This is particularly true where specific market places and political and cultural spaces coincide to some extent.

It is also worth noting that, in an age of international sport and transnational media, a traditional fixture such as the Glasgow derby between Celtic and Rangers can attract, in 1998, a capacity crowd of 60,000 to watch the game, with a further 30,000 willing to pay to sit in a stadium to watch live television pictures!

Conclusion

Debates around the global and the local cannot simply be framed in the context of individuals or groups being located in either one space or the other. As Schlesinger notes when he argues for an actionist perspective on identity formation:

> Such a perspective requires us to see identity not as a prior condition of collective action but rather as a continually constituted and reconstructed category. (Schlesinger, 1991, p. 173)

It becomes necessary in this perspective to be aware of the position that the media occupy in such a process, and to be alert that, at particular times, in specific circumstances their importance will vary considerably.

There is also the extent to which that, given the pace of political change in Scotland and in the UK as a whole over the last few years, sporting and broadcasting institutions at times appear to lag behind. A month before the elections in May 1999 to the first Scottish parliament for almost three hundred years, the BBC launched a briefing document *The Changing UK,* aimed at helping south-east English members of that organization to deal with covering political events in Scotland.

Interestingly, one of the areas highlighted was sports coverage, which was deemed 'particularly sensitive'. Readers were warned not to assume England meant Britain and that the national team in Scotland was not the same as in England. In addition to these revelations, it also noted that hooligans following the England football team were to be described as English not British!

Against this changing political backdrop and the growing competition for audiences in an increasingly competitive sports–media marketplace the hyping of national rivalries as one way of appealing to and attracting an audience, is, we would suggest, as likely to increase as disappear. As the globalization of the media industries (in all its complexities and contradictions) continues apace, sport will continue to be an important cultural, political and commercial marker of boundaries, identities and markets.

CHAPTER 9

Sportspages

Journalism and Literature

Nowadays the soccer writer sits at home watching *Match of the Day* with a glass of hemlock in his hand knowing that if he has got it wrong then ten million people will know it too.

Willis Hall and Michael Parkinson (eds.) (1973) Introduction, *Football Report*: An Anthology of Soccer

The language of sport is the language of war, love, politics, religion, business and of life itself . . . Its goals are recognised universally. Sport is about commitment and compassion, pressure and participation, highs and lows and the everyday.

Desmond Lynam and David Teesdale (1994) *The Sporting Word*, p. 9

After more than thirty years of writing on sport it is still possible to be assailed by doubts about whether it really is a proper job for a grown person. But I console myself with the thought that it is easier to find a kind of truth in sport than it is, for example, in the activities covered by political or economic journalists. Sports truth may be simplistic but it's not negligible.

Hugh McIlvanney (1991) 'Sportswriter', *Arena*, BBC TV

Introduction

Despite living in a highly visual media culture, the print media remain an important source of information, gossip and insight for the sports fan. Reading about sport remains a pleasure for millions of newspaper readers and during the 1990s, as media sport has expanded, so to has the interest in sport among newspaper editors keen to find a new audience. In the UK this has been accompanied by a boom in sports publishing as sports writing in this country has come of age.

The first part of this chapter examines the area of sports print journalism, outlining the economic and cultural factors which have shaped its distinctive development within journalism in general. The second focuses on the way sport has been treated by writers and journalists operating outside the confines of the newspaper marketplace. It traces the differing traditions within US and British writing on sport and suggests reasons why there has been such a publishing explosion in the arena of sports writing in the UK during the 1990s.

Sports journalism

As we have already observed in Chapter 2, the introduction of televised sport had a profound effect on the role of sports reporters as they found themselves passing on second-hand news. The sporting press had been central to the rise of modern commercialized sport and sports journalism had done much to promote and service the various organized sports that established themselves in the nineteenth century.

Professional ideologies

Sport gave newspapers a constant source of news and gossip as well as a new corps of journalists, who specialized solely in the field of sport. Historically, the sports scribe often had to work in extreme conditions, from cramped press boxes to suffering the vagaries of the British weather. Moreover, in the newspaper hierarchy, sports reporters battled against a stereotypical image of the failed journalist, their status in the newsroom often suffering from the perception that sport was a trivial matter in the wider scheme of news values.

Often underpinning these assumptions were issues related to social class. Journalists covering working-class sports such as football, were often viewed differently from those associated with more middle–upper class sports such as cricket. In Britain a particularly literary approach to cricket or rugby writing was deemed acceptable, while no such pretensions would be allowed to inform coverage of mass spectator sports such as football.

The flip side of this slight to the sports journalist's trade was the increasing allocation of resources for foreign travel to cover the growth of international sport. More often than not, the sports correspondent would travel incognito with British teams on foreign jaunts around the world.

Before the introduction of scheduled long-haul flights this invariably meant spending weeks away on board a ship filing reports back via telegraph or, in the case of an Ashes cricket series from Australia, via a

courier service to North America and then on to Britain via transatlantic
cable. With the global scale of contemporary sports events the demand
on resources has continued to increase. As Jeremy Tunstall (1996,
p. 211) has observed in his study of the British press in the 1990s:

> Sport, in the tabloid papers, tends to be the most expensive department.
> A typical daily sports desk in the early 1990s had an annual budget of
> £4 million and a staff of some sixty journalists. Foreign travel – with
> British teams playing abroad – is a major cost.

The establishment of sports desks in local and national daily newspapers was premised on the need to offset the costs of sports reporting
through the application of a 'beat' system. 'The beat' is a method of providing a predictable supply of information from reporters in the field.

Different sports have developed their own formal practices, assign-
ing reporters to particular organizations or events. It is rare, therefore,
for sports journalists to cover more than two or three sports, and, in
many instances, journalists will report on the same sport throughout
their careers, never seeking or being required to broaden their horizons
in other sporting fields. This places severe restrictions on material and
human resources. Furthermore, it dictates the breadth of coverage any
newspaper can give to the varied environment of sport.

In the British daily and Sunday press professional sport has dominance over amateur sport, team sports get more coverage than individual sports, men's sport receives more attention than women's sport,
heavily commercialized sport will gain a privileged status over large
participation sports, urban sports are covered to the virtual exclusion
of countryside or 'outdoor' sports, and new or imported sports are subordinate to historically traditional sports.

Some of these distinctions and formalized conventions of the sports
page operate within sports as well as across them. For example, Championship athletics will gain more coverage than para-Olympic athletics
in spite of the widely acknowledged achievements of disabled athletes
within the sport itself.

Similarly, as noted above and in Chapter 7, there is a marked gender
bias in favour of men's professional sports that impacts on the com-
parative status of women in the same field (particularly noticeable in
the virtual myopic coverage of women's team sports). As Cramer (1994,
p. 169) has observed in the North American context:

> Because women's sports on the whole receive the least amount of
> coverage, being deemed not very newsworthy, having a women's sports
> beat carries almost no weight for professional advancement.

In spite of the prejudicial parameters set by the sports press, there never appears to be a shortage in sports news itself. The routines of the sports reporter are such that there is always a daily supply of items, regardless of the extent to which sport is in the wider public eye.

The emphasis on which sports are reported, when and from where, clearly depends on seasonal changes, although the ubiquitous nature of football on the back pages of newspapers fifty-two weeks of the year belies the traditional division between winter and summer sports. This process, accelerated by the increasing role that television plays in sporting development, is likely to increase as the global commercialization of sports such as football, tennis and golf continues.

Indeed, the intrusion of the football season into the months of June and July during World Cup or European Championship years has somewhat distorted the cycle of sports news in favour of football and to the detriment of cricket, tennis, golf and athletics. There is now no rest from the latest hearsay regarding transfer deals and the latest exploits of stars, which places more strain on the ability of sports journalists to sustain the newsworthiness and exclusivity of their columns.

Old sources, new sources

The drive for exclusivity and a 'good nose' for a story are the pressing demands of contemporary sports journalism. Here the 'beat' system comes into its own and each reporter can expect to have developed their own network of contacts within any given sport. In horse-racing a major part of a journalist's work is geared towards being a tipster. This may require contacts with owners, trainers, stable hands and jockeys so that a journalist can gain an insight into how a particular horse is performing. In order to get a feel for individual races it could also help a journalist to get information on the ground or the 'running' from insiders at the course as well as up-to-date information on the latest odds from the bookmakers.

The routine sources of the sports journalist provide the bread and butter of sports news and are not only fed from a network of contacts that a journalist attempts to develop over his or her career, but more and more through the public relations arms of commercial sports organizations.

In the 1990s, contemporary governing bodies of sport and both individual clubs and athletes manage their news output in a much more structured way than previous generations. In order to keep their sport in the media spotlight sports organizations have become more competent at producing press releases and staging press conferences.

A prime example has been the employment by the English Football Association of an ex-sports journalist David Davies, who has transformed the relationship between the governing body and the media. A catalogue of economic, political and personal transformations and scandals during the mid-to-late 1990s has propelled the FA into the media spotlight for issues not always directly concerned with the playing of the game.

Like a sporting spin doctor, Davies has frequently taken the helm of managing the FA through torrid times. In January 1999 Davies was elevated to the role as deputy Chief Executive of the FA after irregularities over the transfer of FA funds to the Welsh FA led to the resignation of then Chief Executive Graham Kelly and Chairman of the FA Keith Wiseman.

However, the ability to control the sometimes cosy symbiotic relationship between a sport and the media can be eclipsed by unexpected events. On the day of the launch of the new governing body of track and field athletics, UK Athletics (which had taken over from the troubled British Athletic Federation), Chief Executive David Moorcroft (himself a former athlete and BBC athletics summarizer) found his hi-tech press conference undermined by news that a British Athlete, Doug Walker, had failed a doping test and was under investigation for the alleged taking of performance-enhancing drugs.

In such cases, sports organizations find themselves fighting fires as heightened media interest distracts the public's attention from any positive image a sport is attempting to portray. This is an aspect of sports 'promotional culture' which is likely to increase in both size and importance as the commercial interface between sport, sponsors and the media, outlined in Chapter 3, continues apace.

Sporting ethics

The American sports journalist Leonard Koppett (1994) has argued that the relationship between the sports organizations or individuals and the journalist deeply affects what news reaches the public. In developing and cosseting news sources, Koppett (1994, p. 150) suggests there are four 'don'ts' which govern a sports journalist's work:

1 Don't take cheap shots.
2 Don't form close friendships.
3 Don't be afraid of arousing anger, but don't pick on people just to show you're not afraid.
4 Don't deny an error, or compound it by looking for justification.

These principles, that set the parameters for 'confidentiality and relevance' of the devoted journalist, are clearly idealized and it is not difficult to recall instances where these codes have been broken or totally ignored by journalists in search of an exclusive story. A good example is the torment successive England football managers have gone through at the hands of certain sports journalists when confidence and privacy issues are betrayed.

Issues pertaining to the relationship between sport and media have pushed the ethical questions of journalistic principles to the fore during the 1990s. Media sport scholars increasingly focus on media ethics in order to understand the corporate relations between the two industries. For example, MacNeill's (1998) research of high-performance athletes in Canada reveals that many athletes are unsure of their rights when dealing with the media, and that governing bodies, event organizers and coaches are often the gatekeepers of information from athlete to journalists and vice versa.

This breakdown in communication between the work of both athletes and journalists has proved a barrier to mutually beneficial relationships between sport and the media which has led to a state where ethical codes of journalism are viewed as 'institutionalised censorship rather than guidelines based on collective wisdom of their field regarding craft style, taste and responsible reporting' (MacNeill, 1998, p. 114). We will now explore what the specific pressures of sports journalism are, and how the structure of the sports page frequently dictates the codes and practices of the sports writer's job.

Constructing the sports page

As Hugh McIlvanney's reflection at the start of this chapter on the fortune of the sports journalist suggests, sports news is perceived as a trivial matter. News organizations, journalists and readers place sport in the wider news media environment and there is undoubtedly a hierarchy of importance given over to different fields of print journalism. Sport occupies a contradictory position of being placed low down the professional ranks of journalism – at times called the Toy department – but enjoying a high status in the daily circulation of newspapers.

On taking over a newspaper, media mogul Rupert Murdoch will focus on the organization of the sports department and the level of sports coverage carried. He believes that getting this section of the newspaper quickly in order and offering extensive coverage of sport are crucial in both delivering readers to advertisers and increasing circulation.

This philosophy has also held true in the growth of his television interests both in the US and the UK, which have been primarily driven by their sports programming.

As we note later in the chapter, one of the key developments in the UK newspaper marketplace during the 1990s has been the expansion of sports coverage within both tabloid and specifically broadsheet newspapers (with sport quite often appearing in its own dedicated supplement). Indeed, a paper's sports coverage may be used in its advertising drive to secure new readers (particularly on Saturday, Sunday and Monday). The recently launched Scottish-based quality broadsheet the *Sunday Herald* quickly extended its sports coverage in response to reader demand. As the UK newspaper trade magazine *Press Gazette* has noted:

> Forget news, forget celebrity gossip, forget hard-hitting investigative reporting. If you want to sell more copies of your newspaper, what you want is more of the f word: football. (*Press Gazette*, 21 August 1998)

So, although sport is 'cast off' to the realms of the back page, away from the world of politics, it does nonetheless drive the sale and readership of many local and national newspapers in the UK.

Interestingly Britain, unlike other European countries, has had until recently no dedicated sports paper. In part due to the expansion in coverage across both the popular and broadsheet press and in the sports magazine section, there does not appear to be a sizeable gap in the market. *Sport First*, launched in 1998, had hoped to establish itself as a sports daily; however, one year on it is a Sunday newspaper with a circulation of around 84,000 (*Press Gazette*, 12 March 1999). While it hopes to expand to become a weekend paper, it faces stiff competition from established newspapers, which appear to be continually expanding their sporting coverage.

Institutional and market pressures

There is, of course, something quite unique about the structure of the newspaper market in the UK. The popular tabloids rely heavily on their populist sports coverage to maintain their circulation figures, while the broadsheet section of the market aims at a higher social class readership which particularly appeals to advertisers. As Rowe (1995, p. 159) notes

> Within the print media, a distinction is made between the 'tabloids' and the 'qualities', a split that is replicated in the typology of 'sports reporters' and 'sports writers'. The 'writer-driven' style of the quality

papers is routinely contrasted with the assumed opposite, the reader-driven tabloid paper seen as cynically exploitative of sport and its personnel according to the demands of market-based profit maximization.

This often has an impact in the type of language used in sports reporting.

Specific to British journalism, the issue of social class runs through the divisions in the newspaper market and the sports historically covered by differing newspapers. Although this is changing, vestiges of this system remain, as sports journalist Brian Glanville has pointed out:

> My thesis was that both the 'quality' and 'popular' writer were in some sense failures. The first because, although he could largely write as he pleased, about mass-interest sports, he reached only a fraction of the public. The second, because although he reached the public at large, he was rigidly confined to a highly stylised, ultimately patronising, form of journalism, which treated the readership with contempt. (Glanville, 1999, p. 257)

He notes that, unlike in the US, France or Italy, the British-based sportswriter is locked into a particular quality–popular dichotomy which still exists today.

What emerged in interviews with football journalists working in the broadsheet market in the UK was the main constraint they felt they worked under wasn't pressure from editors, but rather gaining access to players and managers. There are exceptions, of course, and it was alleged, during BSkyB's securing of the rights to English Premier League football in 1992, that the football correspondent of the Murdoch-owned *Sunday Times*, was opposed to the deal; however, he was discouraged from airing this position in the newspaper.

The distinguished football journalist Patrick Barclay, who has written for the broadsheets *The Independent*, *The Observer* and more recently the *Sunday Telegraph*, encapsulated the differing pressures between a football journalist working for a tabloid newspaper and one working on a broadsheet as being: 'If I see a boring match I can say it's boring, whereas a popular journalist would have to find a booking or something, and his intro would be Trouble Flared at Ewood Park last Night, when it didn't'.

This pressure to embellish or sensationalize has also increased as a proliferation of media outlets, particularly in the UK, covers sport, and there is more media sport around to comment on. As in other areas, such as rolling television news, it remains highly debatable whether more outlets actually means better information for the viewer.

Sporting news and vested interests

This also raises the issue of sports news values. As sports rights and patterns of viewer access to sports changes (see Chapter 11) there is also a re-orientation in the level of sports news self-promotion among channels, or differing media outlets within an organization. This means that what sports the media deem to be worthy of covering in their sports news or mainstream news output increasingly reflect events to which they have access, rather than those being covered by another channel. For example, in 1999 Channel 5 in the UK, with exclusive coverage of the football European Cup Winners Cup competition, will deem this competition newsworthy, while BBC television news may not.

In another context, the range of both tabloid and broadsheet newspapers owned by Rupert Murdoch in the UK will extensively promote and cover sporting events exclusive to BSkyB, of which he is the major shareholder. This is not to suggest that there are not sports stories, such as the sacking of the national football coach or manager, which all news outlets will strive to cover or take an angle on, rather that what gets covered and the priority it is given increasingly reflects both the access that organization has to an event, and also the degree to which the news coverage will act as promotion for an event to which that organization has exclusive rights.

Given this explosion in the sporting media profile which television coverage in particular has facilitated, new opportunities also exist to extend the range of print sports journalism. The increasing influx of money into sport, from television, has also offered print journalists the opportunity to expose corruption in sport, such as the apparent increase in drugs/doping scandals.

The recent exposure during 1999 of alleged corruption involving the International Olympic Committee (IOC) in the awarding of the Olympics to Salt Lake City and other city venues was print media lead, with television following on behind. This has allowed the tabloid press to position itself as the defender of the ordinary fan and to occupy the moral high ground, as they expose 'the villains' who are corrupting sport. However, this 'exposure' of corruption appears to be pursued more vigorously by newspapers when they have no direct links to the organizations which own the sports rights to the particular sporting event in question.

The notion that the 'sports chatter' of the sports page is ideologically adrift from the 'realities' of the world is a familiar retort for those that feel sport is a distraction from the democratic process of citizenship

(Eco, 1986). However, as corporate interest in sport, driven by television and sponsorship money, grows apace, the political economy of sport increasingly intrudes on the daily reportage of sport. Political battles over the governance and finance of sport are fought out amid the sports pages, as mergers and acquisitions become embedded in the language of sports reporting.

Models of sports news

However, the manner in which issues of commerce and political affairs are dealt with by the sporting press is distorted by the various frames in which sports journalists operate. The clearest analysis of these different frames is given by Rowe's (1992) four typologies of sports journalism. Just as the wider field of journalism has its various modes and frames, sports journalism operates by producing 'hard news', 'soft news', 'ortho-dox rhetoric' and 'reflexive analysis'. Hard news may be characterized as the flip-side to the current affairs dealt with at the front of the paper.

The sports headline mirrors the lead story of the front page, to cre-ate virtually a second headline that may attract the reader to buy the paper. Here, sports photo-journalism also plays a distinctive role in the character and layout of the back page, not only as a pictorial representa-tion of an event, but as part of the narrative that helps the abbreviated description of the action.

Hard news, then, records events, including match analysis, score-lines and results in an apparently objective description of what has occurred. As Rowe argues, this invokes an air of authority to the serious business of sports reporting and will be constructed in the third person, with rare exception. However, in the British press the pretence to object-ivity is masked by the subjective interpretation of events and, as Blain and O'Donnell (1998, p. 45) in their analysis of English tabloid coverage of Euro '96 reveal, interpretation of events is frequently framed by lan-guage that is 'restricted, adolescently masculine, and idiomatic, often deploying spoken modes and mixing them with what have now become codified tabloid habits'. This markedly contrasts with the specialized sporting press of continental Europe, where the analysis offered is more focused and technically sophisticated (Blain and O'Donnell, 1998, p. 46).

Reports on the latest commercial deals in sport will play a marginal role in the hard news of tabloid and broadsheet coverage, but will enter the more 'soft news' focus of the sports page. *Soft news* trades in the star gossip and biographical focus of key individuals within sport, whether they be athletes, managers, coaches, directors or administrators. Work-ing within the realms of 'infotainment' soft news produces the latest 'scoops' or exclusives and, as mentioned above, provides the mainstay of the 'beat' reporters' daily routine. The emphasis here is on hero worship and, as we discussed in Chapter 5, it is the main vehicle for the construction and reaffirmation of celebrity status.

Star athletes may be placed in wider cultural terms, as reflecting the age in which they perform, but rarely are they situated in the political matrix of sport and, if at all, only in the context of representing the nation and thus causing it to resonate with some wider 'feel good factor' (as in the pride engendered in the triumphs of Tim Henman or Greg Rusedksi in tennis). Star profiles may also be an occasion where cross-promotion of sponsors and advertisers can piggy-back on the focus on their star man or woman.

This may be a competition to win sports equipment used by the celebrity athlete or, as is more likely the case, a chance to reflect on the riches sport can bring to its élite, including a catalogue of endorsements and prize money from lucrative sponsored events.

Sport does not always get an easy ride. A high degree of critical comment is chewed over on a daily basis by a range of lead writers and sports columnists. A third category Rowe alludes to is that of *'orthodox rhetoric'*, where the authorial subjectivity of the sports journalist comes to the fore. The trade of the sports columnist is to develop a distinctive voice that adopts a form of advocacy. This mode of writing deploys a different form of authority to that of 'hard news' that stems from the experience or celebrity status of the columnist.

It is not unusual for ex-professional sports stars to continue their sporting careers by becoming the adopted pundit of any given paper. With their inside-track to the business of sport they can often reveal the latest comings and goings in their specialized field or pass comment on a particular issue without fear of accusation that they lack knowledge or experience.

Orthodox rhetoric may also come from the seasoned sports journalist to pass judgement on the health of sport, casting a critical eye over the latest scandals and transformations. This form of reporting does, at least, admit the politics of sport. Revelations over irregular payments or administrative procedures in sport, such as the bribery scandal involving members of the IOC and bidding Olympic cities, tangibly reveals moments where the political economy of sport is of direct consequence to a sports readership, and judgement has to be passed.

Yet, rarely are such moments of criticism acutely problematized in any sociological way. Issues often appear clear-cut and polemical. The moral order of sport, historically embedded in the philosophy that sport is a socio–cultural good, is often imposed or reasserts itself to protect sport from wider political pressure for change.

The final mode of sports writing, involving what Rowe terms *'reflexive analysis'*, addresses the problematics of sport head on, eschewing any simplified celebration of sport. The reflexive analysis of sport critically questions the phenomenology of sporting practices and discourse reconciling the celebration of sport with the particularized subjective position of the writer.

As we discuss below in our review of the new trench of sports writing and writers, the reflexive writer questions his or her relationship with sport, psychologically, morally and economically to reveal the way in which sport operates in our culture and society. It is quite rare for this form of writing to appear on the sports pages and it is more likely found within different sections of a newspaper, either in a review section or magazine. Reflexive analysis is also inherent in many sports-related fanzines (Haynes, 1995), an alternative sporting press where the political struggle over the meaning of sport is most acutely realized (see following chapter).

Interestingly, broadcast investigative sports journalism has been re-invigorated not by television in the UK, but by BBC radio. This aspect of sports journalism has been poorly served historically by television journalism as sporting historian Tony Mason once remarked:

> Anything on which the BBC is prepared to spend almost half of its summer schedules' budget deserves the sort of penetrating analysis never found on *Sportsnight*. (*The Listener*, 5 June 1986)

Aside from the fact that it is doubtful whether the BBC would spend that proportion of its budget on sport today, it is worth noting this new strand of radio investigative sports journalism as the BBC re-positions itself in the new sports marketplace (see Chapter 11).

The new sports writing

> There was a time when the football shelf in your local bookstore was one of the dustier corners of the literary world . . . Nick Hornby changed all that.
>
> **Scotland on Sunday (22 March 1998)**

> Ten years ago the suggestion that a market might exist for a daily newspaper aimed at the generality of sports fans would have been scoffed at. Today, it seems that the growth of sports journalism will never end.
>
> **Dave Hill, *The Observer* (25 January 1998)**

Born in the USA

Sports writing in the US has never suffered from the class-bound ethos which has influenced its position within the journalistic hierarchy in Britain. In America sports were seen as an important aspect in forging, defining and reflecting the wider values and ideals which helped define 'America' throughout the twentieth century. Sports were part of the fabric of American (usually masculine) experience and identity and as such worthy of scrutiny.

To this extent sports were seen as a natural terrain to be explored by American literature and to be written about with style and intelligence. Thus American writers viewed exploring sport as a way of understanding not only their own passions and interests, but of talking about what sport told us about the state of America and American culture and identity. This continues today, where writers such as Richard Ford, Philip Roth, John Updike will all integrate sport into their work, and more recently Don deLillo will open his novel *Underworld* at a baseball match, using it as a starting point from which to propel us through fifty years of American history.

As noted earlier, much of sports journalism argues that politics should be kept out of sport; the reality as David Rowe (1992) notes is that:

> Sports journalism is addressed to a popular cultural realm which, while saturated with politics and power, is commonly apprehended as transcending or bypassing the structured conflicts of everyday life. Most sports writing colludes in this misrecognition of sport's place in the reproduction of social inequality. (Rowe, 1992, p. 110)

While this has been recognized in a sports-mad US, where the very 'naturalness' of sport makes it such an ideologically and politically potent arena, it has not been widely acknowledged in Britain.

Sporting class

As we have argued throughout the book, sporting cultural forms in part reflect wider economic and cultural realities. With the exception of cricket with its middle-class and élite associations, sports writing historically in Britain has been confined largely to the back pages with many traditional working-class sports deemed subjects unworthy of serious attention. This situation began to change during the 1990s.

As noted above, sports journalism has always been viewed as a key component in the make-up of the popular press. However, one of the most striking features of sports journalism in the UK over the past decade

Sports Final! – The 1990s has seen a dramatic growth in the coverage of sport in the British press.

has been the growth of this sector of journalism at the broadsheet end of the market. All the major broadsheet newspapers, both dailies and Sundays, from the *Daily Telegraph*, through *The Times* to *The Guardian*, have all expanded their sports coverage significantly in the last few years, and in addition have focused much of their advertising drive around the launch of dedicated sports sections within their newspapers.

In part this expansion has been driven by wider shifts in media markets. The expansion of television sport through Murdoch's BSkyB network has been vigorously supported and hyped by his newspapers who occupy both ends of the marketplace. In addition, this more competitive television marketplace means that all sports attempt to sell and market themselves more aggressively and this is partly done through newspaper coverage.

Peter Preston, former editor of *The Guardian*, also suggests that broader global shifts helped to accelerate this expansion of sports writing within the UK newspaper market. He argues that the collapse of the Berlin Wall at the end of the 1980s resulted in 'a perceptible shift of quality newspaper reader interest – away from politics and heavy diplomacy and towards lifestyle, leisure, and the panoply of sport . . . There was a natural stirring in the marketplace and the talent to fill it' (*The Guardian*, 21 June 1996).

As argued above, sport remains a vital part of a newspaper's armoury, as it seeks to deliver a young male audience with a disposable income to advertisers. In a market where newspapers fight over a declining audience, the broadsheets have realized the importance that sports coverage can play in attracting a sports-fan readership.

Unlike other European countries such as France and Italy, Britain seems to have resolutely refused to support a daily all-sports newspaper. Attempts in 1998 to launch dedicated sports dailies have had mixed fortunes. Part of the problem lies in the extensive coverage devoted to sport in the broadsheets, plus the plethora of sports magazines which have mushroomed in the 1990s to complement increased television exposure of sport and exploit developments in desk-top publishing and industry practice.

New and older titles

During the 1990s there was an explosion of sports titles in the magazine sector which developed alongside a more general growth in titles aimed specifically at a male readership. Thus glossy monthly magazines such as *Loaded* inspired a generation of sporting titles such as *Total Sport, FourFourTwo* and *Goal.* However, it was in the upmarket men's magazine sector of the early 1990s, in publications such as *Esquire* and *GQ*, that the model of sportswriting, for many years established in America, began to appear aimed at a UK audience.

Of course, there have been journalists in Britain writing about sport in an intelligent manner (many influenced by the great US sports journalists such as Budd Schulberg and Damon Runyon), and there are non-football books which appeared during the 1980s which drew heavily on the US model of sportwriting epitomized by Norman Mailer's poetic commentary on the boxing industry. Perhaps the most interesting was by Gordon Burn. His book *Pocket Money: Bad-Boys, Business-Heads and Boom-Time Snooker,* was published in 1986 at the height of the popularity of the sport in Britain.

Burn took the reader on a behind the scenes tour of the global snooker circuit, dominated by television, sponsors and money. However, in keeping with the US tradition, this is a book which tells us as much about Britain during the mid-eighties as about the sport of snooker. Here is a sport dominated by working-class players being transformed by television and sponsorship and being driven by the entrepreneurial Thatcherite skills of Barry Hearn.

The book is as much about class and shifting class mobility as about sport. This type of revelatory, investigative behind the scenes look at aspects of the sport–media relationship, part of the staple diet of US writing, is one of the areas which other British writers have developed in recent years. Richard Williams' year spent on the Grand Prix circuit is recounted in *Racers* (1998) and Lawrence Donegan's *Four-iron in the Soul* (1998) involved the author caddying on the European golf tour. Both are excellent books which would have found difficulty getting published in Britain ten years ago. Yet, while we talk of sports publishing, fundamentally it has been football – which has been reshaped by the money and exposure invested in it by BSkyB – that has kick-started the boom in sports publishing over the last decade.

A whole new ball game?

[Football] a slum sport, watched by slum people.

Sunday Times, 18 June 1985

I think it's got a bit too trendy actually.

Mark E. Smith, football supporter and lead singer with *The Fall* speaking on *The Ball is Round*, a documentary which was part of an entire evening devoted to football-related material by BBC2, *Goal TV*, 30 May 1994

Over the last number of years the volume and quality of written material related to football has increased considerably. In the 1990s football has become popular again and in the process gained a 'respectable' middle-class audience. Writer and journalist Jim White outlines the key changes:

> From the mid-70s, through the 80s, there was nothing smart or amusing about football; the only literature was sociological . . . Then, after the nadir of Heysel and the awful tragedy of Hillsborough, things began to change. The hooligans largely gave up, seats replaced terraces, the football authorities realised that the future lay not in treating customers like cattle, but like consumers. And, slowly, the literature returned. It began with the fanzine movement, acidic, abrasive and funny home made publications written for the fan by the fan. (White, 1994, p. 43)

As a result of the increased middle-class interest (itself accelerated by the commercialization of the sport which is financially squeezing its traditional working-class supporters, base), the broadsheet press extended its coverage of football, while books and magazine articles began to appear related to the various aspects of the sport and its fan culture.

There also appeared to be a distancing of the fans (old and new) from the tabloid newspaper culture which had come to dominate writing about the sport, and from which supporters felt increasingly distant.

While there had been (and still is) an English class-bound tradition which saw writing about cricket elevated to a literary status, football's popular working-class support was ill-served by the tabloid press mercilessly lampooned by the growing fanzine movement as fans attempted to set their own agenda for discussing football in a new 'culture of defence' about the game (Haynes, 1995).

Nick Hornby's book, *Fever Pitch: a fan's life*, published in 1992 is a useful starting-point in any examination of what has become known as the 'new' football writing. In the book he articulates for many those emotional feelings associated with being a fan and following football. While its popularity can be explained by its universal theme (particularly for male readers) of fan/football obsession, it is also very much rooted in an English culture preoccupied with class.

Discussing novelist Martin Amis's review of *Granta* editor Bill Buford's book *Among the Thugs*, Hornby attempts to explain the new-found appeal of football to middle-class writers:

> Some [people] like it because they are sentimental socialists; some because they went to public school, and regret doing so; some because their occupation – writer or broadcaster or advertising executive – has removed them far away from where they feel they belong, or where they have come from, and football seems to them a quick and painless way of getting back there. It is these people who seem to have the most need to portray football grounds as a bolt-hole for a festering, vicious underclass . . . a wise man called Ed Horton wrote in the fanzine *When Saturday Comes* after reading Amis's review. 'Writers are welcome at football – the game does not have the literature it deserves. But snobs slumming it with "the lads" – there is nothing we need less'. (Hornby, 1992, pp. 96–7)

What Hornby and others are talking about is the middle-class appropriation of a traditional working-class area of popular culture.

While Hollywood in the 1940/50s used the sport of boxing as a short-hand way to introduce the viewer to 'a seedy criminal underworld', so some contemporary writers use football to demonstrate their knowledge of a male working-class environment, usually for the benefit of their middle-class readership. One of the main reasons why media coverage of football has expanded is because of the growth of this middle-class market.

The market for all things football-related has not only expanded, but also become more affluent, and thus deemed worthy of being served by the commercial media. Julian Germain's (1994) *In Soccer Wonderland*, is a good example of what could be called the coffee-table-style football book. A book which attempts to re-position football within the clearly defined middle-class realms of the art world.

Both the tabloid and broadsheet press offer coverage of the sport to different markets, a well-developed fanzine movement has fans talking to fans, and a publishing cottage industry has developed which serves the fans, old and new, drawn to a sport which is now deemed respectable by a previously disdainful middle class (although it should be noted that some middle-class people have always watched football, and that some of the middle class still view football and its supporters with suspicion).

England and all that . . .

Much of the writing on football offers an insight into aspects of national character and identity, not by divorcing football from its cultural and political context, but by making the connections between popular culture and politics (often in an amusing and entertaining manner). However, it could also be argued that perhaps some of the writing offers insights into the state of contemporary English culture unintended by the writers.

Among those in the former category are Dave Hill's (1989) *'Out of his Skin': The John Barnes Phenomenon*, whose exploration of football, racism and English society and his consistently challenging journalism for the broadsheets and various magazines mark him out among the most interesting of the new breed of writers. The fact that Hill isn't ghettoized into writing solely about sport, but regularly writes about politics and current social issues adds depth to his engagements with sport.

Novelist Pete Davies' ground-breaking book (1990) *All Played Out: the full story of Italia '90*, which centred on the Italia '90 World Cup and the English role in it, offered a portrait of: a nation in decline isolated on the periphery of Europe; its media and fans fixated with the Second World War; and the motivation behind the young males who follow the English national football team abroad (who in turn are a product of the political and economic changes that have occurred in English society during the 1980s). He notes:

> when the sociological wisdom is extended to the England following as a whole, excluding the racist/nationalist hardcore fanatics, the picture develops of a predominantly young, white, urban, male section of

The New Sports Writing – Following the success of Nick Hornby's *Fever Pitch* the boom in sports literature has opened up the market for new innovative writers.

> England's following whose home environment . . . is, culturally, economically, politically, morally, all played out.
>
> So that there's little civil restraint left.
>
> So they will descend, they will steal, they will be offensive and difficult. And is this football's problem? (Davies, 1990, p. 64)

Novelist Davies has developed his passion for writing about sport, by following up with books on women's football and cricket.

Journalist Simon Kuper's (1994) *Football Against the Enemy*, developed this broader concern when he examined the relationship between football and politics in twenty-two different countries. Among other things it offered a fascinating insight into the differences between Dutch and English national character (and particularly working-class culture), demonstrating how these differences informed the footballing cultures of both countries. He also examined how political relations between the Dutch and the Germans are mediated through international sport:

> It all began in Hamburg, on a summer night in 1988, when the Dutch beat the Germans 2–1. Back in Holland, the staid nation surprised itself: nine million Dutchmen, over 60 per cent of the population, came on to the streets to celebrate. Though a Tuesday night, it was the largest public gathering since the Liberation. 'It feels as though we have won the war at last', a former Resistance fighter said on TV. (Kuper, 1994, p. 4)

All these books offer a view of football and its attendant media culture which is inextricably linked to the social and political culture of modern society.

They look at the familiar afresh and make connections with wider influences in society: in short they are writers who appreciate the importance of sport beyond its immediate boundaries. Indeed, such has been the commercial success of these books that Kuper has edited a softback review of new sports writing called *Perfect Pitch* (1998), which is published twice a year on various themes related to football.

In addition, the re-issue of books such as Hunter Davies's *The Glory Game* (originally published in 1972), Arthur Hopcraft's *The Football Man* (originally published in 1968), and collections such as Stephen F. Kelly's (1993) *A Game of Two Halves* and in particular *McIlvanney on Football* (1995) serve to remind us that journalists such Hugh McIlvanney have been offering insightful and stylish quality writing about football (and other sports, boxing in particular) for longer than may often appear.

There is also little doubt that, within a UK context, bookstores such as SportsPages, originally based in London, have helped to promote, feed and foster the growing market for books about sport, often making material available which has been out of print for a number of years. In addition, publishers such as Mainstream, based in Edinburgh, have provided an outlet for a growing number of books centred around oral histories of football clubs in particular. Often these books are meticulously researched and sensitively written by life-long fans.

New writing, old concerns

There are broadly two strands in much of this new writing about sport. In part due to the success of Hornby, many of the books centre on the individual and his or her relationship with sport. They use sport as a vehicle through which other emotional areas of their lives are examined. The other, heavily influenced by the US model, is concerned with the broader sweep of the place of sport within the cultural and political life of a country.

Again they use sport as an entry point which allows them to examine sections of society, and often allows the voices of people to be heard in their actual context. Thus a book such as Geoffrey Beattie's *On the Ropes : boxing as a way of life* (1997), rooted in the boxing gyms and culture of the north of England town of Sheffield, tells us much about the pressures and experiences of young men growing up in that part of Britain during the 1990s.

At its best sports writing offers sport and fandom a context that goes beyond the sport itself and helps make sense of the emotional and rational attachments that are formed between fans and sport. McCarra's and Woods' (1988) *One Afternoon in Lisbon*, which chronicles the hopes, fears and emotions of the Celtic players who formed part of the first British team to win the European Cup in 1967, is one such example.

It is a book full of passion and insight, and aware of the broader position and importance that a club like Celtic occupies in the culture of the west of Scotland. To this end, Peter Preston (*The Guardian*, 21 June 1996) has argued that there is 'not really something called *sports* writing, only great writers describing sport in the same breath as they tackle life itself'.

Hornby (1992) is at his best talking about the complexities of class and gender identities in what all too often is unproblematically called a 'man's game'. When he talks about the Germans as 'Jerries' he is also articulating aspects of an English insecurity regarding the European 'other' which runs deep through both the cultural and political life of that country. In the same way a Scottish fixation with seeing the English beaten in sport can be read as indicative of a politically immature nation which views itself as being dominated politically by a larger neighbour.

To many people, sport and sports writing are ephemeral and insignificant in the social and cultural life of British society. Yet, when examined closer, in all its various forms and contexts, sports writing may offer an insight into the relations of gender, class, region and ethnicity which exist in modern Britain, and tell us more about politics and culture than we may care to admit.

Conclusion

There can be little doubt that the increasing synergy between sporting and media interests which has so marked the development of sport during the 1990s has impacted on sports journalism. At one level it has helped sustain and carve out new markets among both live and armchair sports fans, while also attracting new readers whose interest in sport has been in part sparked by the extensive media coverage. It has also seen the development of the reporting of the media–sport relationship moving outside the traditional back pages of the newspaper.

As mentioned at the beginning of the previous chapter, much of the most enlightening coverage surrounding the France 98 football World Cup was to be found in the sections of the press covering the financial and cultural dimensions of this media event. Anyone interested in tracking the business and commercial aspects of sport in the 1990s finds themselves needing regularly to trawl the media and business sections of the broadsheet press.

However, a note of caution is also worth sounding. As television's stranglehold on sport increases (see Chapter 11) it is still only some sports which generate most of the huge amount of inflated press interest. These sports, such as football and the footballers themselves, are often subject to the same scrutiny given to others in related entertainment industries, such as television.

Ironically, at a deeper structural level, this means that, while we may know more about the private sexual peccadilloes of individual players, the closer media–sports business links often mean that the exposing or investigating of this aspect of the sports business is in fact the terrain of a relatively small section of the media. It is also less likely to be found in an organization with a vested interest in the sport, or among journalists who are not prepared to risk the contacts and relationships they have built up and which are crucial in allowing them to do their jobs. Increasingly it may be that these sports journalists will not be drawn from the domain of sports, but have a background in business and financial journalism.

A worrying trend, and one which raises the issue of the increasing usage of promotional or public-relations techniques by sporting bodies, is the attempt to increase direct sponsorship of events and competitions by sections of the media. This clearly has the potential to lead to a conflict of interests. Recently (1998/99) the Scottish Premier League (SPL) entered a deal with the *Scottish Daily Express* in which they came on board as sponsors and in return were given access to a certain number of exclusive stories from both the organization and the individual football clubs within the league.

One might argue that for the supporter these close ties will make it less likely that any criticism of that sporting body will come from this particular section of the press. It is at this changing relationship between the fan and sport in an increasingly media-saturated environment that we look next.

CHAPTER 10

Consuming Sport

Fans, Fandom and the Audience

> The game is a marketing tool; its players are protagonists in a tabloid soap opera. In saving itself from an abyss of brutish squalor, football has become an ersatz business, a corporate bunfight with fans as involuntary extras. The only difference between football and a film set is that on a film set the extras get paid.
>
> Pete Davies, author of *All Played Out*, writing in *Broadcast*, 19 March 1999

Introduction

Being a sports fan in the 1990s has become an expensive passion. Much of our attention in this book has focused on the history, political economy and textual analysis of media sport. However, central to both the media and sporting industries is, of course, the fan and/or reader/viewer, the people who consume sport, either in its relatively raw form, or in its increasingly mediated form. Part of what we want to do in this chapter is to examine the consumption of mediated sport, and attempt to develop an empirically grounded theory of audiences for televised sport.

In the latter part of the book we have also been interested in the relationship between sport, media and identity-formation. To this end it is also worth saying something about how fandom relates to this process and to re-emphasize the extent to which the media are not the sole agents shaping the process of identity-formation among fans and other collectivities.

The masculine ritual of sport

In a TV ad for the ubiquitous soft drink Coca-Cola, stylized black and white images of thousands of men intensely caught up in the ritualized, carnivalesque behaviour of the football terrace are twinned with the up-tempo music of the pop band Collapsed Lung whose track 'Beat My Goal' pays homage to the sport. The tag line for Coca-Cola's promotion is 'Eat Football, Sleep Football, Drink Coca-Cola', a motif that runs throughout the advert. The rhetoric which underlies this campaign – initially broadcast in the UK during the run-up to Euro '96 – envisages football as a communal masculine culture which consumes the energy, time and imagination of men (hence the eat–sleep–drink metaphor) within which Coca-Cola, as a sanctioned sponsor of the sport, seeks to exploit its own association with this specific target market.

Within this contemporary view of the sports fan, the idiosyncrasies of sport as a popular cultural form are writ large: in this case, football is perceived as integral to men's everyday lives, born of an essentialist discourse which reiterates a distinction in masculine and feminine forms of sporting experience. This heavily stylized display of a tra-ditionally male-dominant pastime is part of a broader fusion of market-ing communications and what has become acknowledged as a culture of 'laddism', serviced by glossy 'new lad' magazines such as *Loaded* (or quasi-sport programmes including *Fantasy Football League*).

The problems of developing an epistemology of watching televised sport becomes immediately apparent as soon as any attempt is made to conceptualize its audience who are characteristically referred to as 'armchair supporters'. This oft-quoted stereotype conjures up images of that other fictional social outcast the 'couch potato': sat in front of the screen with a 'four-pack' of beer and munching away at copious amounts of 'fast food'. One consequence of this characterization is the creation of a social and psychological pathology of televised sports audi-ences which conflates the individual viewer with an élitist perception of fandom as a deviant cultural phenomenon.

As Jenson (1992, p. 9) has suggested with regard to images of fan-dom in general, this behaviour can frequently be seen to be obsessive, where 'Fandom is seen as a psychological symptom of a presumed social dysfunction.' The perceived slothful nature of this mode of con-suming sport – isolated, lonesome and narcissistic – works to stigmatize individuals and groups seeking relief from the anxieties of modern life. Moreover, by defining fandom in this way, Jenson argues that it allows a form of self-aggrandisement for those demarcated outside the fanat-ical, supporting 'the rational over the emotional, the educated over the uneducated, the subdued over the passionate, the élite over the popular, the mainstream over the margin, the status quo over the alternative' (Jenson, 1992, p. 24).

While these overtly conservative images of fandom would not appear to relate in any way to the four million or so regular viewers who watch a programme like BBC television's *Match of the Day* on a Saturday night, certain dichotomies are invoked by the phrase 'armchair supporter'. Perhaps the most ubiquitous dichotomy would be between the passive experience of watching televised sport and the active experience of being among the supporters in the sports arena.

This separation of the spectating experience has been at the heart of administrators' fears about the effect broadcasting would have on attendances at sport. For its part, television has gone out of its way to lure the 'armchair supporter' to the screen, and it is to the process by which the coverage of sport invokes a masculine mode of spectatorship that the analysis now turns.

Male spectatorship and televised sport

Influenced by feminist psychoanalytical film theory, recent critiques on male spectatorship have emerged to study the processes by which masculine subjectivities are constructed through visual pleasure and narrative structures (Nixon, 1996). Here, the spectator is constituted as a gendered subject, the dominant male gaze being characterized as voyeuristic, linear and contemplative.

Drawing upon this theory of spectatorship which focuses on the 'interpellation' or mode of address of film discourses, Morse (1983) suggests that televised sports spectatorship elicits homoerotic desire as it involves a 'gaze at maleness'. Moreover, as we have seen with the commentator's narrative (Chapter 4), the vernacular of televised sports invites the male spectator to participate in the 'world of sport' which confirms sport as a male preserve.

TV sport as male soap opera

In a critique of this dominant position on classical male spectatorship, Rose and Friedman (1994) have argued that, while a degree of fetishization of the male body constitutes the 'hermeneutic process of reading and evaluating athletic performances', the 'analytic discourse' on the male spectator of televised sport should 'ultimately be qualified by the *melodramatic*'.

In other words, as Morse herself realized but did not develop theoretically, televised sport can be viewed as a 'male soap opera' with multiple narratives which highlight 'personal struggle', 'social tension' and 'moral conflict'. Appropriating the theory of 'distraction' from the film theorist Kracauer (1926) and reinterpreting the notion of a 'rhythm of reception' from Modlenski (1983), Rose and Friedman state:

> What is ultimately at stake in our argument, then, is a reconceptualisation of masculine modes of consumption and production: we are suggesting that the distracted, decentred and other-oriented consumption of sport by television spectators reflects and reifies the patterns of perception and the skills required of the postindustrial male worker. (Rose and Friedman, 1994, p. 26)

As suggested in Chapters 2 and 3, television was integral to the standardization and commodification of sport, as new technologies were continually introduced to 'make sense' of the action for the viewers.

The sports commentator places the spectator in relation to the melodrama of the event which, like a serial, is ongoing and continually fragmenting into new stories about players, managers, clubs and nations. While the main commentator provides the narrative within the action – heightening the sense of actuality and 'liveness' – the co-commentator, or in-match summarizer, provides and draws upon wider narratives, which are far more speculative, and function, according to Rose and Friedman (1994, p. 27) 'like the gossip of soap opera'. It is in the frame of this latter discourse, specifically, that the male spectator is interpellated to identify with sport as a masculine domain.

Identification with the re-representation of the action is central to the popular pleasures produced by televised sport. The familiarity with the form and style of commentary and emotional identification with specific players and teams combine to dissolve the boundary of the television screen, and invoke participation from the viewer. Again, we can recall early attempts to develop commentary techniques in radio and television which sought to address the listener as a friend.

However, it could be argued that the 'friend' in question is distinctly male and, as O'Connor and Boyle (1993, p. 116) suggest in terms of football: 'If women are accommodated with the discourses of televised football . . . it is in a marginal and trivial manner'. By engaging with this discourse, men view televised sport as an extension of their world and, as we will argue later in a case study of boxing, the metatexts of televised sport provide social tools with which men can operate in public domains, as part of a 'hegemonic masculinity' (Connell, 1987).

Therefore, instead of analysing male spectatorship as distinct from a feminine mode of spectatorship, televised sport can be read as an 'open text', in which the 'dialogic activity' of spectating involves absorption into multiple identifications with characters, settings and narratives of the 'world of sport', in a 'rhythm of reception' which is distracted, partial and interrupted (a masculine counterpart to the standard reading of women's reception of soap opera).

That fans should make paradigmatic readings of televised sport, focusing on the play of possibilities between stars, stories and action, should not, however, deflect from the actual, historically constructed power relations between men and women (and men and men) which are realized in televised sport, and are characteristic of a dominant 'gender order' (Connell, 1987). As we suggest in Chapter 7, televised sport practices and discourses continue to connote maleness. It is in this way that male images of sport, equating male sporting prowess with masculine superiority, contribute to the social reproduction of dominant cultural values.

Sport remains a contradictory domain in which male emotions, culturally silenced in wider society (Rutherford, 1996), are legitimately expressed: the image of Paul Gascoigne's tears at Italia '90 being the most public 'show' of male grief in recent memory (later self-parodied by the England player in an advert for Walkers crisps in 1996). The imaging of such personalized moments within televised football attempts to invoke an emotional attachment from the viewer and, in the case of Gascoigne, his tears were shed for his country. His actions, therefore, conflate masculinity, sporting pride and national identity – all familiar points of reference with which football fans can identify.

The feminist study of 'women's genres' has placed gender at the centre of understanding television spectatorship in terms of wider relational connections and 'interpretive communities', which are characterized by a gravitation towards certain discursive modes of interpreting media content (Radway, 1984). In following this contextualizing of media reception, we can employ similar modes of analysis to research the reception of televised sport by men. The interrelationships between gender, genre and fandom become important dynamics to the study of men watching televised sport.

As Livingstone (1996, p. 445) has argued, how these variables are negotiated by the viewer has 'consequences for their critical responses, their participation and involvement, and their motivations for viewing'. Having provided an overview of the discursive address of televised sport, and the construction of the male spectator, the analysis now turns to the social and cultural consumption of the genre by men – this was conducted as part of the project *Men Viewing Violence* (Schlesinger *et al.*, 1998) in which both authors were involved.

Sport in the digital age – Sky Sports has been at the forefront of transforming media sport in the 1990s. © *Sky Sports*

Men viewing boxing

Qualitative audience research has sought both to understand the ways that viewers use television, in the belief that individuals have the power to engage actively with media to 'gratify' psychological needs and, on the other hand, to understand how a viewer's interpretation of television is informed by social group membership.

Why study men? Why study violent sport?

In the Broadcasting Standards Commission research project *Men Viewing Violence*, fifteen focus groups were conducted among men from various backgrounds to simulate broadly 'the ways in which people talk about what they see on the screen when presented with a common topic' (Schlesinger *et al.*, 1998, p. 5). Participants viewed a range of violent programming so that how interpretations and reactions were influenced by social status, ethnicity, age, sexual preference and general life experiences could be studied. The study built on the research design of a previous project, *Women Viewing Violence* (Schlesinger *et al.*, 1992), where programmes were chosen to stimulate group discussion on depictions of violence against women. In the men's study, we were acutely aware of the need to widen the range of programmes to include not only violence by men against women, but also men against men, including violence in sport.

The introduction of sport, in particular boxing, to the screenings became important for several reasons. Firstly, it allowed the investigation of men's identification with forms of aggressive masculinity. As we noted in Chapter 7, the connection between sport and masculinity is central to understanding the genre of media sport, and the researchers were eager to explore the various myths that connect gender with particular types of programming.

Secondly, it enabled the exploration of men's reactions to various aspects of violence in sport: brutality, arrogance, drama and spectacle. To this end, men viewed two contrasting boxing events, one representing the competitive thrill and destructive violence of the sport (Nigel Benn against Gerald McLellan); the other, representing the glitz and glamour of contemporary boxing on pay-television (Prince Naseem Hamed against Remigio Molina).

A third reason for choosing sport as a stimulus was methodological. Audience studies of men remain a neglected field of media research, partly due to the problems associated with researching groups of men. In conducting focus groups with men, not only is the process of recruitment often difficult, but the moderating process can often be stifled by intransigence of male participants to open up discussion and express their views and feelings. However, sport offers one field of enquiry where men freely cooperate in a controlled group setting because, if managed properly, discussion can soon come to simulate the informal conversation familiarly associated with the social relations men experience in everyday life. Finally, and connected to this last point, the study was interested to explore men's general consumption of televised sport and examine how knowledge of sport carries currency in everyday social relations.

Before conducting the focus groups respondents were also asked to complete a questionnaire that surveyed their media consumption and sporting interests. The overwhelming response, more than 80 per cent of the 88 men in the study, highlighted sport as the favourite type of television programme. However, fewer than 10 per cent had subscriptions to Sky Sports channels in the home, and only two respondents had paid for a pay-per-view sports event.

The men's media consumption and preferences pointed to a stereotypical association between gender and genre, with evidence from the survey supporting the recognition of televised sport as a masculine domain. The notable exceptions to this dominant finding came from two groups of gay men, from Glasgow and Manchester. These two groups showed a stark contrast to the other groups in the survey, in both the participation in and viewing of sport. Gay men in the study equated contact and team sports with dominant hegemonic masculinities that exemplified the macho, often violent, ideology displayed through sport by a large proportion of the male population.

A general abhorrence of violence was crystallized through a specific dislike and avoidance of contact sports. While the feeling of anti-sports violence was by no means exclusive to the gay men in the study, it did suggest that the way different masculine identities are constructed do have a significant bearing on the experiences and interpretative strategies of viewing violent sports on television.

The excitement of brutality

In the group discussions gay men continued to press home their dislike of boxing, with some participants equating violence in sport to other forms of violence in both public and private domains:

> I think in some people it will evoke thoughts of violence towards either their partner or somebody else who is watching at the time . . . because people who are immature may get some kick out of it and think, right, well, your missus is giving me some grief, or a partner . . . smack, I'll wallop you one. (Gay white man, 30–39, Manchester)

The sense that boxing could initiate violence among groups of men was not widely held, although one young working-class man did note that 'It always kicks off [trouble starts] in pubs when there's a boxing match on'. However, it was generally agreed across the groups that boxing could act as a cathartic outlet for male aggression:

> I've been to a couple of boxing matches and the crowd do generally get worked up, I think it does, I think that is one sport that does bring out a bit of aggressiveness in people.
>
> . . . and watching it on TV?
> I feel aggressiveness but I wouldn't necessarily say I would get aggressive, but you feel that aggressiveness there. (Middle-class white man, 30–39, Glasgow)

The notion that boxing represents a legitimate field of violent confrontation was widely understood, although not all men found the sport entertaining. For some men boxing presented something of a paradox, it could be engaging and challenge their moral outlook on violence in sport, at one and the same time:

> I see boxing as purely entertainment but even though I say that, after a
> fight, I can sit back and say, 'Oh shit, this is brutal!' You know? but
> when I am watching it, I see it as purely . . . I mean you feel the
> adrenaline you know . . . almost . . . sometimes you find you are
> moving about. (West African man, 18–29, Glasgow)

The dramatic intensity of the Benn/McLellan fight was viewed by
men in the study to be central to the excitement of boxing. As we have
argued above, and in previous chapters on the presentation of sporting
narratives, a key aspect to people's enjoyment of media sport are the
contingent aspects that rely on the unknown outcome of events and the
importance of characterization in the unfolding story. Identification
with winners and losers, favourites and underdogs is, therefore, an
important aspect of the viewer's experience of televised sport.

Again, as one middle-class man from Manchester responded to viewing the Benn fight:

> I think it was the fact he was swinging from like . . . both sides . . . it
> looked like one guy was going to win, then it was the other guy. It kept
> swinging backwards and forwards so you were in limbo really. And it
> was action all the time. What I was thinking was, action, action, action,
> wasn't it? (Middle-class man, 30–39, Manchester)

The majority of the men in the study had a knowledge of the
Benn/McLellan fight and were aware of the damage caused to the
American boxer. This was viewed as an inevitable aspect of the sport,
and it was widely held that boxers understood the dangers ahead of
them in the ring. It was clear from the research that a significant number of men enjoy boxing because of the raw excitement it engenders.
Moreover, while many of the men found the brutality of the sport
abhorrent, they found no favour in wanting the coverage of the sport on
television regulated or banned.

Boxing as spectacle and entertainment

We noted in Chapter 7 how the celebration of boxing by the media can
serve to mask the brutality and violence associated with the sport. In the
study, the discussion of how men engaged with television coverage of
boxing led on to questions regarding the entertainment values of televised sport. In particular, the research focus turned to men's perceptions of BSkyB's coverage of boxing, which was discussed through a
case study of the featherweight boxer Prince Naseem Hamed. Even for
those men who disliked boxing, it was agreed that the entertainment
values built into the coverage of the sport legitimized its appeal.

Men above the age of thirty could remember the days when televised boxing was dominated by the BBC during the 1970s and 1980s. It was felt by some of the men that television coverage had dramatically changed over time. The intensive coverage given over to boxing on Sky Sports was considered to be overtly voyeuristic, in the sense that the camera dwelt on every punch and blow. For some, this had turned them away from viewing boxing. Again, particular examples were used to illustrate the point:

> Years and years ago, I would have enjoyed a big Mohammed Ali fight, and I would have been a typical sort of prime-time TV fan, wanting to watch it for the excitement. But as I got to know boxing and more about what goes on in boxing, in terms of moves and punches and that, I don't find it that entertaining. (Middle-class man, 30–39, Manchester)

> I think they've got to be very careful with Sky, in that now you've got the action replays, so close and so slow and so accurate, you can have different camera angles. It becomes very disturbing, to me personally. (Middle-class man, 30–39, Glasgow)

The hype that surrounds contemporary boxing and the spectacle garnered by television for stars like Prince Naseem Hamed was understood to be part and parcel of big-business sport.

Some men believed Hamed was deliberately 'mismatched' to ensure his longevity at the top, placing emphasis on 'showbiz' rather than sport, 'pulling in the punters . . . the audience who would not normally watch boxing' (Middle-class man, 40+, Leeds). It was noted that Hamed's fights tended to be short, and some concern was raised regarding the cost of viewing boxing on subscription channels where there was no guarantee of value for money. The introduction of pay-per-view boxing also drew criticism from those who subscribed to Sky Sport, but were forced to pay extra to view major fights:

> I must admit, it goes against the grain with me, this pay per view thing. Because up until recently we did have Sky, more or less full packages, but I was determined not to pay an extra £10 for boxing matches, because I thought if you are paying for sports channels, why should you have to pay extra? (Middle-class man, 30–39, Glasgow)

Resistance to paying for televised sport was clearly a big issue for men in the study, even when they had subscribed to specialist sports channels. Although pay channels are now well established in the UK, it can still be argued that subscription to Sky Sports represents a material and symbolic marker of status.

As Brundson (1991) observed at the dawn of satellite television in Britain, the display of satellite and cable hardware carries ambiguous meaning and the message communicated is dependent on class distinctions of taste and geography. As the study of men viewing boxing further illustrates, the extent to which new vistas of consuming televised sport are opened up heavily depends on social relations of age and gender. Younger men were far more likely to live in a household that subscribed to Sky Sport, and were also more likely to view sport in social settings like the pub. It was also apparent that discussion about boxing opened up men's imaginary connection to a wider popular culture, where sport was an important aspect of male cultural capital.

Sport, then, provides a quintessential example of men's relationship to the public and private domains: where men's active engagement with televised sport, in this case boxing, connects with men's domination in public life.

Tribal instincts: fandom and the media

As the 1998/99 football season came to a close, ten years after the tragic loss of life at Hillsborough Stadium in Sheffield, the vibrancy of football fandom was as strong as ever. Times had changed: new and refurbished all-seater stadiums in England, Scotland and Wales; large television screens to replay goals and near misses to the spectators in the ground; more supporters wearing team colours and replica shirts (including the sponsor's logo) – many last season's design because not everyone can afford to upgrade every year; a noticeable level of affluence among supporters – if not rich then certainly 'comfortable'; and an increasing number of women and young girls at the games – albeit still constituting a distinct minority.

However, the passion play that draws people to the game still underscores any transformation fans may have experienced in their ritual trail to the match. Fans no longer have the ability to choose where they watch the game as they did in the era of open terraces, something that certain fan groups believe has been detrimental to the atmosphere of British football. Yet, having to sit in a pre-designated seat week in week out, often next to a total stranger, is not necessarily a prerequisite to a loss of an imagined communal identity football fandom engenders. As we have expressed elsewhere in this book, identity formation in and around football (or any sport) is an important site for understanding the relationship between sport, media and popular culture.

The 1990s has also seen a noticeable reappraisal of the role fans play in sporting cultures. As has been well documented in academic and popular writing on football supporters, for much of the 1970s and 1980s any association with the game immediately brought up issues of violence and hooliganism. This, we believe, is no longer the case, and for several reasons.

The media perception of fans underwent a complex transformation after the events at Hillsborough, largely motivated by supporter activism through the Football Supporters Association, club-based independent supporters' organizations and football fanzines (Redhead, 1991; Haynes, 1995; Brown, 1998). While the level of democratic control fans have at their disposal remains negligible where decisions really count, football culture has certainly enjoyed more favourable public relations in the 1990s thanks to its fans.

The celebration by the media of the carnivalesque subculture of international events like the World Cup, the European Championships and the African Nations Cup are reminders that the sport is a global enthusiasm, of mass appeal and the builder of affective relationships between different nation groups. Italia '90, USA '94, Euro '96 and France '98 may have been the ultimate marketing communication events, but they also signal a marked reverence being held for fan subculture. Fans are constantly used as the ultimate symbol for 'flagging' the nation (Billig, 1995), drawing on an array of geopolitical stereotypes. The 'samba' sounds of the Brazilians and the 'Reggae Boys' of Jamaica contrast with the boisterous party spirit from the Danish 'Roligans' and the gregarious 'craic' enjoyed by the Irish.

On balance, British fans have also received a more sanguine representation in the media since 1989. Scottish supporters ubiquitously known as the 'Tartan Army' are paraded on our television screens at every available opportunity during major tournaments involving Scotland. Reporters and journalists are even allocated the role of following the fans in order to report 'home' the latest views and opinions from the unofficial 'Scottish camp' (see Chapter 8).

The 'Tartan Army' as it is perceived by the media – and possibly by those who consider themselves as members – is qualitatively different to that of the traditional associations with England fans. Where Scots are a contingent body that show bonhomie and good humour, the English are considered menacing, chauvinistic and potentially violent. As Finn and Giulianotti (1998) have observed, the gregarious fan style of Scotland supporters not only trades off the negative stereotypes of England fans, but also benefits from the self-congratulatory tone of the Scottish media who praise the ambassadorial role performed by the fans.

The changing mood of domestic football fandom in England has also prompted media speculation that hooliganism is unfashionable or being stamped out by the authorities. Football-loving political figures like David Mellor or Tony Banks during the 1990s have professed a sea-change in the behaviour of England supporters, denigrating the 'minority' who 'spoil it for the rest of us'. Equally, the reportage of football-related violence has become more muted during the 1990s.

In September 1991, after the number of arrests at football in England was seen to be on a remarkable downturn, the BBC programme *Newsnight* gave an example of this sea change in the perception of fans. The programme ran a ten-minute feature on the new culture of football fandom in which the sports correspondent Kevin Geary proclaimed 'it's no longer hip to be a "hooly"', suggesting that the spread of 'rave culture' had done much to 'mellow out' the mob mentality of young male supporters. Paradoxically, hooliganism is now viewed as a public relations opportunity as much as a blight on the game. Before every major tournament 'dawn raids' by police forces up and down the country, drawing on covert intelligence compiled on hooligan activity by the National Football Intelligence Unit, are given prominent treatment in television news programmes as evidence of 'cleaning up the game'. In the 1990s, football is considered a safer place to be, a temple of unrestrained hedonism for the love of the game.

All together now?

Such rhetoric clearly oversimplifies the nature of fandom in the late-1990s. As we discuss below in the case of the Glasgow 'Old Firm', rivalry remains entrenched throughout domestic football. The unassailed success of Manchester United during the 1990s has prompted new and old fissures of animosity to surface, not least among Liverpool and Leeds United supporters. However, not all supporters feel and act the same. What we believe we can see in the highly commodified game of football are myriad fan subcultures that express their affective ties to the club they support in various and intriguing ways.

One area where these differences are visibly displayed is in the sustained subculture of football fanzines and the rapid growth of football-related websites. As one of the authors has previously noted, fanzines grew out of a 'culture of defence' when the pathology of fandom reached its lowest ebb, and processes of modernization threatened to undermine the bond many fans had for the game (Haynes, 1998).

In turning consumption into production, fanzines opened up new avenues to challenge symbolically and actively the governance and media representation of the sport. Furthermore, fanzines also made real the plight of football clubs in the lower divisions of the Football League. The fight for survival has often been led by fan activism, drawing on the irreverence of fan subculture, politically mobilizing what Raymond Williams referred to as the 'structure of feeling' many supporters have for their club.

Football-related websites on the Internet have taken up the verve and spirit of fanzines to communicate their love for the game electronically with the well-established fan magazine *When Saturday Comes* one of the first to introduce a multimedia alternative to the standard printed publication (http://www.wsc.co.uk/wsc/).

Tradition and history among football fans

Much of the recent debate regarding the future of football in Britain (and Europe) has centred around the perceived tension between the 'traditionalists' and the 'modernizers'. The first group is usually portrayed as supporters who invest the club with a symbolic significance, and the latter encompass the business and commercial community who view football as part of a wider media/leisure economy in which supporters are viewed as consumers (see Boyle and Haynes, 1996).

In Simon Kuper's examination of football culture in over twenty different countries, he noted that in his experience it was only in British fan culture that history and tradition were deemed to be so important:

> British fans are historians. When two British sides play each other,
> their histories play each other too. This is especially true in Glasgow.
> (Kuper, 1994, p. 216)

He argues that, while this fixation with tradition is mirrored in British political culture, with continual debates about the dangers to British life of losing specific traditions (usually threatened by Europe), in Glasgow this concern is driven by specific ethnic and religious concerns unique to that city.

Research carried out among fans by one of the authors in both Glasgow and Liverpool identified the role of the clubs and their positioning within ethnic and city identities as different and reflected by the supporters' concerns with their club and what they understand to be that club's tradition. Even in a media-saturated culture, football's emphasis on competition and rivalry at local, regional and national levels, allied with its close association with urban working-class culture and its attendant concern with the demarcation of territory, make it a potent cultural form for the expression of individual and collective identities.

Embedded in this cultural form is the centrality of tradition in informing how supporters come to think about their team, themselves and other supporters. As in the 'imagined community' of the nation, football culture celebrates its heroes and triumphs by weaving them into a powerful narrative which connects the past with the present. This draws on not only myths that exist within club histories, but also connects with deeper myths that circulate beyond the parameters of football and are embedded in wider society. This process is mediated through a number of institutions, including the media, family, school, supporters' clubs and so forth.

Many official club histories (and indeed much history writing in general) attempt to map out and impose a narrative structure on past events. In so doing they also help to make sense of (or legitimize) aspects of the present. John Thompson has commented on how 'narrativization' is an important element in this process of legitimization:

> claims are embedded in stories which recount the past and treat the
> present as part of a timeless and cherished tradition. Indeed traditions
> are sometimes invented in order to create a sense of belonging to a
> community and to a history which transcends the experience of
> conflict, difference and division. (Thompson, 1990, pp. 61–2)

History is a process of forgetting, as well as remembering, of legitimizing the present through one particular version of the past.

This process helps sustain the collective group identity among supporters and their allegiance to a particular club. The linkage between tradition and the selective interpretation of history is important, as it sustains particular discourses and allows them an ahistorical position: they become 'given' and 'natural'.

Many of the discourses relating to national or cultural characteristics are represented through various forms of narrative as 'given' or 'fixed'. For example, many of the discourses relating to Irish immigration in nineteenth-century Liverpool and Glasgow are very similar to those which exist in certain social and political circles with regard to the position of the immigrant population in Britain in the 1990s. It is 'our' traditions, 'our' jobs, 'our' heritage that is threatened by the 'wave' of immigrants. In this instance, aspects of 'tradition' are mobilized to legitimize current thinking and political actions.

In addition, traditional aspects of culture are perceived to belong to an earlier more innocent time. They become symbolic events that connect us with the past, and hark back to a more secure, less complex society. In part this stems from a dissatisfaction with the modern world, allowing particularly comforting views of the past to function as nostalgia: a sense of longing for a more secure 'golden' era, which of course in reality may never have existed.

As Chase and Shaw note with regard to modern human life experience:

> The only certainty is uncertainty, so that in this view nostalgia is the attempt to cling to the alleged certainties of the past, ignoring the fact that, like it or not, the only constant in our lives is change. (Chase and Shaw, 1989, p. 8)

Popular culture, and football – even mediated football, for to some extent all the fans' experience of the game comes through various channels of communication – in particular in the cities examined, becomes a site for this social process. It is not simply a case of one version of history versus another, but of how the clubs come to symbolize a sense of history, place and belonging to supporters who often view themselves as an integral part of the club and its historical narrative.

A sense of belonging in an era of change

For many fans, versions of tradition and history associated with football clubs and their cities provide a tangible link between the past and present. Football teams are always changing (players, managers and the like all come and go), yet the club exists in a space that is in part untouched by these changes (it is often remarked at Liverpool and Celtic that no one player is bigger than the club). To supporters the club offers a projection of a community which signifies, among other things, stability and continuity. If in Glasgow the centrality of the importance of religious and ethnic identities has been evident in the continuing rivalry that surrounds the position of Celtic and Rangers in the culture of the west of Scotland, by contrast in Liverpool it appears that football occupies a less divisive position in the cultural life of that city, and instead it provides a specific city identity which is placed in opposition to other regional and English national identities.

In both cities there is another element of symbolic significance in the attachment and devotion of the supporters to their clubs. The crisis in

British football in one respect personifies a deeper concern about the future relationship of the individual to the wider collective in society.

Among many supporters there exists a sense that yet another area of popular culture is being subjected to commercial pressures and interests which misunderstand the symbolic importance which football carries for many people. This is particularly true for those groups to whom football is interwoven with a range of other identities and experiences, and is not viewed as some optional extra which can be purchased as another part of the leisure economy.

Stan Hey, talking about the seating of the Kop at Liverpool FC, encompasses this clash of tradition and change, and how this process is bound up with a sense of a specific place, identity and moment in history coming to an end. While aware of the dangers of lapsing into an uncritical account of contemporary society fuelled by nostalgia, it is worth quoting at length, touching as it does on a number of issues keenly felt among the supporters interviewed:

> As the factories die and their docks become shopping malls or art galleries, and the sea-faring, music-making past becomes part of the heritage industry, Liverpudlians, like most of the country, are bemused and wounded by the feeling of having lost a sense of community. The paradox of progress losing us more than we gain, of advancement for some, but not for all, may not be restricted to the streets if the Kop does indeed go. 'People have had some of the biggest moments of their lives there,' says Rogan Taylor. 'Moments they'll put in the big box, the one you take down to your death. The Kop has been the site of all this.' (Hey, 1993)

Despite television and sport increasingly addressing their fan base as consumers, for many people sport – even in its highly mediated forms – still carries with it a more rooted symbolism which connects with other areas of social life such as class and community. Understanding fandom means always attempting to locate it within that broader social context.

Conclusion

As we examined in Chapter 5, another impact of the increasingly close links between the media and sport, and how it is funded, is the growing financial gap between those who watch and those who play. This is particularly acute in the football industry, where the traditional supporters of the game, while still important, are no longer the major financial backers of the sport. While this differs from club to club and fans still matter when they are asked to consume vast quantities of officially endorsed club products, it is television, and the money which flows from it into the game that has fuelled a massive increase in players' wages and media-related endorsement earnings.

In a sport such as football which historically has been a working-class sport, a new generation of footballers, still drawn from this section of the community are in a very short time moving in very different financial, social and often media-related circles. This gap, which has characterized sport in the US, is very much becoming the norm in the new age of satellite-backed and media-hyped football in Britain.

Despite the globalization of major sporting events, the distinctive locale in which viewers engage with these events remains vital. The Lyons and Ticher (1998) collection of essays from 25 countries which examined how the world watched the 1998 football World Cup, demonstrated that, while we may watch the same games, the context in which they are understood is more often than not determined by a country's wider political and cultural context.

There is also an argument which suggests that the difference between watching sport live and watching live sport on television is breaking down. This suggests that all-seater stadia, with giant video screens and a constant supply of food and drink provided for the spectators has turned these venues into extensions of your front room.

As Trevor Fishlock discovered on his tour of America back in the 1980s, it brings a very literal meaning to the marketing principle that fans should be viewed as consumers. At a baseball match in New York he commented on:

> the relentless mass chewing of junk food, an anorexic's nightmare of bulging squirrelly cheeks. . . . Soon our shoes were hidden in a litter of expended sachets, paper beer cups, ice cream cartons, peanut shells and ketchup-stained napkins. That evening the stadium had a crowd of 55,000 people and I calculated that the median fan was consuming three [hot] dogs . . . The reeking stadium sent up a thermal of sausage vapour. (Fishlock, 1986, p. 138)

While there have been major developments in football stadia in Britain, replicating many of the characteristics found in America, the actual stadia experience remains quite different. Even in all-seater stadia, fans in Britain do not go to football or rugby simply to spectate, they go to *participate* in the event, believing, with some degree of justification, that they may be able to influence the result of the game by supporting their team, or creating an intimidating atmosphere for the opposition.

Thus, while similarities exist, patterns and levels of fan intensity differ between sports and between countries. In many ways the notion of the global sports fan remains something of a media and marketing myth. In addition, of course, sport increasingly appears to be an adjunct of the entertainment media industry and, as we argue in the final chapter, this appears to involve the sports fan being asked to pay extra for the privilege of viewing the mediated event.

CHAPTER 11

Conclusion

The State of Play, Sport in the New Media Age

> What are we in sport? We are completely controlled by television.
> Let's not kid ourselves.
>
> **Barry Hearn, sports manager and promoter, *Fair Game,* ITV, 1 June 1995**

> ENGLAND V SCOTLAND NEXT SATURDAY. THERE'S ONLY ONE SIDE TO WATCH . . . SKY SPORTS 2
> SKYdigital: the home of sport
>
> **Newspaper advert., promoting the 1999 Five Nations rugby union international**

Introduction

At the beginning of the book we suggested that sport, and its relationship with the media, have become key markers of late twentieth-century popular culture. We also noted that sports media have increasingly encroached on the domain of business and politics, to such an extent that even governments cannot ignore its significance. What then are the key pressure points around which the battle for control of sport is taking place?

Power play: regulating media sport

In the spring of 1999 the UK government's Department of Trade and Industry blocked the controversial attempt by BSkyB to merge (or merge-over) with Manchester United football club. The decision was based on an independent enquiry by the Monopolies and Mergers Commission (now the Competition Commission) which had taken evidence from a range of organizations and individuals from the sport and media sectors. Among the evidence to the MMC was a submission from the United Shareholders Against Murdoch, headed by journalist Michael Crick, who had lobbied hard against the proposed merger.

From a Media Studies perspective, it is interesting to note that the main criteria for the decision were based on media issues, the most dominant one being that ownership of United would give BSkyB an unfair advantage during the negotiation of the future television rights to the English Premier League (the existing contract runs until 2001). This 'toe-hold effect' was given as a major reason for the DTI's decision, in spite of assurances from Mark Booth, the then Chairman of BSkyB, that United's representatives would withdraw from the negotiating table to allow the remaining 19 clubs to make such decisions on their behalf.

BSkyB clearly understood the potential conflict of interest that may arise in such cases, where they are both the buyer and part seller of sports rights. In this respect, BSkyB had followed the concessions made by Fox in the United States, also controlled by News Corporation, who had bought control of the Los Angeles Dodgers, the American Football team, after giving similar assurances to United States regulators.

The DTI also made an issue of the effect the merger might have on smaller clubs in England. This had been a major fear of fans, sports journalists and sports-minded politicians who had lobbied hard against the threat of widening the gap between the rich and the poor clubs. As the Trade and Industry Secretary, Stephen Byers argued:

> [T]he merger would damage the quality of British football by reinforcing the trend towards growing inequalities between the larger, richer clubs and the smaller, poorer ones and by giving BSkyB additional influence over Premier League decisions about the organisation of football leading to some decisions which would not reflect the game's long term interests. (Quoted by Netscape Netcenter, 9 April 1999 http://www.excite.uk.netscape.com/news/)

In many respects, that divide is already an almighty chasm, and a large number of clubs outside the Premier League (and several within it) have been developing strategies to cope with the momentous shifts in wealth that have occurred during the 1990s.

Sport plc

Perhaps more significant was the immediate effect of the decision to block the merger on the stock market. The public flotation of football clubs has increased towards the end of the 1990s, following the original example of Tottenham Hotspur who were the first British club to become a plc in 1983 (Boyle and Haynes, 1996). The process has placed more pressure on clubs to perform well financially in order to reward their investors. Although many private shareholders of the club may well own shares for the love of the team, not necessarily expecting a return on their investment, large corporate backers do expect clubs to cash in on the various media, promotional and merchandizing opportunities that emerge in the sport.

Key to the excitement over football-related shares was the prospect of new partnerships between sport and the media, in particular the projected revenues available to clubs from an introduction of pay-per-view. However, from an initial upturn in football-related shares in 1996 and 1997, the novelty of football-shares soon wore off as clubs hit various troubles on and off the pitch. The decision to knock back the BSkyB merger with Manchester United dealt a further blow to the market. United's shares had rocketed when the merger was first mooted but, on the DTI announcement, its shares fell from 218.5p to 186p, wiping £85 million off the market capitalization of the share value (*Sunday Business*, 11 April 1999).

Other clubs that had also come under scrutiny from media companies were equally effected. The shares of Newcastle United and Aston Villa both dropped as the promised riches of sport–media ties were stalled. Conversely, BSkyB's share price had consolidated itself during the week before the DTI announcement due to News Corporation's deal with Liberty Media who sold its 50 per cent holding of Fox/Liberty Networks, an American television sports programmer, to Rupert Murdoch. The failure to capture the deal with Manchester United merely knocked 1p off the BSkyB price.

Of more concern for the television industry as a whole was that the block from the DTI may have set a problematic precedent. The natural synergies of vertical integration between sports organizations and media conglomerates is easy to recognize when one understands the centrality of televised sport in the contemporary media environment. With the proliferation of television channels, and heightened competition for an increasingly fragmenting audience, quality programme content is at a premium. Sport, in particular football, has provided a ready-made supply of attractive programming. One consequence of this shift in the economics of broadcasting markets, is that a widening spectrum of delivery methods has placed more power in the hands of content providers.

Long gone are the cosy days of the 1980s in British television when both the BBC and ITV carved up sport between them, paying as little for the rights as they could get away with. This cartel for sports rights was broken up with the introduction of cable and satellite services in the major television markets of the world and the cost of televised rights to sport have been pulled by an inflationary spiral causing economic rents to escalate at alarming rates.

For broadcasters, the power remains in the hands of sporting bodies and organizations who now strike far tougher bargains for exclusive rights to their product. On the other hand, for those sports that have sold to the highest bidder, the remuneration involved is large enough to hand over a significant amount of responsibility in running sport. Hence, sporting events get moved to all manner of days in the week, times of the day and, in the case of rugby league's shift to a summer season, time of the year, to suit the needs of television. As we argued in Chapter 4, those who chastise television for taking over sport, may be misplacing their criticism. Blaming television for controlling sport misses the subtle complexities of what the political and economic dynamics of the sport–media nexus actually are.

Power play: convergence in media sport

It is the latent power of sport to withdraw altogether from the television arena, and the phenomenal hike in sports rights, that has urged media companies to look at sports organizations, not as partners, but as integral units of their business strategies.

It would appear that one of the key submissions to the MMC came from the broadcasting regulator, the Independent Television Commission (ITC). Before the release of the report it had been widely reported that the chairman of the ITC had publicly decried the merger as damaging to the UK market for televised sport. Other companies, apart from BSkyB, have also shown an interest in owning football clubs and were withholding their full commitment until the DTI's decision on the matter.

NTL, the American cable operator, had moved to buy Newcastle United, but dropped this in the light of the decision regarding BSkyB and Manchester United. However, at the same time they were busy securing a major sponsorship deal with the top two clubs in the Scottish Premier League – Celtic and Rangers. Other UK media companies, such as Granada, have begun to invest in clubs such as Liverpool.

As we argued above, the integration of sport–media businesses is a way of shortcutting the costs of sports-rights negotiations. However, the timing of these decisions coincides with the establishment of new digital platforms for the delivery of multi-channel television (via satellite, aerial and cable). Furthermore, new structures of packaging programmes, combining subscription with pay-per-view services, have allured the capitalist eye to new streams of income.

These developments are new to UK sports business, but they have their precedents on the European continent, and North America. One of the most famous football club sides in Europe, AC Milan in Italy, is famously owned by Silvio Berlusconi, who has controlling interest of the media group Mediaset and interests in the Canal Plus Italian subsidiary Telepui which controls the pay-television football market in that country. Canal Plus, the giant French media company owns the successful French team Paris Saint Germain – the Chairman of the media company Pierre Lescure is also President of the football club – as well as having interests in other European soccer markets, and Disney, Time Warner and Fox all have several sporting links with various clubs across the United States.

One of the contra-arguments to the government's decision on BSkyB's bid for Manchester United has been that media companies are one of the few businesses able, and willing, to invest the large sums of money required to maintain successful sporting concerns.

Bolt from the sky: transformations in terrestrial sports broadcasting

The rapid transformations that have impacted on the 'sporting triangle' we reviewed in Chapter 3 have left the pioneers of sports broadcasting in the UK, and public-service broadcasters of other nations, under growing pressure to adapt to the paradigmatic shift in the market for television sport. Cut-throat competition for sports rights and its corollary, costs, have stretched the purses of many traditional broadcasters of sport.

The extent to which public-service broadcasters can juggle their responsibilities to all their viewers, to include both mass and minority audiences, has placed further pressures on their ability to meet the needs of exposure-hungry sport. Conversely, the multi-channel age, with its dedicated niche programming, operates in an environment that affords expansive scheduling for sport and in-depth coverage. As we noted in Chapter 4, the quantity of dedicated television coverage can often lead to overkill and is not necessarily a marker of quality. Broadcasters with long traditions in sport, like the BBC, often fall back on the belief that they cover sport better than anyone else because of their impressive track record.

However, such rhetoric can often pale in significance when sports bodies are seeking new arrangements with television. European television executives and sports administrators have jealously observed the revolution that struck the US sports broadcasting market in the early-1980s with the rise of ABC's dedicated sports channel ESPN. Ted Turner's Home Box Office had also pioneered the pay-per-view market through its promotion of heavyweight boxing, bringing new riches to the worlds top fighters and their promoters.

Broader shifts in broadcasting regulation had given early signs that British television would be following the US example. Shaped by the Thatcher government's free-market ideology, the 1990 Broadcasting Act pushed through under the tutelage of David Mellor as a member of the Major government (who both promoted their sporting credentials), did much to enable BSkyB to gain a foothold in the UK broadcasting market (Horsman, 1997). New terrestrial channels have also widened the market for televised sport.

The cosy duopoly between the BBC and ITV companies was given initial competition from Channel 4 in the 1980s, particularly with the introduction of non-indigenous sports like American Football and later with the introduction of Football Italia in 1992 (built on the back of Paul Gascoigne's ill-fated move to Lazio, but still going strong). The introduction of Channel 5 in 1997 added further competition for football, with the channel gaining its first coup when it screened England's World Cup qualifier against Poland during the first month of its launch. The channel has gone on to compete successfully for European club football, tracking Chelsea's successive seasons in the European Cup Winners Cup.

Power play: public-service sport and the BBC

The BBC, whose budget for sport has struggled to match the inflated prices being negotiated for live sport (in particular football), has found its sports portfolio shrinking year-on-year. The Corporation has not screened live domestic English league football since 1988 when ITV brokered a four-year deal with the Football League. When negotiations began for live coverage of the newly formed Premier League in 1992, the BBC was not even a viable player.

The BBC has also lost rights to several 'blue chip' events like the Ryder Cup, England's Five Nations Rugby Union and Rugby League to Sky Sports; Grand Prix motor-racing and the FA Cup Final to ITV; and England's home Test Matches to Channel 4. The BBC still points to its success in maintaining rights to the Grand National, Wimbledon and the remainder of the Five Nations matches. Furthermore, it also ensured the rights to the Olympic Games until 2008, thanks to its membership of the European Broadcasting Union, and repeatedly outperforms its rival ITV in the ratings for the World Cup finals held every four years.

The loss of certain sports rights has led to a 'bleeding' of sports broadcasting talent. Murray Walker, who joined the BBC in the immediate post-war years following in the footsteps of his father Graham, left to join ITV's team once the contract for Grand Prix racing switched channel. Similarly, presenters Des Lynam and Jimmy Hill, stalwarts of the BBC's coverage of football during the 1980s and 90s have moved to ITV and Sky Sports respectively in search of live football on which to comment. Even sports producers and editors are not immune from jumping ship; one of the BBC's top sports executives, Brian Barwick, left in 1997 to head up ITV's renewed attempts to claw back its own reputation in sport. The ageing profile of many of the top commentators has also caused the BBC to lose some of its 'cosiness' in the production of sport, with figures like Harry Carpenter in boxing and Peter O'Sullivan in horse-racing hanging up their lip microphones at a time of rapid transformation in the coverage of sport.

The BBC has had to change its strategy in the televised sport environment to stabilize its position, often through some 'unholy' alliances with the very competition that has placed its role in the genre in jeopardy. When BSkyB won the rights to English Premier League football, the BBC operated as secondary partners in the deal capturing the rights to screen edited highlights of the top-flight English game, allowing it to reintroduce Match of the Day. This manoeuvre has been duplicated in Scottish league football and one-day Sunday League cricket.

The market for sports rights, therefore, has become far more complex in the way rights are 'bundled' or 'unbundled' between live coverage, delayed transmission and recorded highlights. Also, public-service broadcasters have forged more and more ties with pay-TV channels in order to secure sports content. Thus, ITV transmits the FA Cup Final and one semi-final, courtesy of its agreement with BSkyB which owns the rights but cannot own exclusive coverage due to broadcasting regulations. Similarly, Channel 4's foray into cricket in a deal worth £103 million over four years was underwritten by an agreement with BSkyB, which now has the rights to the Lords Test in any given series for the duration of the deal.

BBC radio sport

The competition for sports also extends to radio. One of the success stories for BBC Sport has been the rejuvenation of its radio sports output. Ironically, it almost marked a return to a time when BBC Sport actually meant radio, as opposed to television coverage. Thanks in part to the UK-wide Radio 5 Live news and sport station, the BBC has been able to command a pre-eminent position in the coverage of sport on radio. Central to this has been the ability of BBC radio to offer live football commentary on English Premier League matches, only available otherwise on the subscription-based Sky Sports television.

The BBC, which has the rights to the Premiership until 2001, was willing to pay almost £12 million for them in 1998, and they have become the cornerstone of the increasing popular Radio 5 Live. In 1999, the station had an audience reach of 5.2 million each week, over 100,000 up year on year (*Broadcast,* 19 March 1999). It also has secured the radio rights to Formula One motor-racing, the Olympics until 2008 and UK athletics.

Radio 5 Live has not only offered more radio sport, supplemented by innumerable radio phone-ins, it has also extended certain areas of sports journalism. In particular its investigative programmes such as *Inside Edge* have become increasingly important in providing a range of sports journalism which goes beyond the mere reporting of sport and examines the broader range of social, economic and even political issues connected with sports.

However, as in television, radio has become an increasingly crowded and competitive marketplace in the UK during the 1990s. The commercial station Talk Radio is also keen to extend its sporting portfolio – although aware of the danger that too much sport may alienate female listeners (see Chapter 7). During 1999, the station successfully bid for a number of one-off sporting events which in the past BBC radio would have been expected to cover. The controversial World Heavyweight boxing match between Lennox Lewis and Evander Holyfield was carried live by Talk Radio and, perhaps more significantly in April of that year, it secured the rights to cover England's 1999/2000 winter cricket tour of South Africa and Zimbabwe.

Even in radio, the old certainties no longer hold and the complexities of the bundling and unbundling of sports rights looks set to continue as new delivery systems all attempt to secure certain sports as core programming. Three crucial developments in sports rights in the future

which are likely to add significantly to this complex picture digital and
pay-per-view broadcasting, and the developing use of the internet.

Power play: digital and pay-per-view sport

The digital revolution that is impacting on sport has once more transformed the power play of media sport. Metaphors of democracy and
open access have greeted the so-called information age since the 1960s,
but it would appear that, as the pace of technological development
reaches a state of hyper-intensity towards 2000, issues around the
liberalization of communication are paramount.

The regulation of new communications technologies has proved
problematic as the pace of change has occurred too fast for state and
supra-state policies to keep up with the often divergent needs of global
corporate interests and end users or citizens (Kofler, 1998). Sport, as a
global enthusiasm that can unite disparate communities, as well as consolidate cultural distinctions, is once more at the cutting edge of these
developments.

The production and consumption of sport cultures are set to change
as these wider shifts in the media and communications industries take
hold both among the traditional broadcasters and the more recent
arrivals in the marketplace.

Terrestrial channels are also investing heavily in digital television as
a means of supporting their tight schedules for screening sport. In order
to gain optimal use of their rights the BBC has begun to screen sport on
its digital channel BBC Choice. This allows it to cover action previously
given restricted airtime in the terrestrial schedule. The arrangement has
proved especially beneficial in the coverage of tennis where there may
be need to cover more than one or two matches at any given time, a tactic
used during the 1999 Australian Open and Wimbledon tournament.

ITV has also utilized its digital channels. Champions League ties that
may now involve two English clubs can be screened simultaneously, with
one game appearing on terrestrial television and the other on either
Granada Plus or Carlton Select. Finally, Channel 4's predicament of eating
up its scheduling with cricket is in part solved by alternating its coverage of the sport with horse-racing on its digital service Channel 4 'B'.

The arrival in the UK sportmarket of pay-per-view television sport
also looks set to make inroads into the consumption patterns of sports
fans (see previous chapter). While boxing has been the sport at the forefront of attempts by BSkyB in the UK to develop a market, the unlikely
setting of Oxford United's Manor Ground saw the first pay-per-view

football match in Britain take place in February 1999. Ironically, the most likely outcome of this development will be to see the large clubs get richer and the smaller clubs, such as Oxford United, struggle to exist in their present form as pay-per-view strengthens the financial position of the teams which can draw a paying television audience.

Despite the various figures which are often given for the potential growth in this market, the amount of money which pay-per-view will generate for both broadcasters and the powerful clubs remains uncertain. However, even given the level of opposition and the cultural arguments made for the centrality of sport in national life – in Spain the showing of Barcelona v Real Madrid on pay-per-view raised concerns about such a 'national game' not being available free to air – the growth looks set to continue, however incrementally.

There are in 1999, 6.5 million pay-TV households in the UK, of which about 600,000 are digital and the vast bulk of these are satellite digital (*The Guardian*, 6 May 1999). While projected growth in uptake is always difficult to predict, there is no doubt that digital television is here to stay, not least because the government will switch off the analogue signal to television sets at some stage over the next 10–15 years. Thus, while the numbers remain relatively small at present, the impact on television's relationship with sport will be substantial.

Longer term, of course, sport relies on competition to flourish and the danger of creating a wealthy minority in any sport is that in the long run competition dies. This has been recognized to some extent in the US, where gridiron football has resisted the temptation to go pay-per-view and remains free to air. As Tom Lappin comments:

> The sport itself stays competitive by ensuring that the best young
> players join the weaker teams, maintaining a system of checks and
> balances. Strange that in America, the bastion of financial
> libertarianism, they should impose such restrictions to keep their sport
> alive. (*The Scotsman*, 25 February 1999).

In the UK this longer-term vision appears to be largely absent.

The packaging of channels and sports rights across other distribution platforms means that television organizations get more 'bang for their buck', effectively selling their product more than once, particularly where advertisers are concerned. The movement into this type of competition also raises questions about the funding of the BBC, and its use of the licence fee to open new markets. It is a problematic that broadcasting impresario Michael Grade picked up on shortly after the Corporation's initial partnership with BSkyB occurred in 1992:

> The BBC may hope that partnership with the Murdoch empire will
> soften the edges of the leaders and comment in the News International
> papers during its argument with government for the renewal of the
> BBC charter and licence. That is a short-term gain to be measured
> against long-term suicide. (Quoted in Haynes, 1998, p. 104)

Further developments in the distribution of television services have
forced the BBC to position itself strategically as one of the leading producers of quality broadcasting content, not just in the UK, but globally.

The BBC's news services in both television and radio have merged to
compete worldwide with, among others, the American news channel
Cable News Network (CNN), in order to capitalize on its 'bi-media' organization. Sport clearly plays a significant role in any news service, and
the 24-hour tracking of major sport around the world, and the immediacy with which it can be delivered to the audience, provides new opportunities for the BBC to consolidate its market position.

Power play: cricket's last stand

The arrival of a multi-channel television age and the convergence of
sports–media interests also has ramifications for sport beyond its historical dalliance with the medium. These changes have not only affected
football. Cricket and both rugby codes have radically transformed their
relationships with the media during the 1990s in what has often been an
ideological struggle between tradition and modernity. We noted in
Chapter 3 that the globalization of sports–media has produced many
conflicts of interest, quite often born of a tension between the historical
ideals of sport and the demands of business.

In 1998 the England and Wales Cricket Board successfully lobbied to
have Test cricket partially removed from government regulations that
restricted their sale of rights to non-pay television channels, placing
the events on a 'B' list that allowed cable and satellite television full-live
coverage with the proviso that highlights must be screened on a terrestrial channel. This was an economic decision as much as a political one,
as cricket needed more leverage in its negotiations with television. It
was also a significant cultural decision, for it signalled that test cricket
no longer had the national resonance it once had alongside the FA
Cup Final, Wimbledon and the Grand National.

Cricket was one of the first sports to find the media taking an interest in the running of the sport back in the 1970s during the 'Packer
Affair' (Barnett, 1990). Since that radical overhaul of the game, the introduction of more regular one-day international games, floodlit matches,

and colourful kits, has promised a series of 'new dawns' that have attempted to transform the image as much as the content of cricket.

The rhetoric of the latest wave of optimism about the game ('Cricket to unleash its full potential', *Sports Business,* January 1999; and 'Cricket's fresh delivery tries to bowl over fans', *Sunday Business,* 11 April 1999), much of it leading up to the 1999 World Cup held in England, has emphasized the need to build a new audience for cricket, away from its male-oriented, ageing demographics.

A major problem for domestic club cricket has been waning interest of spectators in the ground and an indifferent television audience. This has turned sponsors away from the sport, with the 1998 sponsor of the one-day Sunday League, Axa Life, terminating its affiliation and turning to the more lucrative field of FA Cup football.

One benefit for the sport, however, has undoubtedly been BSkyB's blanket coverage of England's tours abroad. The broadening of spectrum and dedicated channels has allowed cricket to dominate the schedule of Sky Sports into the small hours of the morning. This level of coverage of England's winter tours was unprecedented before satellite television took an interest.

The coverage has proved very popular for a specialist audience and has breathed new life into the actual spectating of the sport. Television has also provided publicity for the growing number of supporters, known as the 'Barmy Army', who travel around the world like a sporting carnival.

In England, a new two-division structure of the County Championship has been aimed at increasing the competitiveness of the sport, cutting out the number of meaningless mid-table matches. The one-day game has also introduced more day–night games as the antiquated stadia at many county grounds have received facelifts and been given permanent floodlights for the first time. The concessions sport gives to television, therefore, can produce quite radical shifts in how sport is managed.

For a sport like cricket, the transformations are born of necessity. The game needs exposure not only to make it financially viable, but to promote the sport to a wider audience and encourage new talent to filter in to its arena rather than another.

Power play: no pay, no play; rugby union

In the world of rugby, both Union and League have made similar transitions to those experienced by cricket. For rugby union, long-awaited professionalization represents a major ideological shift in the ethics of the sport from the era of 'gentlemen and players' (Dunning and Sheard, 1979).

The migration of star players from Union to League during the 1980s and 1990s forced the amateur ideals of the former to collapse. Rugby union in the nations of the Southern Hemisphere had long since taken the step towards payment for play that had sustained the appeal of the sport and made Australia, New Zealand and, latterly, South Africa the dominant forces in world rugby (News Corporation holds the rights to all three nations in a combined deal worth £350 million over ten years).

In England, the transition to professional clubs and a more struc-tured league system was aided by a five-year television deal between the Rugby Football Union (RFU) and BSkyB worth £87.5 million from 1996 to 2001. The bulk of this money secured exclusive live coverage of England's internationals in the Five Nations Championship. The dis-appearance of England's games from their historic association with the BBC programme Grandstand prompted further political outrage from sporting traditionalists that 'the nation' was being deprived of a signi-ficant cultural event. While the remaining fixtures involving Scotland, Wales, Ireland and France (and, from 2000, Italy) continued on the BBC, England's decision to chase increased streams of revenue from television capitalized on the new era of rights management and promo-tional culture in sport.

Like cricket, rugby union has suffered from too much mediocrity at club level, where a few clubs dominate and the remainder merely survive. New tournaments, such as the European Cup inaugurated in 1995/96, have attempted to introduce new levels of competition to the sport. While this may produce further income for rugby, including a £40 million deal with BSkyB, the Europeanization of the game has also produced a further congestion of fixtures, stretching the traditional playing season into summer months, as it caters to the global needs of television (Maguire and Tuck, 1997).

Furthermore, in spite of wider television coverage, enabling the sport to double the level of sponsorship courting the game, from £10 million in 1994 to £22 million in 1998 (*Sports Business*, April 1999), the linkage of sponsors to rugby union, in terms of public perception, has been negligible (a survey in 1998 showed that less than ten per cent of 20,000 people interviewed could identify the sport with a particular brand – *Sports Business*, February 1999). In Scotland, the poor profile of the sport and continuing political wrangling over the governance of the game caused the main brand sponsor 'Famous Grouse' to end its association with the national team.

'Mad dogs and League players go out in the midday sun'

Rugby league has undergone equally dramatic change in its attempt to build its appeal beyond its traditional constituency in the North of England. The sport has been in a state of flux throughout the 1990s, again driven by television money from BSkyB. The transformation in the coverage of rugby league, such as the hype that surrounds the Allied Dunbar Premiership discussed in Chapter 4, illustrates the new promotional culture that has sharpened the business ethics now prevalent in mainstream sport.

As the chief executive of the Warrington Wolves, Peter Deakin, has commented:

> You have to play fair by Sky, who are major sponsors as well as
> broadcasters. You can't sell them the rights and then want to change
> the rules. (*Financial Times*, 5 March 1999)

The realization that the sport had to adapt to the needs of television, and not necessarily the other way round, parallels a process happening in the whole of sport. Strategies to remove the 'cloth cap and ferret' image of rugby league have brought the game to the South-East of England with the founding of the London Broncos, fronted by well-known stars like Martin Offiah.

In only its second season the club managed to reach the showcase event Challenge Cup final at Wembley in 1999. In many respects, new ventures such as this confirm the portability many team sports now have to exhibit. Traditional ties to locality and community are not necessarily key to sporting success, especially when the target audience is television viewers not spectators at the ground. Rugby league has attempted to confront these shifts in the identity of the sport, where global audiences are as important, if not greater than, those closer to home.

Further evidence of the repositioning of rugby league to suit the global strategy of media–sport interests can be seen in the shift of the league season from autumn/winter to spring/summer. Images of rugby players covered from head-to-toe in mud are long gone. The movement of the league programme was instigated by the scheduling demands of television, and the new structures the globalization that the governing body of the sport imposed.

The new system allows the British game to alternate with the season 'down-under' in Australia, so that the global 'footprints' of each do not collide, producing a virtually twelve-month diet of the sport for television. The mobility of teams is matched by the mobility of the entire league structure, an unprecedented level of manipulation in media sport.

Power play: the Internet: a new sporting superhighway

The globalization process that has transformed the organization of sport is also affecting the traditional ways in which media sport can be produced, delivered and consumed. Information and communication technologies (ICTs) have opened up new possibilities for sport to convey its message and create new markets. The rhetoric that accompanies the interactive era of digital telecommunication suggests a new 'computer age' in a rich equality-laden 'information society'.

Sport, as well as other facets of our daily lives, is set to be dramatically affected by the growing importance of the Internet, virtual reality and other multimedia applications, placing more control in the hands of the consumer who may choose from a vast array of services through many-to-many communication. However, the rampant optimism that drives the promotional strategies of large computer-based corporations, is only heard and acted upon by a small technological élite (Loader, 1998).

In analysing the rapidly expanding 'online' services for the sports fan, we must guard critically against any oversimplified linear approach to technological change in media sport and its promise to empower its audience. While the interactive possibilities of the World Wide Web of sport are exciting, as we have argued throughout the book, any deeper understanding of media technologies of sport requires a concern for social, economic, political and cultural processes in order to appreciate the complex ways in which power is structured and manipulated.

An interesting case study comes from one of the most original producers of sport on the Internet, Quokka Sports. Founded in 1995, Quokka Sports describes itself as a 'digital sports entertainment company' that uses ICTs to develop a form of 'immersion' within the event. The promotional text on the company's website provides a description of what it considers the future of media sport will be like:

> Quokka Sports Immersion™ seeks to remove the barriers to the most immersive or intense experiences. We want our audience to know it in their heads and feel it in their stomachs. We would like to measure our success in their adrenal glands. The opportunities are as obvious as the challenges. By telling the story from the inside out – by giving the world a glimpse of the inner workings of the event from the unique perspective provided by technology, we can create a next generation spectator experience that is as informative as it is engaging. We give sports fans what they are always screaming for – more.
> (http://www.quokka.com/company/immersion.html)

Behind the advertising rhetoric it is clear that the company is seeking to transform the one-to-many communication of televised sport. The process of 'immersion' is illustrated by one of the company's most successful ventures, the production of a website for the 1997–8 Whitbread Around the World Yacht Race. The nine-month challenge to navigate the world's oceans successfully was obviously too long and too dispersed for coverage by television. In a unique experiment daily updates were provided on each crew, posted on the Internet by the boats themselves.

Regular e-mail was accompanied by audio and visual material, and other information of consequence to the race, such as the weather, was used to produce a broader picture of what the competing crews were experiencing. The multimedia experience provided a more enriched narrative of events, allowing regular users of the site to become emotionally attached to the crews, enabling them to identify with the ups and downs of the race in a quite personal way.

This case study is evidence of how innovations in media sport have evolved quite rapidly in the late 1990s. One interesting feature of the Internet is that it places the power and responsibility of communication in the hands of competitors themselves. This unparalleled access to sports performers has rarely occurred in mainstream television, with the rare exception of video-diaries produced by athletes themselves. However, as we have suggested, these innovations that warrant new avenues of engagement with our sporting heroes remain firmly embedded in the interests of big business.

As with any commercial operation, Quokka Sports sells its audiences to advertisers and sponsors, whose logos adorn and frame the various web pages on view. The company has found investment from established sports organizations, such as the IOC, and multi-national digital media companies, including the Intel Corporation, to help fund the new media sport venture. Leading sports–media organizations, from ESPN to News Corporation, have also invested heavily in new ICTs, developing their own ancillary sports sites to bolster and cross-promote their regular television output.

In the UK, the BBC has also pioneered the convergence of traditional broadcast media and the Internet to produce new ways to consume sport. This has included audio and visual information from Radio 4's *Test Match Special* team covering England's tour of Australia in 1998, to Radio 5 Live football commentaries on the 'Old Firm' match in Glasgow to a global audience via the Web in May 1999. These examples of a paradigm shift in the cultural experience of media sport may well be transformative, but the main players in the economic and political success of sport on the Internet remain those with global corporate interests.

Endgame

As we enter a new century, sport has become intertwined with the media to a greater extent than at any other time during the last 100 years. As we write, alliances between various media companies throughout Europe – such as BSkyB and Canal Plus – are being negotiated in an attempt to secure a stranglehold of any pan-European pay-television market. In Italy, for example, a consortium of football clubs has secured a 12 per cent stake in the pay-TV company Stream, in which the largest shareholders are News Corporation (part of Murdoch's media empire) and Telecom Italia. Football clubs such as Manchester United and Barcelona have also set up television channels in order to maximize any revenues which they can derive from the digital television revolution.

This jockeying for position will continue as long as sport, and football in particular, is viewed as the bridgehead which will allow new delivery systems to establish the patterns of market domination required to make them profitable.

Anybody who wishes to understand sport, whether an academic, a fan or a journalist, needs to understand the economic and political forces which are shaping and reshaping the contemporary sporting experience. For the media industries, sport offers a 'product' which can be transformed into a valuable commercial entity delivering readers, viewers, advertisers, customers and subscribers. Sport, it appears, is often only too happy to oblige as a willing victim in this process.

However, media sport is too important to be left solely to the political economists. It also offers a rich arena of myth, image, narrative and a compulsive world of story-telling. At a cultural and textual level the images that a community project onto the sporting field, and the manner in which that image gets refracted through various media, tell us much about our individual and collective identities. They also expose in a very public manner our values, priorities, hopes, dreams and aspirations like few other cultural forms. It is a publicly mediated arena which can be exciting, exhilarating, yet also inconsequential, but all the time saturated with the social forces and ideological energies which run through society.

Any analysis of the sport–media nexus needs to be alert to the importance of both approaches to the subject. Studies of the cultural dimension of sport often require sporting development to be placed within the context of a changing and increasingly complex media infrastructure. At the same time, the sensitivities people often bring to sporting identities more often than not originate in social spaces outside the media and can be rooted in deeper structures of class, gender, ethnicity and nationality. It remains important to locate media sport within the wider political, economic and cultural context within which it is both produced and consumed.

A study of media sport involves locating it firmly within the evolving cultural industries. Sport is now part of a wider business infrastructure which includes the audio-visual industries, music, publishing and new media. Of course, in the US, sport has been part of this entertainment nexus for a considerable length of time and aspects of this relationship are beginning to emerge in Europe, despite resistance from more traditional forms of sporting organization and fandom.

Specific patterns of media development both in the UK and elsewhere in Europe have seen the extension of market forces and increased competition within this, and other public-service sectors of the economy. The market lies at the centre of the new economic orthodoxy. In addition, the rise and increasing integration of the service and cultural industries both within and across economies has helped to propel professional sport into a closer relationship with media.

Having helped create the political and economic climate in which global entrepreneurs and conglomerates could harness developing information technologies to make inroads into the previously closeted world of broadcast media, governments are only now becoming aware of some of the cultural implications of such a process. The result has been that arguments about the need to regulate or intervene are becoming more central to political debate in both the UK and Europe.

National governments and, to an extent, the EU are aware of the cultural and, by association, political importance of sport. However, they also see the cultural industries as increasingly key drivers in the economy, and as a source of employment and wealth creation. It is that balancing act between commerce and culture that sports have to confront as they become ever more closely identified with the media. As the television rights to top sports are sold to the highest bidder Will Hutton has noted that:

> for viewers the entry ticket to this world is the money to afford the
> subscriptions that are three times higher than the BBC licence fee . . .
> Great national sporting events . . . cease to be shared by us all . . .
> Both the sport and national life are therefore diminished.
> (Hutton, 1995, p. 222)

The longer-term danger is of course that what makes sport culturally different and commercially viable in the first place may be eroded over a period of time if short-term financial interests are prioritized.

Into tomorrow

We began this book by arguing that what appeared to mark the progress of sport throughout this century was the extent that it mattered to people. We also suggested that one of the significant characteristics of contemporary sport was the way in which it now appeared to matter to a wider range of publics, many of whom view sport as something to be used commercially as part of the media entertainment industry.

We would argue that throughout the century, despite various trials and tribulations, sport's relationship with the media has been one of mutual benefit. The broadcast media in particular have helped create truly national and international sporting events, and in the process given democratic access to millions of people, consumers and citizens. We now stand on the brink of both a new millennium and a new era in the sports–media marriage. However, it appears, unlike the century that is passing, that we are entering an era based on media exclusivity rather than universal access. We now have a media landscape which, while dominated by the rhetoric of extending viewer choice, none the less addresses us not as citizens, but rather by our ability to pay for the consumption of new – and not so new – services.

The national and international governing bodies of sport, governments and media regulators need to be aware that, without a change in political will and a commitment to look further ahead than simply the next season, this process of fragmentation will continue apace.

It has proven to be notoriously difficult to predict future developments in both the media and sporting industries. As we demonstrated at the beginning of the book, few people could have foreseen the transformation of sport which has occurred in the last decade. As we look towards the next decade and a new millennium we can perhaps say with some degree of certainty that for fans, media executives and even academics, sport – in the fields of politics, economics and culture – will continue to matter.

Bibliography

Abel S. and Long A. (1996). Event Sponsorship: does it work?, *Admap*, December

Aldgate A. (1979). *Cinema and History: British newsreels and the Spanish Civil War*. London: Scolar Press

Anderson B. (1991). *Imagined Communities: Reflections on the Origin and the Spread of Nationalism* (2nd edn). London: Verso

Aris S. (1990). *Sportsbiz: Inside the Sports Business*. London: Hutchinson

Arlott J. (1968). Over now to . . . The story of cricket on the air. In *Armchair Cricket* (Johnstone B. ed.). London: BBC

Arundel J. and Roche M. (1998). Media Sport and Local Identity: British Rugby League and Sky TV. In *Sport, Popular Culture and Identity* (Roche M. ed.). Aachen: Meyer and Meyer

Baillie R. ed. (1994). *100 Years of Scottish Sport*. Edinburgh: Mainstream

Bairner A. (1994). Football and the idea of Scotland. In *Sport in the Making of the Scottish Nation: Ninety-minute patriots?* (Jarvie G. and Walker G. eds.). Leicester: Leicester University Press

—— (1999). Sport, Politics and the Press in Northern Ireland, paper presented at *Sport, Media and National Identity* conference, Stirling Media Research Institute/Sports Studies Department, University of Stirling, Scotland, 5 February.

Baker A. (1997). A Left/Right Combination: Populism and depression-Era Boxing Films. In *Out of Bounds: sports media and the politics of identity* (Baker A. and Boyd T. eds.). Bloomington and Indianapolis: Indiana University Press

Barnett S. (1990). *Games and Sets: The Changing Face of Sport on Television*. London: BFI

Beattie G. (1997). *On the Ropes: boxing as a way of life*. London: Indigo

Bellamy R.V. Jnr. (1998). The Evolving Television Sports Marketplace. In *MediaSport* (Wenner L.A. ed.). London: Routledge

Billig M. (1995). *Banal Nationalism*. London: Sage

Biscomb K., Flatten K. and Matheson H. (1998). Read the Paper, Play the Sport: A Decade of Gender Change. In *The Production and Consumption of Sports Culture* (Merkel U., Lines G. and McDonald I. eds.). Brighton: LSA

Blain N. and Boyle R. (1994). Battling Along the Boundaries: Scottish identity-marking in sports journalism. In *Sport in the Making of the*

Scottish Nation: Ninety-minute patriots? (Jarvie G. and Walker G. eds.). Leicester: Leicester University Press

—— (1998). Sport as Real Life: Media, Sport and Culture In *The Media: An Introduction* (Briggs A. and Cobley P. eds.). London: Longman

Blain N., Boyle R. and O'Donnell H. (1993). *Sport and National Identity in the European Media*. Leicester: Leicester University Press

Blain N. and O'Donnell H. (1998). European Sports Journalism and its Readers during Euro 96. In *Sport, Popular Culture and Identity* (Roche M. ed.). Aachen: Meyer and Meyer

Bough F. (1980). *Cue Frank!* London: MacDonald Futura

Bourdieu P. (1988). *Distinction: A Social Critique of the Judgement of Taste*. London: Routledge

Boyle R. (1992). From our Gaelic fields: radio, sport and nation in post-partition Ireland. *Media, Culture and Society*, 14 (4), 623–36

—— (1995). Football and Cultural Identity in Glasgow and Liverpool. PhD. Thesis. University of Stirling, Scotland

Boyle R. and Haynes R. (1996). 'The grand old game': football, media and identity in Scotland. *Media, Culture and Society*, 18 (4), 549–64

—— (1998) Modernising Tradition? The Changing Face of British Football. In *The Production and Consumption of Sports Cultures*, Lines G. and McDonald I. (eds.). Brighton: LSA

Bradley J. (1994). Ethnicity; the Irish in Scotland – football, politics and identity. *Innovation*. 7 (4), 423–39

Brewer J.D. (1992). Sectarianism and racism, and their parallels and differ-ences. *Ethnic and Racial Studies*, 15 (3), July

Briggs A. (1961). *The History of Broadcasting in the UK*. Vol. 1: *The Birth of Broadcasting*. Oxford: Oxford University Press

Brown A. (1998). *Fanatics: Power, Identity and Fandom in Football*. London: Routledge

Brown C.G. (1993). *The People in the Pews: Religion and Society in Scotland since 1780*. Dundee: Economic and Social History of Scotland

Brunsdon C. (1991). Satellite Dishes and the landscape of taste. *New Formations*, 15, 23–42

Bryant J., Zillmann D. and Raney A.A. (1998). Violence and the Enjoy-ment of Media Sports. In *MediaSport*. (Wenner L.A. ed.). London: Routledge

BSkyB (1998). *Annual Report 1998*. London

Buford B. (1991). *Among The Thugs*. London: Secker and Warburg

Burn G. (1986). *Pocket Money: Bad-Boys, Business-Heads and Boom-Time Snooker*. London: Heinemann

Buscombe E. ed. (1975). *Football on Television*. London: BFI

Butcher M. (1999). Football in chaos over 'New Bosman' ruling. *The Observer*, 10 January

Butler B. (1997). 1948: the Way It Was. In *50 Years of Sports Report* (Adams A. ed.). London: CollinsWillow

Cashmore E. (1982). *Black Sportsmen*. London: Routledge & Kegan Paul

—— (1996). *Making Sense of Sports* 2nd edn. London: Routledge

Chase M. and Shaw C. (1989). The dimensions of nostalgia. In *The Imagined Past: history and nostalgia*. (Shaw C. and Chase M. eds.). Manchester: Manchester University Press

Clapson M. (1992). *A Bit of a Flutter: Popular gambling and English society, c.1823–1961*. Manchester: Manchester University Press

Clarke A. and Clarke J. (1982). Highlights and action replays. In *Sport, Culture and Society*. (Hargreaves J. ed.). London: Routledge & Kegan Paul.

Clarke J. and Critcher C. (1985). *The Devil Makes Work: Leisure in Capitalist Britain*. Basingstoke: Macmillan

CNN/Sports Illustrated (1999). Up in the air *<http://cnnsi.com/basketball/ nba/news/1999/01/07/nba_comebac/index.html*

Cohen P. (1988). Tarzan and the Jungle Bunnie: Class, Race and Sex in Popular Culture. *New Formations*. 5, 25–30

Conn D. (1997). *The Football Business: Fair game in the '90s?* Edinburgh: Mainstream

Connell R. (1987). *Gender and Power: Society, the Person and Sexual Politics*. Cambridge: Polity Press

—— (1997). *Masculinities*. Cambridge: Polity Press

Corner J. (1995). *Television Form and Public Address*. London: Edward Arnold

Cosgrove S. (1998). The Tartan Army, France 98. *The Observer Guide to the World Cup*, 7 June

Cramer J.A. (1994). Conversations with women sports journalists. In *Women, Media and Sport: Challenging the gender order*. (Creedon P. ed.). London: Sage

Creedon P. (1994). *Women, Media and Sport: Challenging the gender order*. London: Sage

Critcher C. (1992). Is there anything on the box? Leisure studies and media studies. *Leisure Studies*, 11 (2)

Cronin M. (1997). Which Nation, Which Flag: Boxing and National Identities in Ireland. *International Review for the Sociology of Sport*, 32 (2), 131–46

Curran J. (1978). Capitalism and control of the press, 1800–1975. In *Mass Communication and Society* (Curran J., Gurevitch M. and Woollacott J. eds.). pp. 195–230. London: Edward Arnold

Davies H. (1990). *The Glory Game* 2nd edn. Edinburgh: Mainstream Publishers (orig. published 1972)

Davies P. (1990). *All Played Out: The full story of Italia '90*. London: Heinemann

Davis R.D. and Harris O. (1998). Race and Ethnicity in the US Sports Media. In *MediaSport* (Wenner L.A. ed.). London: Routledge

Deford F. (1999). A Man For His Time, *Sports Illustrated: Michael Jordan A Tribute*. 20 January

Denney R. (1989). *The Astonished Muse*. New Brunswick, Canada: Transaction Publishers

Donegan L. (1997). *Four-iron in the soul*. London: Penguin

Duke V. and Crolley L. (1996). *Football, Nationality and the State*. Manchester: Manchester University Press

Dunning E. (1989). The Figurational Approach to Sport and Leisure. In *Leisure for Leisure: Critical Essays* (Rojek C. ed.). London: Routledge

Dunning E., Murphy P. and Williams J. (1988). *The Roots of Football Hooliganism: An historical and Sociological Study*. London: Routledge

Dunning E. and Rojek C. eds. (1992). *Sport and Leisure in the Civilising Process*. London: Macmillan

Dunning E. and Sheard K. (1979). *Gentlemen, Barbarians and Players: A Sociological Study of the Development of Rugby*. Oxford: Oxford University Press

Dyson M.E. (1993). Be Like Mike?: Michael Jordan and the pedagogy of desire. *Cultural Studies*, 7 (1), 64–72

Easton S. and Mackie P. (1998). When football came home: a case history of the sponsorship activity at Euro '96. *International Journal of Advertising*, 17, 99–114

Eco U. (1986). Sports Chatter. *Travels in Hyper-Reality*. London: Picador

Fielding R. (1972). *The American Newsreel, 1911–1967*. Norman: University of Oklahoma Press

Finn G. and Giulianotti R. (1998). Scottish fans, not English football hooligans!: Scots, Scottishness and Scottish football. In *Fanatics! power, identity and fandom in football*. (Brown A. ed.). London: Routledge

Fishlock T. (1987). *The State of America*. London: Faber & Faber

Frei M. (1997). *Italy: The Unfinished Revolution*. London: Mandarin

Fynn A. and Guest L. (1994). *Out of Time*. London: Simon and Schuster

Gardiner S. (1998). The Law and Hate Speech: 'Ooh Aah Cantona' and the demonisation of 'the other'. In *Fanatics!: power, identity and fandom in football* (Brown A. ed.). London: Routledge

Germain J. (1994). *In Soccer Wonderland*. London: Booth-Clibborn Editions

Gilroy P. (1993). *Small Acts: Thoughts on the Politics of Black Cultures*. London: Serpent's Tail

Giulianotti R. (1991). The Tartan Army in Italy: The Case for the Carnivalesque. *The Sociological Review*, 39 (3)

—— (1994). The Patriots' Tour of Duty, *The Herald*, 22 January

Giulianotti R. and Williams J. eds. (1994). *Games Across Frontiers: Football, Identity and Modernity*. Aldershot: Arena

Glanville B. (1999). *Football Memories*. London: Virgin

Goldlust J. (1987). *Playing For Keeps: Sport, the media and society*. Melbourne: Longman

Goodwin P. (1998). *Television under the Tories: Broadcasting Policy 1979–1997*. London: BFI

Guinness Sports Yearbook (1994). London: Guinness

Guttmann A. (1994). *Games and Empires: Modern Sports and Cultural Imperialism*. New York: Columbia University Press

Hall A.E. (1985). How should we theorize sport in a capitalist patriarchy? *Internatioal Review for the Sociology of Sport*. 20, 1

Hall W. and Parkinson M. (1973). *Football Report: An Anthology of soccer*. London: Sportsmans Bookclub

Hamilton I. (1994). A Victory of Sorts. *Weekend Guardian*, 4 June

Hargreaves Jen. (1994). *Sporting Females*. London: Routledge

—— (1997). Women's Boxing and Related Activities: Introducing Images and Meanings. *Body & Society*, 4 (1), 77–98

Hargreaves John (1986). *Sport, Power and Culture*. London: Polity

Haynes R. (1995). *The Football Imagination: The rise of football fanzine culture*. Aldershot: Arena

—— (1998). A pageant of sound and vision: Football's relationship with television, 1936–60. *The International Journal of the History of Sport*, 15 (1), 211–26

—— (1999). 'There's many a slip twixt the eye and the lip': An exploratory history of football broadcasts and running commentaries 1927–39, *International Review of the Sociology of Sport*, 32 (2)

Hearn J. (1994). Research in Men and Masculinities: Some Sociological Issues and Possibilities. *Australian and New Zealand Journal of Sociology*, 30 (1), 47–70

Hey S. (1993). The Kop's Last Stand. *The Observer*, 2 May

Hill D. (1989). *'Out of his Skin': The John Barnes Phenomenon*. London: Faber and Faber

Hoberman J. (1984). *Sport and Political Ideology*. London: Heinemann

—— (1997). *Darwin's Athletes: How sport has damaged black America and preserved the myth of race*. New York: Mariner Books

Holland B.L. (1997). Surviving leisure time racism: the burden of racial harassment on Britain's black footballers. *Leisure Studies*, 16, 261–77

Holt R. (1989). *Sport and the British*. Oxford: Oxford University Press

Hopcraft A. (1988). *The Football Man* 2nd edn. (orig. published 1968). London: Sportspages

Hornby N. (1992). *Fever Pitch: a fan's life*. London: Victor Gollancz

—— ed. (1993). *My Favourite Year*. London: Witherby

Horne J., Jary D. and Tomlinson A. eds. (1987). *Sport, Leisure and Social Relations*. London: Routledge & Kegan Paul

Horsman M. (1997). *Sky High: The inside story of BSkyB*. London: Orion

Hoskins C., McFadyen S. and Finn A. (1997). *Global Television and Film*. Oxford: Oxford University Press

Houlihan B. (1994). *Sport and International Politics*. Hemel Hempstead: Harvester Wheatsheaf

—— (1997). Sport, national identity and public policy. *Nations and Nationalism*, 3 (1), 113–37

Hudson R. (1968). The Commentary: Radio. In *Armchair Cricket 1968* (Johnston B. ed.). London: BBC Publications

Humphries T. (1996). *Green Fields: Gaelic Sport in Ireland*. London: Weidenfeld and Nicolson

Hutton W. (1995) *The State We're In*. London: Jonathan Cape

Inglis S. (1987). *Soccer in the Dock: A history of British football scandals 1900 to 1965*. London: Willow Books

James C.L.R. (1963). *Beyond a Boundary*. London: Hutchinson

Jarvie G. and Maguire J. (1994). *Sport and Leisure in social thought*. London: Routledge

Jarvie G. and Reid I. (1997). Race Relations, sociology of sport and the new politics of race and racism. *Leisure Studies*, 16, 211–19

Jarvie G. and Walker G. eds. (1994). *Sport in the Making of the Scottish Nation: Ninety-minute patriots?* Leicester: Leicester University Press

Jarvie J. (1991). Sport, Racism and Ethnicity. In *Sport, Race and Ethnicity* (Jarvie G. ed.). London: Falmer

Jefferson T. (1998). Muscle, 'Hard Men' and 'Iron' Mike Tyson: Reflections on desire, Anxiety and the Embodiment of Masculinity. *Body & Society*, 4 (1), 77–98

Jenson J. (1992). Fandom as Pathology: The Consequences of Characterization. In *The Adoring Audience: Fan Culture and Popular Media* (Lewis, L.A. ed.). London: Routledge

Johnston B. ed. (1968). *Armchair Cricket 1968*. London: BBC Publications

Jones S.G. (1992). *Sport, politics and the working class*. Manchester: Manchester University Press

Jordan M. (1994). *Rare Air: Michael on Michael*. San Francisco: Collins Publishers

Katz D. (1994). *Just Do It: The Nike Spirit in the Corporate World*. Holbrook, MA: Adams Media Corporation

Kelly S.F. ed. (1993). *A Game of Two Halves*. London: Mandarin

King A. (1998). *End of the Terraces: The Transformation of English Football in the 1990s*. Leicester: Leicester University Press

Kofler A. (1998). Digital Europe 1998: Policies, Technological Development and Implementation of the Emerging Information Society. *Innovations*. 11 (1)

Kolah A. (1999). *Maximising the Value of Sports Sponsorship*. London: Financial Times Media

Koppett L. (1994). *Sports Illusion, Sports reality: A Reporter's View of Sports, Journalism and Society*. Urbana and Chicago: University of Illinois Press

Kraucaur A. (1926). The Cult of Distraction. Reprinted in the *New German Critique*, 1987, 40

Kuper S. (1994). *Football Against the Enemy*. London: Orion

—— ed. (1998). *Perfect Pitch: Foreign Field*. London: Headline

Larson J.L. and Park H.S. (1993). *Global Television and the Politics of the Seoul Olympics*. Boulder, CO: Westview Press

Leigh D. and Vulliamy E. (1997). *Sleaze: The Corruption of Parliament*. London: Fourth Estate

Loader B.D. ed. (1998). *Cyberspace Divide: Equality, Agency and Policy in the Information Society*. London: Routledge

Lowerson J. (1989). Golf. In *Sport in Britain: A social history* (T. Mason ed.). pp. 187–214, Cambridge: Cambridge University Press

—— (1993). *Sport and the English Middle Class, 1870–1914*. Manchester: Manchester University Press

Lowes M.D. (1997). Sports Page: A case study in the manufacture of sports news for the daily press. *Sociology of Sport Journal*, 14, 145–59

Lyons A. and Ticher M. (1998). *When Saturday Comes: The first eleven*. London: WSC

McCarra K. and Woods P. (1998). *One Afternoon in Lisbon*. Edinburgh: Mainstream

McChesney R.W. (1998). Media convergence and globalisation. In *Electronic Empires: Global Media and Local Resistance* (Thussu D.K. ed.). London: Arnold

MacClancy, J. ed. (1996). *Sport, Identity and Ethnicity*. Oxford: Berg

McCormack M. (1967). *Arnold Palmer: The Man and the Legend*. London: Cassell

McIlvanney H. (1995). *McIlvanney on Football*. Edinburgh: Mainstream

MacKay A. (1997). How it All Began. In *50 years of Sports Report* (Adams A. ed.). London: CollinsWillow

MacNeill M. (1998). Sports Journalism, Ethics and Olympic Athletes' Rights. In *MediaSport* (Wenner L.A. ed.). London: Sage

MacPherson A. (1991). *Action Replays*. London: Chapman

MacRae D. (1997). *Dark Trade: Lost in Boxing*. Edinburgh: Mainstream Publishers

Maguire J. and Tuck J. (1997). Global Sports and Patriot Games: Rugby Union and National Identity in a United Sporting Kingdom. In *Sporting Nationalisms: Identity, Ethnicity, Immigration and Assimilation* (Cronin M. and Mayall D. eds.). London: Frank Cass

Malac M.A. (1995). *The Social Roles of Sport in Caribbean Societies*. Luxembourg: Gordon & Breach

Malik S. (1998). Race and ethnicity. In *The Media: An Introduction* (Briggs A. and Cobley P. eds.). London: Longman

Mann M. (1992). The emergence of modern European nationalism. In *Transition to Modernity* (Hall J.A. and Jarvie I.C. eds.). Cambridge: Cambridge University Press.

Mangan J.A. (1981). *Athleticism in the Victorian and Edwardian Public School*. London: Cambridge University Press

—— ed. (1996). *Tribal Identities: Nationalism, Sport, Europe*. London: Frank Cass

Mangan J.A. and Park R.J. (1986). *From 'Fair Sex' to Feminism*. London: Frank Cass

Mantle J. (1999). Luciano's magical drive. *EuroBusiness*, April

Martineau G.D. (1957). *They Made Cricket*. London: The Sportsman's Bookclub

Martin-Jenkins C. (1990). *Ball By Ball: The story of cricket broadcasting*. London: Grafton Books

Maskell D. (1988). *Oh I Say!* London: Collins

Mason T. (1988). *Sport in Britain*. London: Faber & Faber

Melechi A. and Hearn J. (1992). The Transatlantic Gaze: youth, masculinities and the American imaginary. In *Men, Masculinities and Social Theory* (Craig S. ed.). London: Unwin Hyman

Mellor A. (1991). Enterprise and heritage in the Dock. In *Enterprise and Heritage: Crosscurrents of National Culture* (Corner J. and Harvey S. eds.). London: Routledge

Messner M.A. (1990). When Bodies Are Weapons: Masculinity and Violence in Sport. *International Review for the Sociology of Sport*, 25 (3), 203–20

Messner M.A. and Sabo D. eds. (1990) *Sport, Men and the Gender Order: Critical Feminist Perspectives*. Champaign, IL: Human Kinetics Publishers

Modlenski T. (1983). *Loving with a Vengeance: Mass-Produced Fantasies for Women*. Hamden CT: The Shoe String Press

Moorhouse H.F. (1991). On The Periphery: Scotland, Scottish Football and the New Europe. In *British Football and Social Change: Getting into Europe* (Williams J. and Wagg S. eds.). Leicester: Leicester University Press

—— (1994). From Zines like These? Fanzines, Tradition and Identity in Scottish Football. In *Scottish Sport in the Making of the Nation: Ninety-minute patriots?* (Jarvie G. and Walker G. eds.). Leicester: Leicester University Press

Morse M. (1983). Sport on Television: Replay and Display. In *Regarding Television* (Kaplan E.A. ed.). USA: AFI

—— (1992). *Power At Play: Sports and the Problem of Masculinity*. Boston, MA: Beacon Books

Nixon S. (1996). *Hard Looks: Masculinity, Spectatorship and Contemporary Consumption*. London: UCL Press

Noble R. (1955). *Shoot First! Assignments of a newsreel cameraman*. London: Pan Books

Oates J.C. (1994). *On Boxing*. London: Doubleday

O'Conner B. and Boyle R. (1993). Dallas With Balls?: Televised sport, soap opera and male and female pleasures. *Leisure Studies*, 12, 107–19

O'Donnell H. (1994). Mapping the mythical: a geopolitics of national sporting stereotypes. *Discourse and Society*, 5 (3), 345–80

—— (1999). France '98: Discourses of Identity. Unpublished paper, Sport, Media and National Identity: One Day Seminar. University of Stirling

Paxman J. (1998). *The English: A portrait of a people*. London: Penguin

Polley M. (1998). *Moving the Goalposts: a history of sport and society since 1945*. London: Routledge

Puijk R. ed. (1997). *Global Spotlights on Lillehammer: How the World viewed Norway during the 1994 Winter Olympics*. Luton: John Libbey

Puttnam D. (1997). *The Undeclared War: the struggle for control of the world's film industry*. London: HarperCollins

Rader B. (1984). *In Its Own Image: How TV has Transformed Sports*. New York: Free Press

Radway J. (1984). *Women read the romance*. Chapel Hill: University of North Carolina Press

Real R.M. (1998). MediaSport: Technology and the Commodification of Postmodern Sport. In *MediaSport* (Wenner L.A. ed.). London: Routledge

Redhead S. (1987). *Sing When You're Winning: The Last Football Book*. London: Pluto

—— (1991). *Football With Attitude*. Manchester: Wordsmith

—— (1997). *Post-Fandom and the Millenial Blues: The transformation of soccer culture*. London: Routledge

Rojek C. (1985). *Capitalism and Leisure Theory*. London: Routledge

—— (1992). The Field of Play in Sport and Leisure Studies. In *Sport and Leisure in the Civilizing Process* (Dunning E. and Rojek C. eds.). London: Macmillan

Rose A. and Friedman J. (1994). Television sport as a mas(s)culine cult of distraction. *Screen*. 35, 1

Rose D. and Wood N. eds. (1996). Introduction. Sport, Globalization and the Media. A special edition of *Media, Culture and Society*, 18, 4

Rose T. (1994). *Black Noise: Rap Music and Black Culture in Contemporary America*. Hanover, NH

Rowe D. (1992). Modes of Sports Writing. In *Journalism and Popular Culture* (Dahlgren P. and Sparks C. eds.). London: Sage

—— (1995). *Popular Cultures: Rock Music, Sport and the Politics of Pleasure*. London: Sage

—— (1996). The Global Love Match: sport and television. *Media Culture and Society*, 18 (4), 565–82

—— (1997). Apollo Undone: The Sports Scandal. In *Media Scandals: Morality and desire in the popular culture marketplace* (J. Lull and S. Hinerman eds.). Cambridge: Polity Press

Rowe D., Lawrence G., Miller T. and McKay J. (1994). Global sport? Core concern and peripheral vision. *Media, Culture and Society*, 16, 661–75.

Rowe D., McKay J. and Miller T. (1998). Come Together: Sport, Nationalism and the Media Image. In *MediaSport* (Wenner L.A. ed.). London: Routledge

Sabo D. and Curry Jansen S. (1998). Prometheus Unbound: Constructions of Masculinity in Sports Media. In *MediaSport* (Wenner L.A. ed.). London: Routledge

Scannell P. and Cardiff D. (1991). *A Social History of British Broadcasting*. Oxford: Basil Blackwell

Schlesinger P. (1991). *Media, State and Nation*. London: Sage

Schlesinger P., Dobash R.E., Dobash, R and Weaver, K. (1992). *Women Viewing Violence*. London: BFI

Schlesinger P., Haynes R., Boyle R., McNair B., Dobash R.E. and Dobash R. (1998). *Men Viewing Violence*. London: Broadcasting Standards Commission

Scully G.W. (1995). *The Market Structure of sports*. Chicago: University of Chicago Press

Silverstone R. (1994). *Television and Everyday Life*. London: Routledge

Sloop (1997). Mike Tyson and the Perils of Discursive Constraints: Boxing, Race and the Assumption of Guilt. In *Out of Bounds: sports, media and the politics of identity*

Smith S.J. (1995). *Women, Sport and the British Press: The Under-representation of Sporting Females* (unpublished BA(Hons) Film and Media Studies dissertation). Stirling: University of Stirling

Steenveld L. and Strelitz L. (1998). The 1995 Rugby World Cup and the politics of nation building in South Africa. *Media, Culture and Society*, 20 (4), 609–29

Strutt J. (1841). *The Sports and Pastimes of the People of England*. London: Thomas Tegg (orig. pub. 1801)

Sugden J. (1997). *Boxing and Society*. Leicester: Leicester University Press

Sugden J. and Bairner A. (1993). *Sport, Sectarianism and Society in a divided Ireland*. Leicester: Leicester University Press

Sugden J. and Tomlinson A. eds. (1994). *Hosts and Champions: Soccer cultures, national identities and the USA World Cup*. Aldershot: Arena

—— (1998). *FIFA and the contest for world football*. Cambridge: Polity Press

Taylor R. (1992). *Football and its Fans*. Leicester: Leicester University Press

Thompson J.B. (1990). *Ideology and Modern Culture*. Cambridge: Polity Press

Toibin C. (1994). *The Sign of the Cross: Travels in Catholic Europe*. London: Jonathan Cape

Tomlinson A. (1986). Going Global: the FIFA Story. In *Off the Ball: The Football World Cup* (Tomlinson A. and Whannel G. eds.). London: Pluto

—— (1994). FIFA and the World Cup: the expanding football family. In *Hosts and Champions: Soccer Cultures, National Identities and the USA World Cup* (Sugden J. and Tomlinson A. eds.). Aldershot: Arena

Tunstall J. (1996) *Newspaper Power: The New National Press in Britain*. Oxford: Oxford University Press

Vamplew W. (1988). *Pay-up and Play the Game: professional sport in Britain, 1875–1914*. Cambridge: Cambridge University Press

Vande-Berg L.E. (1998). The Sports Hero Meets Mediated Celebrityhood. In *MediaSport* (Wenner L.A. ed.). London: Routledge

Wacquant L. (1995). Pugs At Work: Bodily Capital and Bodily Labour Among Professional Boxers. *Body & Society*, 1 (1), 65–93

Waddell S. (1979). *The Book of World Darts*. London: BBC Publications

Wagg S. ed. (1995). *Giving the Game Away: Football, Politics and Culture on Five Continents*. Leicester: Leicester University Press

Wakelam H.T.B. (1938). *Half Time: 'The mike and me'*. London: Nelson

Weight R. (1999). Raise St George's standard high. *New Statesman*, 8 January

Wenner L.A. (1998). Playing the MediaSport Game. In *MediaSport* (Wenner L.A. ed.). London: Routledge

Whannel G. (1991). Grandstand, the sports fan and the family audience. In *Popular Television* (Corner J. ed.). London: BFI

—— (1992). *Fields in Vision: Television Sport and Cultural Transformation*. London: Routledge

—— (1998). Reading the Sports Media Audience. In *MediaSport* (Wenner L.A. ed.). London: Routledge

White J. (1994). They Thought it was all over. *Radio Times*, 28 May–3 June

—— (1999). One for the Ghettto. *The Guardian Weekend*, 23 January

Whitson D. (1998). Circuits of Promotion: Media, Marketing and the Globalization of Sport. In *MediaSport* (Wenner L.A. ed.). London: Routledge

Wignall T. (1936). Introduction. In *Daily Express Book of Popular Sports* (Knowles Hodder T. ed.). London: Daily Express Publications

Williams C.L., Lawrence G. and Rowe D. (1985). Women and sport: A lost ideal. *Women's Studies International forum*, 8 (6), 639–45

Williams J. (1991). Having an away day: English football supporters and the hooligan debate. In *British Football and Social Change* (Williams J. and Wagg S. eds.). Leicester: Leicester University Press

—— (1994). The local and the global in English soccer and the rise of satellite television. *Sociology of Sport Journal*, 11 (4), 376–9.

Williams Raymond (1974). *Television, Technology and Cultural Form*. London: Collins

Williams R. (1998). *Racers*. London: Penguin

Willis P. (1982). Women in sport in ideology. In *Sport, Culture and Ideology* (Hargreaves Jen. ed.). London: Routledge & Kegan Paul

Wilson B. (1997). 'Good Blacks' and 'Bad Blacks': Media Constructions of African-American Athletes in Canadian Basketball. *International Review for the Sociology of Sport*, 32 (2), 177–89

Wilson B. and Sparks R. (1996). 'It's Gotta Be the Shoes': Youth, Race and Sneaker Commercials. *Sociology of Sport Journal*, 13, 398–427

Wolstenholme K. (1956). *Sports Special*. London: Stanley Paul

Wynne-Jones G.V. (1951) *Sports Commentary*. London: Hutchinson's Library of Sports and Pastimes

Index

ABC   56, 58, 59, 69
AC Milan   151, 210
Ackerman, Val   130
Adams, Victoria   103
Adidas   46, 51, 58, 103, 131
advertising   25–8, 49, 68–9
African Nations Cup   198
Ali, Mohammed   44, 80
All England Croquet Club   27
Allied Dunbar Premiership rugby   77, 219
Allison, George   37, 82
Alliss, Peter   85, 95
Alston, Rex   38
amateurism   25
American Airlines   58
American football   45, 54, 207, 211
American sports stars in the UK   98–9
American sports writing   20, 177
Amis, Martin   181
Anderson, Rachel   129
Andrews, Eamonn   37
Anheuser Busch   56
Arlott, John   37, 38, 81
Arnold Palmer Enterprises   95
Arsenal FC   40
Ascot   41
Ashes series   22
   (1921)   29
   (1998/99)   76
Associated Rediffusion (AR)   43
Associated Television   43
Association for the Protection of Copyright in Sport (APCS)   42
Aston Villa FC   208
Athletic News   27
athletics   167
Atlanta Braves   61
attendances   48–9
audiences   68–9
Australian Open (1999)   214
Australian Rules Football   66
Axa life   217

Banks, Tony   199
Barcelona FC   215, 222
Barnes, Simon   132
Barnett, Dave   114
Barnett Press Weekly Newspaper   84–5
Barwick, Brian   212
baseball   65, 103
basketball   98–9
BBC   69–71, 211–14
   Audience Research Unit   78
   radio sport   33, 34, 213–14
   television sport   39–41
BBC Handbook   36
BBC Scotland   133, 162
bear-baiting   24
beat system   167, 168
Beattie, Geoffrey: On The Ropes: boxing as a way of life   115, 183
Beaverbrook, Lord   27
Becker, Boris   132
Beckham, David   2, 92, 103
Bell, Ian   120
Bell's Life in London   26
Benetton, Luciano   50
Benetton Formula One   50
Benn, Nigel   116, 117, 138, 139, 193, 195
Benson and Hedges   50
Bentley, J.J.   27
Berlusconi, Silvio   61, 150, 151, 210
Biograph company   30
Bird, Larry   96–7, 105
blood-sports   25
Boat Race   35, 36
Bolton Wanderers FC   35, 82
Booth, Mark   207
Borg, Bjorn   80
Bosman, Jean-Marc   101, 102
Botham, Ian   76
Bovril   48
boxing   31, 137–41
   men viewing   192–7
   sponsorship   54
   women   141–2
   world heavyweight   80

Braveheart   156
bribery   106–7
British Boxing Board of Control (BBBC)   141
British Movietone News   31
British Open Golf Championships (1998)   90
Broadcasting Act (1990) (UK)   60, 211
Brown, Calum   120
Brown, Craig   155
Brundle, Martin   75, 76
Bruno, Frank   18, 116
Brylcreem   103
BSkyB   60, 61, 69, 70, 74, 75, 102, 172, 173, 178, 180, 195, 206–12, 215, 217–19, 222
Buford, Bill: *Among the Thugs*   181
Burn, Gordon: *Pocket Money: Bad-Boys, Business-heads and Boom-Time Snooker*   179
Butler, Bryon   33
Byers, Stephen   207

Cable News Network (CNN)   216
Campbell, Naomi   113, 132
Canal Plus   210, 222
Canon   59
Cantona, Eric   106, 107–9
Cardus, Neville   29
Carling, Will   92
Carlton   209
Carlton Select   214
Carpenter, Harry   212
Cavalcade of Sport   43
CBS   69, 96
Celtic FC   43, 111, 119, 120, 122, 123, 200, 209
centrifugal interplay   79
centripetal interplay   79
Challenge Cup   219
Champions European Cup   55
Champions League   55, 214
Changing UK, The   164
Channel 4   44, 69, 70, 77, 98, 133, 211, 212, 214
Channel 5   70, 77, 173
Charlton, Jack   52
Charlton Athletic FC   82
Chelsea FC   211
Cheshire County Express   84
Chicago Bulls   104
Christie, Linford   92
cigarette advertising   49

class, social   177–9, 180–2
CNN/Sports Illustrated   98
Coca-Cola   56, 58, 59, 60, 95, 131, 187–8
Cock, Gerald   35, 36, 39
Coghlan, Eamon   153–4
Coleman, David   42, 84, 85
Collapsed Lung   188
Collins, Steve   138, 139
Collymore, Stan   114
Colomiers   19
commentating mode of address   85–7
Committee on Copyright   42
Conn, David   100
copyright   41–2
Cosgrove, Stuart   123
Couch, Jane   141
Coventry City FC   106
Cowes, yachting   31
Coxon, J.W.   34
CPS Emitron cameras   41
Crick, Michael   207
cricket   31, 216–17
 Sunday league   54
 Test Match   32, 35, 211
 village   25
 World Series   54
 see also under names of events
Cricket Reporting Agency   28
Crooks, Garth   107
croquet   27
Cultural Studies approach   5–6
cycling   28

Daily Express   27, 29
Daily Mail   27, 28
Daily Mirror   27, 29
Daily Record   107, 122, 123, 124, 158
Daily Telegraph   90, 178
darts   73
Dassler, Horst   58
Davies, Barry   84, 85
Davies, David   169
Davies, Hunter: *Glory Game, The*   184
Davies, Pete: *All Played Out: the full story of Italia '90*   182
Davis, Steve   73
de Lotbiniere, Seymour Joly   37, 81, 82, 86
Deakin, Peter   219
deLillo, Don: *Underworld*   177
Denney, Reuel   66

Derby   35, 36
   (1896)   30
Desgrange, Henri   28
digital television   87, 214–16
Dimmock, Peter   42
Disney   210
Donegan, Lawrence   91
   Four-iron in the Soul   180
Douglas, Jill   134
Drummond, Rose   91
Durex   50
Dyson   97

Ecclestone, Bernie   64
Economist, The   65
Edison, Thomas   30
Edward, Prince of Wales   30
Edwards, Billy   30
El Mundo Deportivo   28
Elias, Norbert   5
Eliminating Racism from Football
   126
Embassy World Championship (1978)
   72
Energizer   59
England and Wales Cricket Board   70,
   216
English Football Association   35, 169
English Premier League   60, 61, 102,
   103, 172, 207, 212
Englishness   152–4
ESPN   58, 59, 211, 221
Esquire   179
ethics   169–70
ethnicity   11
   media bias and   121–5
Eubank, Chris   114, 116, 138
European Broadcasting Union (EBU)
   43, 44, 212
European Champions League   69
European Championships   198
European Court of Justice   101
European Cup (football)   43
   (1967)   185
European Cup (rugby)   218
   (1999)   19
European Cup Winners Cup   173, 211
European Football Championships
   (Euro '96)   56, 57, 154–9, 188,
   198
European Union   65
Eurovision   43
Evans, Gavin   140

Event Agency and Marketing AG, The
   (TEAM)   55

faking, film   30
Famous Grouse   218
fans, football
   media and   197–200
   tradition and history   200–3
Fantasy Football League   188
Fashanu, John   106
Fédération Internationale de
   l'Automobile (FIA)   64
feminist critiques of sport   128
Field magazine   26–7
FIFA   2, 57, 58, 59, 129
figurational sociology approach   5–6
Fishlock, Trevor   100
Five Nations Rugby Union   35, 211,
   212, 218
floodlighting   43
football   31, 65
   attendances   48–9
   domestic   55
   flotation   207–9
   premier   55
   televised   11–12
   see also under names of events and
      teams
Football Association   43
Football Association Cup Final   32, 85,
   211, 213, 216
   (1929)   35
   (1938)   82, 83
   'Matthews Final' (1953)   42
   English   35, 69
   Scottish   35, 69
Football Association of Ireland (FAI)
   51, 52
football fanzine sub-culture   12
football hooliganism   11
Football Italia   211
Football League   27, 42, 43, 211
Football on Television   11
football pools   27
Football Supporters Association   198
Ford, Richard   177
Ford Motors   52
Forman, George   44
Formula One Administration   64
Formula One Constructors' Association
   64
Formula One motor racing   61, 64, 68,
   70, 74–5, 213

Forza italia movement   150
FourFourTwo   179
Fowler, Robbie   103, 135, 136
Fox   207, 210
Fox/Liberty Networks   208
France-Soir   161
Franco, General   145
Fuji Film   59

Gaelic Athletic Association (GAA)   52, 119
gambling   25–8
Gascoigne, Paul (Gazza)   92, 102, 105–6, 191, 211
Gaumont   31, 32
gay men   135–6, 194
Gazzetta dello Sport   28
Geary, Kevin   199
gender   5, 127–42
   see also women
General Motors   51–3, 59
Germain, Julian: *In Soccer Wonderland* 182
Gillette   59, 60
Giro Ciclistico   28
Glanville, Brian   172
Glasgow 'Old Firm' rivalry   199
Glasgow Evening Times   157
Glasgow Herald   157
Glendenning, Raymond   37
globalization   161–4
Goal   179
Goldlust, John   66
golf   90–2
   Senior Tour   96
   see also under names of tournaments
Good Friday Peace Agreement   126
Goram, Andy   124
Gower, David   78
GQ   179
Grade, Michael   215
Gramsci   146
Granada   209
Granada Plus   214
Grand National   32, 35, 68, 80, 212, 216
Grand Prix motor-racing   211, 212
   Japanese (1998)   74
Grandstand   12, 42, 72, 218
Graydon, John   43
Greyhound Racing Association   42
Grisewood, Fred   82
Grobbelaar, Bruce   106, 107

Guardian, The   62, 63, 113, 140, 161, 178
Gunnell, Sally   92
Gutteridge, Reg   138

Hakkinen, Mikka   75
Hall, Willis   165
Hamed, Prince Naseem   114–16, 140, 193, 195, 196
Hancock, Nick   78
hard news   174
Hargreaves, John   87
Harvey, Len   41
Havelange, Joao   57, 58
Hearn, Barry   62, 179
hegemonic masculinity   135
hegemony   9–10, 145–7
Hendry, Stephen   73
Henley Regatta   31
Hey, Stan   203
Hill, Damon   75
Hill, Dave   176
   'Out of his Skin': The John Barnes Phenomenon   182
Hill, Jimmy   155, 212
Hillsborough tragedy   14, 123, 180, 197, 198
Hingis, Martina   132
Hoddle, Glen   16, 20, 124
Holyfield, Evander   2, 213
Hopcraft, Arthur: *Football Man, The* 184
Hornby, Nick   176, 185
   Fever Pitch: a fan's life   181, 183
Horse and Hound   26
horse-racing   25, 26, 31, 41
Horton, Ed   181
Houston Rockets   104
Howe, Darcus   159
Hudson, Robert   38
Hulton, Edward   26, 27
Hunter, Nick   72
hunting   26
Hurst, Geoff   78, 80
Hutton, Will   223

identity, sport and   12–14
Il Ciclista   28
Independent   138, 172
Independent Television Authority   42
Independent Television Commission (ITC)   209
IndyCar series   65

Ingle, Brendan   115
Inside Edge   213
Intel Corporation   221
International Management Group
   (IMG)   53, 93, 94
International Olympic Committee (IOC)
   56, 221
   corruption   2, 173, 175
International Sport and Leisure
   Marketing (ISL)   53, 56, 57–8, 59
Irvine, Hazel   85
ITV   61, 69, 70, 73, 74, 148, 211, 212
ITV sport   43

Jameson, Andrew   62
Jeffries (prize-fighter)   30
Jewell, Jimmy   83
Jockey Club   25
Johns, Hugh   85
Johnson, Ben   106
Johnson, Magic   96–7, 105, 106
Johnston, Brian   38
Johnston, Maurice   123
Jordan, Joe   155
Jordan, Michael   11, 18, 89, 96–9, 104,
   105
Juventus   69
JVC   59

Katz, Donald   89
Kelly, Graham   169
Kelly, Stephen F.: *Game of Two
   Halves, A*   184
King, Don   139
Klammer, Franz   80
Klener, Martin   63
Knight, Phil   89
knur-and-spell   24
Kodak   56
Kuper, Simon
   Football Against the Enemy   183
   Perfect Pitch   184

L'Auto-Velo   28
L'Equipe   28, 48, 143, 159
LA Dodgers   61
La Tripletta   28
Lady's Magazine, The   25
Lancashire County Cricket Club   29
Lappin, Tom   157
lawn tennis   27
   see also Wimbledon Championships
Lawn Tennis Association   131

Lawson, Mark   67, 68
Lazio   211
Le Saux, Graham   135–6
Leach, J.P.   157
Leeds United FC   199
lesbianism   135–6
Lescure, Pierre   210
Levi-Strauss, Claude   56
Lewis, Carl   80
Lewis, Denise   132
Lewis, Lennox   2, 116, 213
Liberty Media   208
Lifetime TV   130
Lineker, Gary   78
Linfield FC   119
Liverpool Echo   122
Liverpool FC   16, 199, 202, 203
Lloyd, Chris Evert   132
Lloyd, Peter   85
Loaded   179, 188
London Broncos   219
Lords Test   212
Los Angles Dodgers   207
Lowe, Ted   72
Lubin, Sigmund   30
Lumière brothers   30
Lynam, Desmond   165

M&M/Mars   59
MacDonald, Ramsay   31
MacIlvanney on Football   184
Mackay, Angus   37
MacPherson, Archie   83, 85
Mailer, Norman   179
Mainstream   184
Major League Baseball   103
Malaja, Lilia   102
male spectatorship
   TV sport as male soap opera   189–91
   boxing and   192–7
Manchester Guardian   29
Manchester United plc   2, 43, 61, 63,
   69, 199, 206, 208, 210, 222
Mandela, Nelson   150
Marshall, Howard   37
Martin, Tony   75
masculinity, sport and   134–7
Maskell Dan   85
Mason, Tony   176
MasterCard International   59, 131
Masters golf tournament   59
Match of the Day   42, 189, 212
Matthews, Stanley   101

Mays, Harold 82
McAvoy, Jock 41
MCC 129
McCarra, Kevin 156
  One Afternoon in Lisbon 184
McClellan 139
McCoist, Ally 156
McCormack, Mark 53, 89, 93, 94, 95
McDonald's 56, 59, 60
McGarry, Ian 157
McGovern, Jimmy 127
McIlvanney, Hugh 165, 170
McKillop, James 157
McLellan, Gerald 138, 193, 195
Media Sports and Leisure Ltd 51, 52
Mediaset 210
Mellor, David 199, 211
Men Viewing Violence 191, 192
Microsoft 57
Mitchell, Kevin 138, 160
Mitford, Mary Russell 25
Molina, Remigio 114, 193
Monopolies and Mergers Commission
   (Competition Commission) 2, 206
Montana, Joe 80
Monte Carlo Rally 43
Moorcroft, David 169
Moore, Brian 83, 85
Morning Telegraph 85
motorsport 28
  see also Grand Prix motor-racing
Motson, John 84, 85, 111, 113
Mullan, Harry 139
Murdoch, Rupert 2, 60, 61, 63, 69,
   170, 173, 178, 208, 216
Murray, David 123

Nally, Patrick 53
National Anti-Gambling League 26
National Basketball Association (NBA)
   90, 96–9, 103, 104
National Football Intelligence Unit 199
national identity 147–54
Nationwide building society 16
Navratilova, Martina 132
NBA 24/7 98
NBC 69, 104
neo-marxist approach see Cultural
   Studies approach
Newcastle United FC 106, 208, 209
News Corporation 69, 207, 208, 221,
   222
News of the World 27

Newsnight 199
Newspaper Proprietors' Association
   (NPA) 33, 35
Newsreel 31
newsreel, sport on 30–3
NFL 45, 103
NHL 103
Nicklaus, Jack 5, 53, 94
Nike 16, 46, 47, 51, 89, 97, 99, 109
Nine O'Clock News 91
Northcliffe 27
Northcroft, Jonathan 114
Nottingham Forest FC 48
NTL 209

O'Rourke, Trevor 52
O'Sullivan, Peter 85, 212
Observer, The 29, 126, 160, 172, 176
Offiah, Martin 219
Old Trafford 29
Oldroyd, Eleanor 133
Olympic Games 43, 53, 80, 212, 213
  (1896) 28
  (1948) 23, 41
  (1960) 43
  (1964) 44, 55
  (1968) 44
  (1976) 56
  (1984) 55–7
  (1996) 59, 130
On The Ball 85
Opel 51–3
Open Golf Championship 35
Orange Order 121, 125
orthodox rhetoric 174, 175
Owen, Michael 2, 103
Oxford United FC 214, 215

Packer Affair 216
Palmer, Arnold 18, 53, 89, 93, 94, 95,
   100
Panorama 47
para-Olympic athletics 167
Paris Saint Germain 210
Parkinson, Michael 165
Pathé 31
Pathé Journal 31
Pathé, Charles 31
patronage, aristocratic 48
Paul, Robert 30
pay-per-view sport 69, 214–16
Pele 44, 80
Pepsi 103

Persimmon   30
Philips   59
Pierce, Mary   132
Pilling, M.J.   44
Player, Gary   53, 94, 95
Player, John   50
Portand Trailblazers   104
Portsmouth FC   35
Post   122
Pot Black   72
power, sport and   4–6, 11
Premier League football   207, 211
   Scottish   186, 209
Press Gazette   171
press
   European   28
   gambling and advertising   25–8
   sporting, origins   24–9
Preston, Peter   143, 178
Princess of Wales   92
prize-fighting   25, 26
Pro-Celebrity golf   95
Professional Footballers Association
   (PFA)   101, 102, 129
Professional Golfers Association (PGA)
   27–8, 91
Pro-Serv   97
Puskas, Ferenc   43

Question of Sport, A   71
Quokka Sports   220, 221

race   111–26
   and ethnicity in televised sport   11
   media representations of   112–14
   sporting behaviour and   5
Racing Calendar   25
racism   112–14
radio   33–8
   commentary   36–8
   continuities of television and   38–9
   outside broadcasts (OBS)   34, 36
   sport rights and   35–6
   production   36
Radio 5 Live   133, 213, 221
Radio Scotland   83
Radio Times   34, 35, 36, 39, 40, 44
Rangers FC   111, 119, 122, 123, 202,
   209
Reagan, Ronald   57
Real Madrid   215
Red Rum   80
Redhead, Steve   100

Reebok   51
reflexive analysis   173, 176
Reith, Lord   34
Republic of Ireland international
   football team   51
Rickman, John   43
Riddell, Lord   33
Robertson, Max   37
Ronaldo   46, 47
Rose, Justin   90, 91
Rosenthal, Jim   75
Roth, Philip   177
RTE   52
Rugby League   74, 211, 218, 219
Rugby Super League   130
rugby union   39–40, 217–19
Rugby World Cup (1995)   150
Runyon, Damon   179
Ruscoe, Sybil   133
Ryder Cup   70, 211

satellite technology   44, 55, 74–8
scandal, sports   106–7
Schulberg, Budd   179
Schumacher, Michael   75
Scotland on Sunday   19, 155, 176
Scotsman   157
Scottish Daily Express   186
Scottish League (football)   83
Scottish Premier League   186, 209
Scottish Television   162
Scottishness   152–4
sectarianism   118–21
Segars, Hans   106
Sharkey (prize-fighter)   30
Shearer   102
Shields   134
Shooting Times   26
Simpson, O.J.   106
Sir Norman Chester Centre for Football
   Research   12
Sky Sport 1   129
Sky Sports   76, 77, 115, 139, 192, 193,
   196, 197, 211, 217
Smith, Mark E.   180
Snead, Sam   93
Snickers   59
snooker   55, 71–3
social history, sport and   6–7
soft news   174–5
Souness, Graeme   122, 123
Southampton FC   106
speedway   36

Spice Girls, The 103
Spiers, Graham 155
sponsorship 27, 46–54
Sport on Friday 107
Sport plc 207–9
Sport Special 86
Sporting Chronicle 26
Sporting Life 26
sports broker 53–4
sports commentary
  codes and conventions 78–87
Sports First 171
Sports Formbook 43
sports journalism 166–70
  class and 177–9
  ethics 169–70
  new 176–80
  professional ideologies 166–8
  sources 168–9
  in the USA 177
sports magazines 179–80
sports page construction 170–6
  institutional and market pressures
    171–2
  models 174–6
  vested interests 173–4
Sports Report 37
Sports Special 12, 42
Sportsbiz 93
SportsPages 184
Sportstour 43
Sportsview 42
sportswear market 46
Springboks 150
Stern, David 98
Stiles, Nobby 155
Stream 222
Strutt, J.: *Sports and Pastimes of the
  People of England, The* 24
Sumo wrestling 45
Sun 63, 106, 123
Sun (Scottish) 122, 155, 156, 158
Sunday Herald 171
Sunday League cricket 212, 217
Sunday Mail 124
Sunday Telegraph 172
Sunday Times 134, 172, 180
Superbowl 59, 80
Sykes Committee (1923) 33
Syncom III satellite 44

Talk Radio 213
'Tartan Army' 152, 155–6, 198

Tattersall's Rings 26
Taylor, Dennis 73
Taylor, Gordan 102
Taylor, Rogan 203
TEAM 55
Teesdale, David 165
Telecom Italia 222
telegraph 26
Telepui 210
television
  continuities of radio and 38–9
  global sport 43–5
  independent 39
  sport and 10–12
  sport, history 38–45
Telstar 55
Test Match Special 38, 221
Texaco 61
Thatcher, Margaret 211
They Think It's All Over 78
Thistle, Patrick 83
Thompson, Peter 83
Time Warner 210
Times, The 63, 84, 178
tobacco company sponsorships 62, 65
Toibin, Colm 120
Total Sport 179
Tottenham Hotspur plc 207
Tour de France 28, 48, 160
Tracey, John 154
Trans World International (TWI) 53
Treaty of Rome 102
Turner, Ted 61, 104, 211
Twentieth Century Fox 31
Twickenham 40
Tyler, Martin 85
Tyrell Formula One 50
Tyson, Mike 109, 117–18, 137

UEFA 55, 56
UK Athletics 169
Ulster (rugby union) 19
Untied Shareholders Against Murdoch
  207
Updike, John 177
US Fox TV 69
US Masters golf 80
US Open tennis championship 59
UVF 123–5

Varsity rugby union match 36
Vaughan-Thomas, Wynford 37
Vauxhall 51

Visa   56
Vitagraph company   30

Wakeham, Captain Teddy   37, 82
Walker, Doug   169
Walker, Graham   37, 212
Walker, Murray   37, 76, 85, 212
Walton, Ken   85
Ward, Bill   43
Warne, Shane   16
Warren, Frank   139
Watt, Jim   138
Webb, Shelley   127
WestNally   53
When Saturday Comes   181, 200
When We Were Kings   44
Whitbread Around the World yacht race
   (1997–8)   221
White, Jim   117
Wignall, Trevor   29
Williams, Richard   75
   Racers   180
Williams, Venus   132
Willis, Bob   76
Wilson, Bob   212
Wimbledon Championships   27, 35, 80,
   131, 212, 214, 216
Wisden, John: *Cricketers' Almanac*   28–9
Wiseman, Keith   169
Wolstenholme, Kenneth   42, 78–83, 85,
   86
Wolves   43
women
   boxing   141–2
   representation in sports   129–34

as sporting heroes   92
sports journalists   85
sports media coverage   131–3
World Championship boxing   141
World Cup football   130
Women Viewing Violence   192
Women's National Basketball
   Association (WNBC)   130
Woods, P.: *One Afternoon in Lisbon*
   184
Woods, Tiger   80, 90, 92
World Boxing Council (WBC)   138
World Cup (cricket)   130
   (1999)   62
World Cup (football)   2, 14, 43, 53, 54,
   80, 90, 182, 198, 212
   (1954)   43
   (1958)   43
   (1962)   44
   (1966)   49, 78, 79, 84, 85
   (1970)   44
   (1974)   11
   (1990; Italia '90)   198
   (1994; USA '94)   47, 57–60, 198
   (1998; France '98)   46, 47, 57–60,
      68, 103, 158, 159–61, 185, 198,
      204
World Federation Wrestling   139
wrestling   43, 139
Wright, Billy   43, 101
Wynne-Jones, G.V.   37

yachting   31

Zidane, Zinedine   46, 161